# HAIL CESAR

# HAIL CESAR
## THE AUTOBIOGRAPHY

## BILLY McNEILL

headline

First published in 2004
by HEADLINE BOOK PUBLISHING

10 9 8 7 6 5

Cataloguing in Publication Data is available from the British Library

ISBN 0 7553 1315 1

Typeset in Garamond by Avon DataSet Ltd,
Bidford-on-Avon, Warwickshire

Printed and bound in Great Britain by
Mackays of Chatham plc, Chatham, Kent

Statistics compiled by Jim Black and Jack Rollin

Headline's policy is to use papers that are natural, renewable and
recyclable products and made from wood grown in sustainable forests.
The logging and manufacturing processes are expected to conform
to the environmental regulations of the country of origin.

HEADLINE BOOK PUBLISHING
A division of Hodder Headline
338 Euston Road
London NW1 3BH

www.headline.co.uk
www.hodderheadline.com

# CONTENTS

To my wonderful wife Liz for the unstinting support she has given me for more than 40 years and to the late Jock Stein for making my dreams come true.

# ACKNOWLEDGEMENTS

I owe so much to my late mum and dad and my wife Liz and our five children for a lifetime of love and support.

I would also like to express my sincere thanks to the other Lisbon Lions – Ronnie, Jim, Tommy, Bobby, John, Jimmy, Willie, Stevie, Bertie and Bobby and the others who were part of our triumph – for making my job as captain easy and for putting up with my bad temper.

Jim Black for all his hard work and patience in collaborating with me to produce my autobiography. Our friendship survived intact because we never forgot how to laugh.

And not forgetting all the team at Headline.

# CHAPTER 1

# LISBON

Surely no other captain of a European Cup-winning team has been bundled into a police car clutching the trophy. Not that I can recall the moment in any detail. Clearly my emotions were such that they blanked out the memory of much of what took place in the immediate aftermath of Celtic's victory over Inter Milan on that historic Thursday afternoon of 25 May 1967.

It was probably ten years later before the enormity of our achievement finally sunk in, when we attended various functions to mark the anniversary of Celtic becoming the first British team to win the European Cup. When I watch film of the incredible scenes that followed at Lisbon's Estadio Nacional, I am reminded of just what Celtic's achievement meant to our fans. As they poured on to the pitch in their thousands, their reaction was a genuine explosion of emotions. It was a wave of sheer joy mixed with relief that the dream had become reality.

The final whistle signalled a green and white invasion and the players were immediately cut off from one another. Incredibly, we recognised many of those who flooded on to the pitch from supporters' functions we had attended over the years, but Ronnie Simpson's dance of delight was cut short when the realisation dawned that he had left his cap lying in the back of the goal net. The cap hardly mattered, but its contents did because it contained several sets of false teeth given to Ronnie for safekeeping by some of the players. Fearing the worst, Ronnie fought his way through the thronging mass in an effort to retrieve his head gear. To his amazement, it was lying where he had left it, despite the fact that the souvenir hunters were having a field day. Fortunately, a well-worn old bunnet held little appeal. Otherwise, a few of the lads would have returned to Glasgow looking decidedly gummy.

Just about every other moveable object was nicked, though, including the jersey I had swapped with one of the Italian players, but it didn't seem to matter. Neither did it matter that our bonus for winning the European Cup was £1,000 – a not inconsequential amount at that time, but loose change compared to the £50,000 to £100,000 players earn nowadays. Few of us have the opportunity to experience such a unique moment in time and it was a day that changed my life and those of my fellow Lisbon Lions forever. Nothing could ever quite be the same again after that.

Hardly a day has passed in the last 37 years when I have not thought of those events in Lisbon or been reminded of what winning the European Cup means to Celtic supporters. Some, who were not even born or who were no more than weeks or months old, talk about the greatest day in the club's history as if they had witnessed it with their own eyes. However, as I say, for me, much of what went on in the immediate post-match free-for-all remains a blank. The adrenaline must have been pumping so hard that certain memories were instantly erased.

I remember the moment when I raised the European Cup skywards in a pose that was immortalised by dozens of press photographers and captured on celluloid by the TV cameras, but how exactly I got there I cannot say with any certainty. I also have to take the word of others that the trophy presentation was made by the president of Portugal. My first clear recollection of the presentation ceremony itself is of the moment when I realised that I was alone. I remember thinking, 'Where are my team-mates? Why am I the only one of the players here?' The Lisbon Lions were a collective. We were a team both on and off the pitch and it felt wrong that we were denied the chance to share such a special moment.

I have often been asked what makes a successful team and I believe the answer is relatively simple. It's about knowing that your mates are standing by your side ready to lend their unqualified support in the belief that there is nothing that cannot be achieved. On our day, we believed that we were capable of beating any team in the world, but fate and the Portuguese police decreed that we were split up in our moment of triumph and celebration. Only Sean Fallon, our assistant manager, accompanied me on the slow walk across the pitch through thousands of jubilant supporters to the section of the stand where the president and the other leading dignitaries were gathered.

Apparently, when my team-mates noticed my absence they wondered where I had disappeared to. They had been taken to the dressing room for reasons of safety, but there was no chance of anyone being hurt, for the supporters were wandering about in a state somewhere between disbelief and sheer delight. Confrontation was the last thought in their minds. As I looked down from the presentation dais, I was able to spot my wife, Liz, and the other wives and girlfriends among the mass of Celtic fans. Many of the Italian fans had also remained behind.

The authorities appeared to care more about the wellbeing of the European Cup than the man carrying it, given the decision to transport Sean and I back to the dressing room by police car, but an astonishing thing happened when we reached the courtyard housing the dressing rooms. Each of the policemen accompanying us insisted on having his photograph taken holding the trophy. Just the trophy, mind you, not the captain of Celtic!

No formal arrangements had been made for a post-match celebration and our wives were not included in any plans. They had, in fact, arrived on the morning of the game and were due to fly home shortly afterwards. They actually travelled with us on the team coach and were dropped off at the airport before we returned to our hotel in Estoril. On the way back, there was a bizarre incident when the coach swerved slightly and our physiotherapist, Bob Rooney, was caught off balance. Bob, who was standing at the front of the coach, conducting a bit of a sing-song, instinctively reached out to grab the nearest support, which just happened to be the steering wheel, and he very nearly forced us off the road. Fortunately, the driver managed to regain control, but, on reflection, a joyous occasion could so easily have turned to tragedy but for the quick reactions of the driver.

With so many Celtic fans having travelled to Portugal, the local airport couldn't cope with the flood and no sooner had we returned to our hotel than we received a call to say that the flight carrying our wives had been delayed until the following morning. Additional space at our hotel was extremely limited, but we managed to squeeze them in somehow, and such was the euphoria that none of us would have been able to sleep anyway.

Jock Stein had selected the Palaçio Hotel, where we had arrived on the Tuesday before the Thursday match, as our base and it proved to be an inspired choice. The place was full of old-world grandeur, the bedrooms were spacious and comfortable, and the setting offered tranquillity and allowed us to unwind. The fact that there were green and white ornamental mushroom-shaped lights fronting the building we took to be a lucky omen. Nothing was left to chance and Jock ensured that every little detail was taken care of in terms of the quality of the food and the facilities, such as a swimming pool. Mind you, we were restricted to just half an hour in it, because Jock feared that if we spent too long in the sun the heat would tire us. So, we spent much of the time playing cards in the shade. Jock was ahead of his time in that sense. The continentals were used to staying at the best hotels and dining off the fat of the land, but, judging from my own experiences prior to Jock's arrival and the stories I heard from other players, British clubs tended not to be overly concerned about home comforts.

The training sessions, which took place on a public park adjacent to our hotel, were short, sharp and fun, and Jock and his backroom team of Sean, Neil Mochan, Bob Rooney and Jim Steele joined in a bounce game along with the club doctor, John Fitzsimmons, which helped create an even more relaxed atmosphere. However, Jock had also compiled an extensive and detailed dossier on the Milan team and we were made aware of the strengths and weaknesses of each their players.

On the eve of the game we were invited to the home of an expatriate Scot from Ayrshire, Brodie Lennox, owner of a local country club, to watch England play Spain at Wembley. I recall that the home side won, 2–0. The day of the game passed reasonably quickly and following a loosening up session we had a light lunch before going for a lie down. But, as you might imagine, the butterflies had begun to flutter and sleep was impossible.

I cannot overemphasise the part played by Jock in ensuring that our preparations were planned to the letter. He was positively brilliant in the build-up to the game. Helenio Herrera, the Inter Milan manager, was used to having his own way and was a formidable opponent when it came to psychological jousting, but our manager was also a master of mind games. Herrera had infuriated Jock by breaching an agreement regarding training on the eve of the final. It had been agreed that we would train first at the stadium, but the Italians arrived before us and after their session stayed to watch us. Herrera might have won that one, but he was in for a shock when he tried to commandeer the home side's bench prior to the kick-off in what was a clear breach of official protocol. Jock marched up to his rival and growled, 'You'll have to find another place,' and Herrera was forced to walk a hundred yards with his tail between his legs. I also recall Sean Fallon threatening to 'set about' Herrera if he didn't shift – and Sean was not a man to be messed with. The bench incident was an illustration of Jock's ability to unnerve the opposition and at the same time convey a sense of invincibility to his players. It was a perfect example of confidence-building.

We also had a twelfth man in the shape of our incredible fans. Looking back, when we set out for the stadium we could have been forgiven for thinking that we were en route for Celtic Park, instead of the Estadio Nacional, such was the volume of Celtic supporters. They heavily outnumbered their Italian counterparts, having arrived in their thousands by car, coach, train and plane and some of them were ticketless. I'm sure that a lot of them had set out from Glasgow by road, not having a clue about exactly where they were headed or how long it would take them to complete what must have been, for many, a nightmare journey. It seems reasonable to assume that there must have been a large number of abandoned cars strewn across the highways of France, Spain and Portugal, judging by the state of some of the vehicles that were waved off from Glasgow's George Square days before. But our fans lit up Estoril and quickly won over the locals to the extent that the Portuguese were on our side when it came kick-off time.

The Inter players must have wondered what had hit them when they walked out into the sunshine to be greeted by the sight of thousands of Celtic fans in full cry. Mind you, they had already been left somewhat bemused by the antics of the Celtic players when we lined up side by side in the tunnel, ready to walk out together. These were the teams: Celtic: Simpson, Craig, Gemmell, Murdoch, McNeill, Clark, Johnstone, Wallace, Chalmers, Auld, Lennox. Inter Milan: Sarti, Burgnich, Facchetti, Bedin, Guarneri, Picchi, Bicicli, Mazzola, Cappellini, Corso, Domenghini.

I suffer a little from claustrophobia and when our arrival on the pitch was delayed for reasons I have never been sure of, the length and narrowness of the tunnel made me feel a touch uncomfortable, so I made an effort to distract myself by looking around at my team-mates and the opposition. I couldn't help smiling. Directly behind me stood this collection of freckle-faced, white-legged individuals. Opposite me I could see a group of handsome Latins with bronzed faces and limbs shimmering under a coating of oil. The contrast could hardly have been greater. The cut of the Inter strips also suggested that they had been handmade instead of mass-produced, adding to the appearance of real quality, and the blue and black stripes made a pleasant aesthetic contrast with our green and white. But while the Inter players certainly looked the part, we didn't suffer from an inferiority complex. There was a cockiness about our team and a real self-belief. I hadn't anticipated what happened next, however. Bertie Auld suddenly began singing *The Celtic Song* and within seconds the rest of us had joined in. The Inter players looked gobsmacked.

But for all that they were clearly not used to rubbing shoulders with a bunch of 'nutters', I don't think our actions unnerved them, because Inter scored after only seven minutes. Jim Craig conceded a penalty when he was adjudged by the West German referee, Kurt Tschenscher, to have bodychecked Cappellini, the Inter striker. The kick was converted by their captain, Sandro Mazzola, and we suddenly found ourselves a goal down.

When Milan were awarded that penalty, one or two of our players wanted to argue with the referee and, in my role as captain, I moved quickly to try to calm the situation for fear of us having someone sent off and losing our discipline. I agreed that the award was harsh, but felt it important we kept our shape in the expectation that Milan would try to pressurise us once they were in front.

Strangely, they didn't press home their advantage and allowed us to take the play to them, which in itself posed a threat because we might be caught if they suddenly broke from defence into attack. That meant it became essential for John Clark and I to maintain total concentration. However, there was no need for me to cajole my team-mates because their commitment was such that each and every one of them gave one hundred per cent. Being captain of the Lisbon Lions was easy in that sense.

We created chance after chance, but we were repeatedly thwarted in our efforts to equalise through a combination of Sarti's outstanding goalkeeping and the woodwork, and I began to worry a little as the minutes ticked away. Jock had earmarked Sarti as a possible weak link, but he chose the occasion to produce probably one of the finest performances of his career and I became increasingly more fearful as the game progressed. It wasn't panic as such, just a nagging doubt niggling away at the back of my mind. That fear was offset, though, by a deep-rooted self-belief that, having come this far, we were not about to fall at the final hurdle and I comforted myself with the thought that the law of averages dictated that we eventually had to convert one of the many chances being created by our aggressive style of play.

Herrera had invented the rigid and boring-to-watch defensive system known as *catenaccio* and that allowed for the opposition to take possession of the ball. Inter were normally comfortable dealing with teams coming at them and hitting on the counter, but Herrera misjudged our pace and the tempo at which we played the game. He overlooked our high level of fitness and also the fact that we were a skilful team. However, at half-time, we were still seething over the award of the penalty and Jock had to calm us down, pointing out that we could have had three or four by that stage and that if we kept playing the same way the goals would come. He was correct, of course, and in the sixty-third minute Jim Craig squared the ball across the eighteen-yard line to Tommy Gemmell and Big Tam powered a perfectly placed shot past Sarti.

The Inter players were clearly rattled and I suspect that they were prepared to settle for a replay, which was scheduled to take place three days later in Lisbon. But we went for the jugular. We were optimistic and confident and continued to attack at every opportunity. There was almost an inevitability about the winner and it came five minutes from time. Bobby Murdoch shot low across the face of the goal and Stevie Chalmers was there to push out his foot and divert the ball past Sarti, who had been caught by the change of direction. I expected Inter to respond with a furious onslaught in the closing moments, but it never materialised. They were a spent force, unable to readjust their game, and we won easily in the end.

The margin of our victory in no way illustrated our overall superiority. Some years later I appeared on a TV programme with Sir Bobby Charlton and he told me he hadn't realised at the time just how well Celtic had performed. 'When I saw the 2–1 scoreline I thought that was a great result for Celtic,' said Bobby. 'But it was only when I watched a recording of the game that I realised you had actually annihilated them.'

The presentation of the medals took place in a restaurant in the centre of Lisbon and the Inter players were so disillusioned that they initially refused to turn up. They did eventually show, but were clearly in a state of shock and didn't stay for long. There were clearly no hard feelings, though. At the 2002 Champions League final between Real Madrid and Bayer Leverkusen at Hampden Park, the Lions were present and Giacinto Facchetti, the Inter and Italy full-back, made a point of seeking us out to talk over the events of thirty-five years earlier.

Although people refer to the Lisbon Lions as the actual eleven who beat Inter, others played a significant part and the contribution of those such as Joe McBride, Charlie Gallagher, John Hughes, Willie O'Neill and John Fallon should never be forgotten. Probably the unluckiest of the players who missed out on a place in the final was McBride. Joe suffered a knee injury playing against Aberdeen at Pittodrie on Christmas Eve 1966 and was out for the rest of the season. By then he had scored thirty-five goals in twenty-six games and was far and away our most prolific goal-scorer. I recall at the time of Jock signing Willie Wallace from Hearts for a £30,000 fee him telling me, 'I think Wallace and Joe McBride could become the greatest striking partnership in the history of the Scottish game, maybe even in Europe too.' Unfortunately, we were never to find out. They played together before and after Joe's injury but much of the potency was lost. However, I can't help thinking that Jock would have been proved right in his assessment had fate not intervened.

Our return to Glasgow the day after the final was a rollercoaster ride of deep emotion. I doubt that the East End of the city has ever witnessed anything like the scenes that greeted our arrival back at Celtic Park. There was no motorway in those days and our journey from the airport to the ground took us past Ibrox. I must confess that I quite enjoyed the moment. All along our route fans turned out to greet the team and when we reached London Road the East End was a sea of colour and people. They were hanging out of windows and flags flew everywhere. We began to realise then just what our achievement had meant to so many people, but it was only later when the Lisbon Lions began to be invited to various supporters' functions that the enormity of our achievement sunk in. To this day, the Lisbon Lions remain special to the Celtic fans.

I was surprised, too, at the impact our victory had south of the border. When I became manager of Manchester City, I was regularly approached by fans wanting to talk about the game and what it had felt like to win the European Cup. We are part of football folklore. Supporters still come up to me and explain how their father or grandfather was at the game in 1967 and how proud they were to be part of what was a truly wonderful experience.

I think it's fair to say that the players themselves have never been able to take on board their iconic status, though, largely because most of us grew up being part of a big club that became hugely successful and we got used to winning trophies. We were a fiercely proud bunch of players but we never allowed ourselves to get carried away. We were fans ourselves and what we have always enjoyed most is the acknowledgement we have received from the supporters. I can honestly claim never to have felt different from the next man. I grew up in the profession and I consider myself very fortunate to have been part of what was a fairytale of sorts. I would also love to see Celtic become champions of Europe again, even if only to take the pressure off us – but the first time round is always the best.

# STARTING OUT

My Lithuanian grandparents boarded an immigrant ship believing that they were bound for the New World, but instead of landing in New York they disembarked at Leith. But for that geographical hiccup I might have been born a Yank on 2 March 1940. I can only assume that my maternal granny and granddad were duped by some unscrupulous wheeler-dealer when they chose to leave their native land to seek a better life in America, but I am rather glad that they were, for I could never envisage myself starring in the NFL or playing major league baseball.

We lived with my grandparents for a time after my dad, Jimmy, returned to my native Bellshill following a short spell of army service at Hereford and I remember them as very proud, kind people. Years later, on a trip to the Ukraine to play Kiev, local journalists were keen to interview me about my family connections behind the then Iron Curtain, although I have to confess that I wasn't able to enlighten them greatly.

Having been born in my mother's parents' house in Bellshill, we lived with them and my Auntie Grace in their miner's row until I was six. There was a kitchen and a front room, with a large black grate, but

I don't recall that we lived in cramped conditions, although I suppose we must have to an extent. Each of the bedrooms had two bed recesses, so I had my own 'space'. My own kids laugh at the notion of an outside toilet, but that was exactly what we had prior to moving to a prefab, which my parents qualified for shortly after World War Two ended. Looking back, I can't remember ever being unhappy or that I missed out on anything. Kids in those days made their own fun and I have fond memories of my childhood. Life in the 1940s was much more austere, but we had never known anything else.

I was already into football before, when I was nine, we moved to Hereford. There I was forced to attend the local rugby-playing high school for two and a half years and I have to confess that I rather enjoyed the oval ball code. I played on the wing and the playing fields, by the banks of the river Wye, were as good as those enjoyed by many professional clubs today. My real love, however, was always football and as a youngster in Bellshill, I played in the streets with my pals for hours on end, late into the evening during the summer. In fact, I can't remember doing much else. Happily, back in Lanarkshire, I attended Our Lady's High School in Motherwell, which had a great football tradition, and I am still in touch with three of my schoolmates – George Tiffney, Arthur McManus and Jimmy Mooney.

Dad, who was as straight-backed at the time of his death in 1998 as he had been during his 22-year army career as a soldier in the Black Watch, and latterly the Army Physical Training Corps, where he attained the rank of Warrant Officer, wasn't a big football fan as such. But my Uncle Frank was. My dad came from Dundee and Frank was a dyed-in-the-wool United fan who loved it when Celtic came to town. If we were playing United, Frank would appear decked out in black and white (United's colours didn't change to tangerine until the early

1970s), but if we were playing Dundee, Frank turned up wearing the green and white of Celtic.

While my dad hadn't been in the habit of going to games, my mum's older sister, Grace, was a football fan. Auntie Grace was the one who introduced me to Celtic at the age of nine. My dad was serving in West Africa at the time and I felt as if I was on a big adventure myself when I paid my first visit to Celtic Park on 15 October 1949. I got off to a winning start when Celtic beat Aberdeen, 4–2, with Mike Haughney scoring two of the goals in the final ten minutes. Bobby Evans and Bobby Collins, who were later to be team-mates of mine for a brief spell, played, but it was Charlie Tully who impressed me most.

Charlie, who had been signed from Belfast Celtic the previous year, was ahead of his time in the sense that he was a personality in the days when footballers were much closer to the fans, both in terms of their standing in the community and the wages they earned. It wasn't unusual to see a Celtic or Rangers player strolling through the centre of Glasgow and being left pretty much alone. Nowadays, it's impossible for Old Firm players to venture out on to the streets without being mobbed by their own fans or abused by the opposition's followers. But Tully was different. He was the Henrik Larsson of his generation and the fans worshipped him for his irrepressible skills and the cheeky tricks he attempted. Tully was also a newspaper man's dream. He always had a quip for the press and the story goes that when the film *Bonnie Prince Charlie* was premiered in Glasgow, Charlie stormed out when he discovered that it was not about him. No doubt he thought that one up himself, but Charlie was certainly my earliest hero and when he died in 1971, at the age of just forty-seven, I had the honour of being one of the pall bearers at his funeral in his native Belfast.

Another abiding memory of that first visit is of my Auntie Grace losing her shoe in the Jungle, when we were lifted into the air and swept forward as the crowd celebrated a goal, but in spite of having to endure the embarrassment of travelling home by bus minus part of her foot wear, it didn't put Grace off and she continued to take me to games.

Although the Aberdeen game was my first at Celtic Park, I had seen Celtic in action the previous year in a First Division match at Cliftonhill, home of Albion Rovers. Coatbridge is only a short distance from Bellshill and I was taken as a treat. I didn't realise it at the time, but Jock Stein played in the match, which finished 3–3.

Being an army man, my dad was strong on discipline and I was made to toe the line. That's not the same as saying that I had to follow a rigid code of discipline, but my old man was strict with me and I was glad in later life that he had been. My parents installed in me strong principles that I have carried with me throughout my life. They stressed to me the need for decent behaviour and consideration for others. They also ensured that there was no religious divide in our home. Ours was a Catholic household, but no distinctions were drawn between Catholics and non-Catholics. Sadly, the same cannot be said of many other homes in the West of Scotland.

My dad didn't have a problem with me supporting Celtic, but I wasn't allowed to wear the club's colours because that was flaunting loyalties in his view. I was also encouraged to support our local team, Motherwell, when I was a kid. I was, in fact, in my early teens before I was permitted to travel to Glasgow with my pals to watch Celtic without adult supervision, and I was still barred from wearing the green and white scarf that I had purchased with my pocket money.

Being an only son, I did not have to share my parents' love and affection with any siblings and my mother, Ellen, doted on me. Such were her feelings that Mum hated watching me play in case I got hurt. But she was always very proud of my achievements and I miss her and my dad.

Naturally, being brought up in a mining community, I inherited the politics of my parents and the community at large. Consequently, I have always been a socialist and I continue to vote Labour. I may live in a beautiful home in an upmarket part of Glasgow, but I have never forgotten my working-class roots or lost sight of the fact that I have been one of the lucky ones in life. I am deeply opposed to any form of exploitation, although I do believe in discipline, order, consideration of others and respect for people's property.

My father always espoused the view that a good education was worth more than gold and, as I've said, I was fortunate to attend Our Lady's High School in Motherwell, where football featured prominently on the sports curriculum. Our team was good enough to reach the Scottish Schools Cup final where we faced Holyrood at Hampden Park. I was seventeen and it was my first national cup final, but unfortunately I scored an own goal and the game finished 1–1, so my excitement was tinged by disappointment. No replay took place because of a dispute over a suitable venue.

Over the next two or three years several clubs showed an interest, including Arsenal, Manchester United, Newcastle, Clyde and Partick Thistle. In fact, Thistle were prepared to pay me £10 a week on the basis of a gentleman's agreement that when I reached the age of sixteen I would sign for them. David Meiklejohn, the former Rangers captain who achieved legendary status at Ibrox, was manager at the time. The money would have come in very handy, but my father would have nothing to do with what was in effect an illegal move. However, when Celtic came on the scene there was no decision to be made other than to sign for my boyhood heroes.

I played for Scotland Schoolboys against England at Celtic Park and Jock Stein was present to watch us win, 3–0. He immediately talked Sir Robert Kelly, the Celtic chairman, into signing me. Jock was accompanied by Eddie McCardle, a Celtic scout, and the pair of them arrived at my home to offer terms. Needless to say, the deal was concluded in record time. So, in May 1957 I signed provisional forms and began an association with the club that has been such a huge part of my life for the past forty-seven years. I also recall Jock, who was coaching the reserves at the time, asking my mum, 'Is it okay if I give him a skelp if he steps out of line?' She instantly agreed.

Coming from the background I did, Celtic was the team most of my friends, family and neighbours supported, so there was quite a buzz when I signed for the club. I suppose I became a bit of a personality in the eyes of some of them, although I never felt that way myself. It really was my dream come true and everyone was delighted for me. In fact, later on, when I began playing for the reserves, I used to think that my father and my friends had more fun than me being able to go to games to support Celtic.

To start with, Celtic 'farmed' me out to junior side, Blantyre Victoria, the club where Jock Stein had launched his career, and I continued my education, also training two evenings a week at Celtic Park. When I was seventeen, I passed Higher exams in English, Maths and Spanish, and Lower exams in French and science, and if I have a regret about that period of my life, it would be that I didn't go on to university, but the pull of becoming a footballer with Celtic proved greater.

The time I spent with Vics taught me a great deal and toughened me up sufficiently that by the summer of 1958 I was considered a bright enough prospect that I won a place in the Celtic squad to go on a close-season tour to Ireland. I had already played a number of games for the reserves, having been handed a baptism of fire in a second string Old Firm match where I faced Don Kitchenbrand, the South African striker known as 'the Rhino'. That was New Year's Day, 1958, and I was seventeen and terrified, both to be playing against Rangers and to be facing Kitchenbrand, who was a giant of a man. To a skinny kid like me, he seemed to stand seven feet eight inches tall. Kitchenbrand was a powerhouse and he let me know pretty quickly what I could expect in terms of his physical challenges. I've probably still got some of the bruises, but I felt that I acquitted myself reasonably well. Fate decreed that I was again in direct opposition to Kitchenbrand when we played a Bohemians Select in Dublin and again I must have handled myself OK because I held on to my place for the rest of the tour and went on to play against a Belfast Celtic select side and Derry.

However, I was still only eighteen and serving my apprenticeship, so I didn't harbour high hopes of continuing my association with the first team once the season got under way. Just a handful of games into the campaign, though, central defenders Bobby Evans and John Jack were injured at the same time and I made my debut proper on 23 August 1958 in a League Cup tie against Clyde at Celtic Park. We won, 2–0, in front of 39,000, and I managed to retain my place, but Celtic were keen to nurse me along and I was in and out of the team, playing right-back, right-half and centre-half, which I preferred, at various times.

I was also still a part-time player with Celtic and remained so for a further three years. During that time I worked first for Lanarkshire County Council and then moved to the insurance company, Stenhouse, in Glasgow. I can't help but wonder if young players nowadays would be better advised to seek similar alternative employment, given the way careers can be ended without warning. It certainly didn't do me any harm having two jobs, even if it meant twelve-hour days because of training at Celtic Park in the evenings.

There was still an element of the star-struck youngster about me and it was marvellous to have the opportunity to rub shoulders with players of the status of Charlie Tully, Bertie Peacock, Bobby Evans, Neil Mochan, Willie Fernie, Bobby Collins and, of course, Jock Stein. Jock had been forced to retire in 1956, at the age of thirty-four, because of an ankle injury, which left him with a slight but permanent limp, but he immediately began coaching young players at the club. Being around these guys was an education in itself. Paddy Crerand, who had signed on the same day as me, listened with the same intensity. Like any other bunch of youngsters we were capable of getting up to mischief, but we didn't step out of line when the senior players were around.

Few players had cars at that time and Jock was no exception. Like the rest of us, he travelled by public transport. John Clark, Jim Conway and I, lived close to one another in Lanarkshire, while Jock stayed in Burnbank, and we used to accompany him to the bus stop at Tollcross Road near Parkhead Cross, a short walk from the ground. Jock had been put in charge of the reserves and having someone of his experience guiding us in the early years was great, but he insisted that we had to wait until his bus arrived. If ours came along first he made us hang on for the next one, because he didn't like being left on his own. Eventually the club gave Jock the use of a Ford Anglia car and he gave us a lift to Bellshill Cross, filling our heads full of fascinating tales and giving invaluable advice along the way.

By the end of the 1958–59 season, I had played a total of twenty-three games for the first team. The following season that increased to thirty-two, but it was in my fourth year at Celtic Park that my career really took off. Bobby Evans's transfer to Chelsea in May 1960 left the way clear for me to establish myself as the first choice centre-half. I like to think that I helped hasten Evans's departure. He was a player I admired and one who gave great service to Celtic and Scotland, making a total of forty-eight appearances for his country, but Bobby wasn't a natural centre-half. He played in the position for Scotland, but in the modern game his talents would have been utilised in a right-sided midfield role. I say that, because Bobby tended to back off the centre-forward and was more adept at starting moves from deep, rather than breaking up attacks.

I think Celtic made a big mistake letting Jock leave in March 1960 to become manager of Dunfermline. Clearly his burgeoning talents as a coach were not fully appreciated by the club, but we youngsters thought the world of him and benefited greatly from his advice and encouragement. He had certainly seemed to take a special interest in my progress and his departure created a void in my life. If Jock had remained at Celtic Park that would have allowed the club to blood him as Jimmy McGrory's successor and the eventual transition would also have been much smoother. Celtic clearly didn't offer him a big enough challenge at the time, but I'm sure that had Jock been given certain guarantees concerning his future and a financial inducement to stay he could have been persuaded to remain where he was.

The 1960–61 season was another unspectacular one for Celtic as we failed to qualify for the latter stages of the League Cup and managed to finish only fourth in the league. Our Scottish Cup final defeat by Dunfermline – now managed by Jock – simply added to the growing sense of frustration, but I had reason to feel satisfied with my own progress. Having managed to establish myself in the Scotland Under-23s team, I was deemed ready to make the step up to full international level, and I was delighted to win my first cap on 15 April 1961. Here

I was, still a part-time player, ready to face England at Wembley. My chest was positively bursting with pride. By the time England had finished with us the dream had turned into a nightmare, but that's another story.

# CESAR

In 1960 a movie called *Ocean's Eleven* hit the big screen. It concerned the exploits of a gang of ex-war buddies trying to pull off a multi-million dollar raid on several Las Vegas hotels. Among the stars were Frank Sinatra, Dean Martin, Sammy Davis Jr and Cesar Romero, and when the movie came to Glasgow a gang of us at Celtic Park immediately headed for the cinema. The reason for our haste was the fact that one of our number, John Colrain, was a huge fan of Sinatra, while another of the lads, Mike Jackson, fancied himself as a bit of a crooner and regularly mimicked Dean Martin. To this day, Mike is known as 'Dino', despite the fact that only he thinks he can sing like the great man.

Paddy Crerand, Bertie Auld and a fellow by the name of Dougie Hepburn, who was a Hearts fan, were also members of our gang. Paddy saw himself in the role of Joey Bishop and Bertie liked to be compared with Sammy Davis, but it was John Colrain who was responsible for landing me with the moniker of 'Cesar'. As I was the only one who owned a car, John decided that I fitted nicely into the role played by Romero and the name stuck. Mind you, it wasn't a flash American-style gas-guzzler. Far from it. My motor was a somewhat more humble Austin A35. It was my first car and I can still reel off the registration. UGE 424 was sky blue and we had a lot of enjoyment bombing about Glasgow in the days when motor cars were considered a luxury rather than a necessity. I may have struck a Caesar-type pose when I lifted the European Cup aloft, but my nickname has nothing to do with Julius. Not that our particular 'rat pack' ever got up to anything as outrageous as plotting a major heist, but we knew how to enjoy ourselves.

Back then package holidays were unheard of and most Scots headed for places like Rothesay, Largs and Saltcoats for their summer holidays. It seemed that only the idle rich and football players went to Spain to soak up the sunshine and a few of the Third Lanark players had sampled the delights of a foreign holiday. When we heard how much they had enjoyed themselves we decided to follow their example and booked a fortnight in the sun. There was only one place we could possibly head for and that was Lloret de Mar. The reason was simple - Sinatra had pursued Ava Gardner halfway across the world and eventually caught up with her in Lloret. John Colrain refused to even consider an alternative destination, so Lloret de Mar it was, but the Costa Brava was very different in those days. Lloret had approximately 100 yards of tarmacadam and the rest was wooden sidewalks, but it was a wonderful experience all the same, even if we did cop a fine from the Scottish Football Association (SFA) when they discovered that we had taken part in an unofficial 'bounce' game.

We didn't think for a minute that anyone would get to hear about our involvement in the game, so on our return, when Mike Jackson and I stepped off the aircraft we were shocked to be greeted by several reporters and photographers. One of them asked, 'Can you give us details of the game?' Initially, we pleaded ignorance, saying, 'Game? What game are you talking about?' But the cat was out of the bag.

A holidaymaker from Glasgow had taken a few snaps and passed them on to the newspapers. When the story appeared in the Scottish press, the SFA immediately took an interest and the upshot was that we were fined £30 each – more than a week's wages at that time.

That same summer of 1961 I met my future wife, Liz. She was Elizabeth Callaghan in those days and came from Whiteinch in Glasgow. Liz was a professional dancer with the BBC's White Heather Club and we were introduced by a mutual friend, Ian Gordon, at a party. I was immediately taken by the attractive blonde and the rest, as they say, is history. We became engaged the following year and were married on 22 June 1963. It was the best move I have ever made. Liz is blessed with an even temper and rarely panics. I would not have achieved half the things I have done if I had not enjoyed my wife's unqualified support and, after 41 years of marriage, I can honestly say that I have never regretted for a single moment the evening in Glasgow when I met the future Mrs McNeill. I am also very proud of my five children – Susan, Libby, Carol, Paula and Martyn. They have had their ups and downs like the rest of us, but we're extremely fortunate to have a close-knit family. Like any other kids, they were capable of getting up to all sorts of mischief and the odd scrape, but I'm glad to say that none of them has let us down.

At the same time as Liz and I were planning our future together, Tottenham Hotspur were the masters of English football. Spurs had achieved the League and Cup double two years previously and had just become the first British club to win a European trophy. The manner of Spurs' 5–1 annihilation of Atletico Madrid in the Cup Winners' Cup final in Rotterdam had been truly breathtaking. Why, given these facts, did I turn down the chance to become part of that outstanding team? I was sorely tempted, but, in the end, it was probably a combination of my love for Celtic and a slight fear of the unknown.

I was just 23 years of age and newly married when the chance of a glamour move to London arose. A former team-mate, Eric Smith, was the Spurs scout in Scotland and he had marked my card for Bill Nicholson. Nicholson, one of the most successful managers in the game's history, was keen to strengthen his squad to compensate for the fact that several of his players were nearing the end of their careers. I was asked by Eric if I would be willing to listen to what Nicholson had to offer and I agreed instantly to a meeting with the Spurs manager at my home in Glasgow. Nicholson was a Yorkshireman, blunt and to the point. He laid his cards on the table straightaway, telling me that he believed I was the sort of player who would fit in at White Hart Lane without too much difficulty.

Celtic would have to be agreeable to selling me, of course, but, provided there were no unforeseen hitches and a deal could be done, I would be on nearly four times the wages I was earning at Celtic Park. That offer was way beyond my wildest dreams. In addition to earning close to £100 a week, there was also the promise of a sizeable signing-on fee. What more could I ask for? Consider, too, the quality of the players at Spurs at that time: Danny Blanchflower, Bill Brown, Dave Mackay, Cliff Jones, John White and Jimmy Greaves had all played in Rotterdam. I knew Brown, Mackay and White as Scotland team-mates and I was very aware of the lifestyles they enjoyed. Compared to the sort of money they were on, I was earning a pittance – just £28 – at Celtic Park. However, it was still considerably more than the average working bloke and Liz and I had been able to buy our first home, a semi-detached costing £3,000, with it. We could have had a bungalow for just £500 more, but I refused to commit myself to a larger mortgage for fear of putting myself under financial pressure.

That will no doubt sound daft to today's younger generation, but back in the 1960s, £3,000 represented a sizeable commitment to someone who had never even met a house owner from Bellshill. Liz was the same. Her dad worked in the shipyards, so, like me, she came from a working-class background where the vast majority were socialists and only the rich Tory voters from the middle and upper classes dabbled in property. The Celtic board included a stockbroker, a lawyer and an accountant among their number, but none of them offered detailed advice about investing for the future. Had they done so, we might not have stumbled about largely in the dark. It was only seven years later when we sold our first home for £6,000 – twice what we had paid for it – that the realisation set in that there was money to be made as a property speculator. With what Spurs were offering me we could have bought another two houses, but we were happy with our lot at the time and life seemed pretty wonderful, all things considered. Mind you, I missed an opportunity to engineer myself a wage increase and I should have told the board that I wanted considerably more in exchange for rejecting Spurs' overtures, although it's always easy to be wise after the event.

I was also a Celtic man through and through. Celtic had been my team since I was a kid and becoming captain of the club I had supported from a young age was a dream come true. So I rejected the chance to further my career in England. Unbeknown to me then there would be several other occasions when I would again have the opportunity to head south, but I remember Dave Mackay saying to me during a Scotland trip that I had made a big mistake turning Spurs down on the grounds that my heart lay at Celtic Park. 'Listen, Big Man, you are not any more Celtic daft than I was Hearts daft,' he said. 'But Hearts were not prepared to pay me the sort of wages I felt I was entitled to and I went where the money was. You would love it at Spurs. They are a great bunch of boys and the lifestyle is vastly superior to what you can afford on the wages Celtic pay you.' Dave had a point. I have often talked to Liz about what such a move would have meant to us in the long term and what sort of life our kids would have enjoyed, but I have never regretted my decision.

Celtic might well have gone on to win the European Cup, even without Billy McNeill, but I would not have wanted to miss the experience for anything. However, I am forced to admit that it was a joke the way players were treated at that time. Provided the club chose to retain your services you were sent a letter informing you that you would be re-signed on the minimum terms acceptable to the Scottish Football Association and the Scottish League. In effect, players were owned by their clubs. Refusal to accept the terms offered resulted in the club retaining your registration, effectively preventing you from playing elsewhere. It was tantamount to white slavery! Short of demanding a transfer and being fortunate enough to have that wish granted, any player who was involved in a contractual dispute risked being left sitting on his backside in the stand without wages. Few players could afford to hold out for long, so the club invariably won in the end. Marc Bosman changed the face of football forever but back in the 1960s, freedom of movement was little more than a dream for most. So, too, was winning the European Cup. If any one at Celtic Park had suggested in 1963 that Celtic would scale such remarkable heights they would have been laughed out of sight.

One by one the experienced players had moved on – Bobby Collins to Everton, Willie Fernie to Middlesbrough, Bobby Evans to Chelsea, Bertie Auld to Birmingham City, Bertie Peacock to Coleraine and Pat Crerand to Manchester United – and Celtic Park was full of youngsters. There was also a dreadful lack of direction at the club. The senior players had taken it upon themselves to offer advice and guidance to the extent that they issued instructions on how we should play, but, with the bulk of them gone, we were forced to provide our own education.

To be frank, several careers were ruined because of the apparent apathy and disinterest that pervaded Celtic Park. The training facilities were practically non-existent and the kit left much to be desired. The reserve players could easily be identified by the red weals on their necks caused by the rubbing of the coarse jerseys. Jimmy McGrory, the manager, was a lovely man, but he was dominated by the chairman, Bob Kelly, later Sir Robert. Bob picked the team and called the shots. Anyone who dared to stand up to him didn't have a future at Celtic, including my close buddy, Mike Jackson. For whatever reason, Mike got on the chairman's wrong side. He was suddenly perceived as being a disruptive influence and, in April 1963, I returned from international duty to find that Mike had been transferred to St Johnstone. This was also an indication of where the power lay. Mr McGrory was the manager, but Bob Kelly was the boss!

Had I been around at the time, I would have done everything in my power to prevent that from happening, because Mike was unjustly treated. Mike and I were inseparable and I regularly stayed at his parents' home in Glasgow. The social life in Bellshill couldn't compare with the buzz of the big city. The so-called swinging sixties were under way and we knew how to enjoy ourselves. But it would be wrong to imagine that we were big drinkers or that we behaved in a reckless manner. We did all the things normal healthy young guys do, but we weren't a couple of wild men. However, Bob Kelly wanted Mike out. Maybe he overheard Mike recounting the story of how he visited the dressing room on three separate occasions prior to a game, after being told that he was in the team, before discovering that he wasn't playing after all. The first time he saw his boots sitting alongside the number four jersey, but when he returned a short time later he noticed that his footwear had been moved to number eight. On Mike's third and final visit his boots were nowhere to be seen.

I was by then an established first team player, having made my debut five years earlier. Eighteen-year-olds may think they know it all, but the reality is somewhat different, and I was fortunate to be surrounded by so many experienced players who were only too happy to give me the benefit of their much greater knowledge. Bobby Collins appeared to take a special interest in my development. We played together only a handful of times, but Bobby was a tremendous help.

He was also one of the hardest players I have encountered. People talk about Ron 'Chopper' Harris, Norman 'Bite Yer Legs' Hunter and Tommy Smith, the Liverpool captain who specialised in intimidating opponents through his very presence, but Collins was the match of any of that trio. In spite of his lack of inches – he stood barely five feet tall – Collins was a pocket dynamo with the heart of a lion. Celtic's loss was very much Everton's gain when he left Celtic Park in September 1958. Originally an inside-right, Collins, christened 'the Wee Barra' by the Celtic fans, played every forward position in a remarkable career lasting nearly a quarter of a century. Collins was strong and full of energy. He also had pace and skill and was precise in his passing. Add to those qualities his versatility and an eye for goal and you had the complete player.

When he moved on to Leeds United, Don Revie was the leader off the field; Collins was the driving force on it. He possessed a remarkable mental toughness that rubbed off on those around him. Collins is credited – rightly so, in my opinion – with creating the incredible will to win that became such a hallmark of Leeds' success under Revie. Leeds did not endear themselves to the football world as a whole, because of their combative nature, and no player epitomised that mentality more graphically than Collins. Johnny Giles, whose 'wholehearted' approach had to be questioned at times, benefited more than most from the influence exerted on the team by Collins. The Irishman is the first to admit that Collins had a great attitude to the game and his role as playmaker in midfield was profound.

It was suggested that the fee of £25,000 Celtic received from Everton helped pay for the installation of floodlights at Celtic Park. If that is true, Celtic also paid a heavy price for agreeing to sell a player whose importance to the club could never be overstated. I suspect that had Collins's services been retained we would have enjoyed a much greater level of success over the next seven years, prior to Stein's arrival, but how often was it the case that the club sold its best players? Far too frequently, I am afraid. Personally, I would love to have had the opportunity to play longer with Bobby Collins. I and the other young players breaking through at the time would have benefited hugely from his influence.

Most of my appearances in that first season had been in the league and we finished in sixth place, a long way adrift of champions Rangers. I did play in the League Cup semi-final against Glasgow rivals Partick Thistle who beat us, 2–1, at Ibrox. As far as the league went, over the next four seasons we finished ninth, fourth, third and fourth again. The closest we came to winning a trophy was reaching the Scottish Cup final in 1961 and again two years later. On both occasions we fell short of the standards required to be winners. Dunfermline's replay win was especially hard to take as we were hot favourites and most neutrals – and I suspect a sizeable percentage of Pars fans – had expected a Celtic victory.

Our defeat by Rangers in 1963 left an even more bitter taste. Our goalkeeper, Frank Haffey, who had endured a bit of a nightmare in the replay against Dunfermline, atoned with an outstanding performance and made several important saves to ensure that the score stayed at 1–1, after Ralph Brand and Bobby Murdoch had scored in quick succession in the closing stages of the first half. Interestingly, Jimmy Johnstone was selected, despite having only two league games under his belt, but 'Jinky', who was to star on so many occasions in the future, was unable to provide the spark of inspiration we required to secure a victory. Jinky was left out of the replay eleven days later and had cause to be grateful. Not to put too fine a point on it, we were completely outclassed. Losing to your closest rivals is bad enough at any time, but the manner of our defeat stung more than usual.

Inspired by wee Willie Henderson and Ian McMillan, Rangers ran over the top of us. Henderson created havoc down the right flank and crossed for Brand to score the opener after only seven minutes. Rangers' other flying winger, the blond-haired Davie Wilson, scored a second just on half-time to end it as a contest in everything but name. However, just for good measure, Brand notched a second goal midway through the second period to our acute embarrassment.

The club's first foray into Europe had been equally unrewarding. Our participation in the 1962 Fairs Cup lasted just one round when we went out to Valencia, losing the away leg in September, 4–2, and drawing the home leg in October, 2–2. In fairness, we had suffered the misfortune to be drawn against the holders, who went on to retain the trophy, but that did not lessen the sense of failure. Coupled with finishing in fourth place in the championship and our failure to qualify for the latter stages of the League Cup, this inglorious baptism in Europe and the Scottish Cup final defeat left us all disillusioned. The fans deserved better – much better.

There was a growing sense of frustration among the players. Celtic Football Club was in desperate need of fresh impetus, but the pace of change was despairingly slow. So much so that by the time 1965 came I had made up mind that I also had to move on. I craved a new challenge. I also felt that I had done my bit for Celtic, but that the club had not shown an obvious willingness to adopt a more futuristic approach. As it happened, Spurs were still interested. Maurice Norman was approaching the end of his career and I was seen as a potential replacement for a player who was good enough to win twenty-three England caps. In the event, Mike England was eventually signed from Blackburn Rovers to take over from Norman. England, too, was a centre-half of real note, as his record of forty-four appearances for Wales underlines. It could have been me. However, I am glad that I chose to remain at Celtic Park, for had I gone to Spurs at that time I would not have achieved the unique distinction of becoming the first British player to hold the European Cup aloft.

Everton were also rumoured to be interested in acquiring my services and there was no shortage of quality at Goodison Park. Harry Catterick had built up a powerful squad of players. I knew some of them; Jimmy Gabriel, a tough tackling wing-half who had begun his career with Dundee, and Alex Young were fellow Scots. Alex and I had, in fact, played together once for Scotland, in a 3–0 win over the Republic of Ireland in Dublin in May 1961. A striker who, before his move away from the capital, was worshiped by Hearts fans, Alex scored one of our goals and deserved the nickname given him by the Everton fans of 'The Golden Vision'. Between them, Gabriel and Young played ten times for Scotland. Nowadays, players of their ability and class would be candidates for a place in the SFA's Hall of Fame for those who have made fifty or more international appearances. Frankly, I cringe when I see the names of some of those who have won twice as many caps. They would not have been able to lace Gabriel's or Young's boots. However, in some cases at least, circumstances have dictated the selection of certain players; Scottish football is no longer blessed with an abundance of talent and needs must on occasion.

Everton, who had been First Division champions in 1962–63, were a team packed with international players. Goalkeeper Gordon West, full-backs Tommy Wright and Ray Wilson (a World Cup winner), centre-half Brian Labone and winger Colin Harvey all represented England at various stages in their careers. I do wonder where I would have fitted in, but it would have been interesting to have found out, especially as Everton went on the win the FA Cup in 1966.

A third club hovered in the wings and I might have found it much more difficult to reject their overtures had Manchester United followed up their initial interest with a firm offer of employment. I hadn't met Sir Matt Busby at that point, but the Manchester United manager was known to both my parents. Matt, whom I was later to get to know well during my exile in Manchester, had attended the same Lanarkshire school as my mother and he and my dad had met during the Second World War when their paths crossed as physical training instructors in the army. Bill Foulkes was getting on a bit and Matt had turned his thoughts to finding an eventual replacement for his centre-half, but while Matt was said to be keen on the captain of Celtic, nothing concrete came of it. Had I gone to United at that time, the events of Lisbon two years later would not have become such an integral part of my life, but the experience of becoming a European Cup winner might have just been delayed for a further twelve months.

As it happened, Foulkes extended his career long enough to be part of the United team that triumphed over Benfica at Wembley in 1968. Apart from Sir Matt, there were several other Scots at Old Trafford. My former Celtic team-mate, Paddy Crerand, had established himself as a key player and, of course, Denis Law was a hero with the Stretford End. Would I have fitted in? I think so. Playing alongside the likes of

George Best and Bobby Charlton could only have made me a better player. Perhaps if I had realised then what United would go on to achieve I might have pushed harder for a move, but it was to be nearly another twenty years before I would discover at first hand just what a wonderful city Manchester is.

The rivalry between United and City fans is every bit as intense as the rivalry that exists in Glasgow, but there is none of the religious baggage that overshadows the Old Firm and, at times, causes such grief – but that's another story. There were to be two more occasions when a move to Manchester United beckoned, but fate decreed that when I played at Old Trafford it was in the hoops of Celtic. The first rumblings of the coming revolution in Scottish football had been felt. Jock Stein was on his way back to Celtic Park and life would never be quite the same again.

CHAPTER 4

# THE SECOND
# COMING

Heaven knows what state Celtic football club would have ended up in had Jock Stein not returned to Celtic Park in March 1965. It would be too dramatic to suggest that the ship was sinking, but it was certainly listing badly to port. The signs of decline were everywhere. The team had not won a major trophy for eight years and there was a growing sense of disillusionment among the players and our supporters. A very fine Rangers team, containing players of the class of Jim Baxter and Willie Henderson, was at its peak and that added to our fans' frustrations.

Jimmy McGrory had been manager for close on twenty years and he was a man who commanded respect. He was a Celtic legend and held a record for having scored 410 goals in 408 league games. His tally of 550 goals was, in fact, a record for British football. But while Mr McGrory – I have never been able to bring myself to call him by his Christian name – was a true gentleman, he was perhaps 'too nice' to enjoy the same level of success as a manager. His almost paternal benevolence meant that some players, at least, took liberties that would never have been tolerated by his successor. In the event, Mr McGrory took on the less onerous task of acting as the club's public relations officer following big Jock's appointment and continued to serve Celtic faithfully almost until his death in 1982.

Jock had already established himself as one of football management's coming men. He had left Celtic, where he had worked as a coach, in 1960, to take up his first managerial appointment with Dunfermline and quickly made his presence felt at East End Park. When Jock arrived Dunfermline had been in grave danger of being relegated from the old First Division, then the top flight, but he managed to get an instant response from the players. Fate decreed that his first match in charge was a home fixture against Celtic and, within one minute of the kick off, Dunfermline were a goal up. I remember the game well. Charlie Dickson shocked us with that lightning strike and we never fully recovered our composure. Having said that, Dunfermline certainly rode their luck and survived several anxious moments before running out 3–2 winners. Dunfermline used that result as a springboard to even better things and went on to survive reasonably comfortably in the end. If my memory serves me correctly, they put together a sequence of six consecutive league wins and no Dunfermline team had done that before.

Jock's star was already shining brightly in the skies over west Fife, but the best was yet to come. A combination of shrewd transfer dealings and Jock's ability to install positive thinking in the players meant that the following season was less fraught. Dunfermline's form varied, but by the time the Scottish Cup began in January, the indications were that it would go down as a successful campaign. Just how successful soon became evident on the back of a quite remarkable cup run. Having disposed of Stranraer, Aberdeen and neighbouring Alloa, Dunfermline found themselves in the semi-final for the first time in the club's history. They weren't fancied to write a fresh chapter in the fairytale but, despite losing their centre-forward, Charlie

Dickson, who was injured early in the second half, the underdogs hung on for a goalless draw with St Mirren at Tynecastle. The replay the following midweek was, by all accounts, an uninspiring affair, so it was entirely fitting that the outcome was settled by an own goal in favour of Dunfermline.

However, not even the most imaginative Hollywood scriptwriter would have dared to suggest Celtic as their opponents in the final at Hampden Park on Saturday 26 April 1961. It was Celtic's first appearance in the Scottish Cup final for five years and the first of a record twelve I played in, but I could not have imagined that my love affair with the cup would get off to such an inglorious start. If the truth be told, we rather fancied ourselves and perhaps, on reflection, that confident air rebounded on us. Who knows? The record shows that a crowd of more than 113,000 watched the goalkeepers, Frank Haffey of Celtic and his opposite number, Eddie Connachan, produce truly outstanding saves to ensure that the scoreline remained blank, even though Dunfermline were down to ten men in the closing stages.

There is a belief that you only get one chance against the Old Firm and the general feeling was that Dunfermline would fall by the wayside the following Wednesday, but the game didn't pan out as the pundits had predicted. Although we put Dunfermline under intense pressure, we simply could not score, due largely to another inspired performance from Connachan. As so often happens when a team is put under the cosh, Dunfermline broke clear midway through the second half and David Thomson, who had not played in the first match, scored with a header. A blunder by Haffey two minutes from time allowed Dickson to seal our fate. Jock, who had captained Celtic to Cup final glory over Aberdeen seven years before, had performed what could only be described as a minor miracle.

In three Scottish Cup finals since 1954, Celtic had lost to Clyde, Hearts and now Dunfermline. It was definitely time for Jock Stein to return, but Celtic waited a further four years before making the approach. By then Jock had moved on to Hibs, after cutting his teeth in Europe with considerable effect and, predictably, the Easter Road side enjoyed an instant revival, winning the Summer Cup during his brief sojourn in the capital.

The news that Jock was to succeed Mr McGrory broke in January 1965, when Hibs released a statement to the effect that the club would be commencing a search for a new manager, adding that as soon as a suitable replacement was found the present incumbent would be allowed to leave to assume his duties at Celtic Park. Despite the fact that Hibs clearly had no wish to lose Jock, I think the directors realised they couldn't stop him from going, given his affection for Celtic and the attraction of a return to Celtic Park. The transfer took place six weeks later when Bob Shankly, brother of Liverpool legend Bill, quit as boss of Dundee, with Bobby Ancell replacing him as manager at Dens Park. The revolution was under way.

Celtic's post-war record up to that point did not make for inspiring reading. The league championship had been won in 1953–54, with Jock as captain, and there had also been two Scottish Cup and two League Cup successes, including the remarkable 7–1 destruction of Rangers, in 1957. But, by and large, the club had been stumbling around in the wilderness for twenty years. That sorry state of affairs was about to change, though, under the first non-Catholic manager of Celtic.

With Jock at the helm, Celtic Football Club underwent an immediate transformation. Crucially, he knew many of the younger Celtic players like myself from his time as coach and that made the task of putting across his message slightly easier. I had never seen Mr

McGrory in a tracksuit; Jock was rarely out of one. Training altered dramatically and it suddenly became a pleasure instead of a chore. Jock dispensed with the tedium of players pounding round the track and replaced these mind-numbing sessions by introducing footballs into our daily fitness sessions! Daft as it may sound, under the previous coaching regime we had prepared in the manner of track athletes, rather than football players, and working with the principal tool of our trade had not figured prominently on the agenda. I felt like a man reborn and all thoughts of a move away from Celtic Park disappeared from my mind.

Jock's knowledge of the game, linked to his strong personality, meant that there was only one boss. For all that he did not suffer fools gladly, however, Jock was a relatively uncomplicated individual when it came to his views on how the game is meant to be played. He kept the basics simple and never asked players to do things that were beyond their capabilities. He quickly recognised that he was working with talented individuals and what we required more than anything at that time was the presence of an influential figure to oversee our development as a team.

The transformation wasn't instant. In Jock's first game in charge we took six goals off Airdrie, with Bertie Auld scoring five of them, but we also suffered several embarrassing defeats, including a 6–2 drubbing by Falkirk. However, on a personal level I enjoyed the distinction of being the first recipient of the Scottish Football Writers' Player of the Year award, a fortnight after helping Scotland draw 2–2 with England at Wembley, and I was also to have the enduring satisfaction of becoming the first Celtic captain, since Stein, to hold aloft the Scottish Cup.

Given the events of four years previously, there was a decided edginess about the team when we lined up against Dunfermline at

Hampden on 24 April 1965. Jock had already made one highly significant change. Bobby Murdoch, known as 'Chopper', was switched from inside-right to right-half. Long term it proved to be something of a master stroke, when he developed into one of the most accomplished midfield players in the game at that time.

In the final itself we twice found ourselves a goal down, but our commitment was such that we managed to fight our way back into the game and, moving into the final period of what was an understandably tense occasion, were set for another replay at worst. Then, with just nine minutes remaining, fate decreed that the Stein years would begin with a victory of considerable significance. Charlie Gallagher swung over a corner kick and yours truly rose to snatch the winner. I have seen that goal described as a 'brilliant header'. Frankly, it wouldn't have mattered had the ball glanced off my backside and struck half a dozen players on the way in. It was the first of three Scottish Cup final goals I scored and easily the most significant.

But they say that pride comes before a fall and just four days later we ended up flat on our faces. Revenge was sweet for Dunfermline in the final game of the season when they thrashed us, 5–1, at East End Park. The result hardly mattered in terms of the championship, for we were in mid-table, but it sure as hell mattered to Jock and all thoughts of our Hampden triumph were washed away on a tidal wave of vitriol from the manager. 'I have not come to this club to win a trophy every ten years,' he stormed. 'The target must be to win every game and every trophy.' There was a further chilling warning. 'Any of you who do not share that attitude can pack your bags right now.'

Our cup success was little more than an hors d'oeuvre as far as Jock was concerned. He had designs on dining on much richer fare in the shape of the championship and Europe. To that end, he realised he would have to strengthen the squad and Joe McBride, a proven goal-scorer, was signed from Motherwell in the close season. Bertie Auld was also a relative newcomer, having been re-signed the previous January from Birmingham City, and the pieces of the jigsaw quickly began to fall into place. A much clearer picture was emerging from Celtic Park and there was a general air of excitement about the place.

There were inevitable casualties, of course. Radical changes on the playing side resulted in Jock releasing around twenty players at the start of May, all of them youngsters, which meant the disbandment of the third team, leaving the coaching staff to concentrate their energies on the senior squad and reserves. Knowing Jock, for all that he did his best at times to give the impression that he was a real tough nut, he would not have enjoyed telling these young players that they no longer had a future with Celtic. But he was a realist and the club was clearly top-heavy with players who were unlikely ever to make the first team.

Every successful general needs tried and trusted lieutenants to ensure that his battle plans are executed in the manner desired. Sean Fallon, who had been a team-mate of Jock's, occupied the role of assistant manager and Neil Mochan, another former player, was appointed coach. It proved an ideal blend. Sean, whose distinct Irish brogue appeared to grow stronger over the years, was both genial and tough. Neilly, on the other hand, was a quiet man who acted as a counsellor for the players. Jock had a ferocious temper when roused and we were capable of being a wild bunch at times, so it was just as well that we had Neilly on hand to take us aside when we were in danger of going over the top.

I recall a trip to Czechoslovakia in March 1964, the season before Jock took over, to play Slovan Bratislava in the European Cup Winners' Cup quarter-final, when we indulged in a water fight lasting several hours. At that time, life in Eastern Europe was austere and it seemed that everywhere we turned there were a couple of KGB 'spies' following behind. I never understood the thinking behind following high-profile football players, but that's just the way it was in those days. Slovan didn't enjoy the luxury of floodlights and the game was played in the afternoon. In the event, we won, 1–0, with a goal from John Hughes late in the game, and booked our place in the semi-final, 2–0 on aggregate.

Travel was much more complicated forty years ago and it was necessary for us to stay overnight before flying home the following morning. That meant we had time to kill and, after taking advice from a couple of locals, we decided to visit a theatre. Of course, the production was in Czech and we rapidly lost interest in what we were watching. Consequently, we decided to return to our hotel and have a few drinks instead. Being fit young athletes with plenty of energy to expend, it didn't take long for further boredom to creep in and that inevitably led to horse play. One of the lads – I think it was Willie O'Neill – kicked it off by flicking water at residents off the end of a straw and the next thing I knew buckets of water were being thrown. I have no idea where the buckets materialised from, but the water fight spilled over into our bedrooms and we were forced to spend an uncomfortable night sleeping in damp beds. However, for all that we indulged in bouts of high jinxes, we never overstepped the mark to bring lasting shame on the club.

In spite of the many duties he faced as manager of Celtic, Jock also agreed to act as caretaker boss of the Scotland international team, following Ian McColl's departure. Scotland had important World Cup qualifying ties against Finland and Poland coming up. We had already beaten the Finns, 3–1, at Hampden to get the campaign off to a positive start and followed that result with a 2–2 draw at Wembley. Poland, in the industrial town of Chorzow, was next on the agenda and Jock's first game in charge coincided with a creditable 1–1 draw.

It didn't take him long, either, to establish a strict code of discipline at national level. On the first evening in Poland some of the players were discovered running a card school well past lights-out. Jock responded with a few well-chosen words before ripping up the cards and chucking them down the toilet! The trip to Poland was as far removed from the good life as you can get. We stayed in what was little better than a youth hostel, where the facilities were almost non-existent, and the atmosphere at the stadium was surreal. There was a full house, but you could have heard a pin drop. The mood of the fans matched the bleakness of our surroundings. There was no cover as such and it poured with rain for the entire ninety minutes.

That game was followed by a trip to Finland and it immediately became evident that reputations meant nothing to the manager; something we would all eventually learn to our cost. John Hughes was a Celtic player and Bobby Collins had been a huge favourite at Celtic Park prior to joining Everton. That mattered not at all to Jock. Both were dropped to make way for two players whose style of play he was familiar with from his time in charge at Hibs, and Willie Hamilton and Neil Martin were introduced in the hope that they would give the team a sharper cutting edge to boost goal average. Jock espoused the view that teams had to be chosen with a specific aim in mind and it was a policy he stuck to throughout his managerial career. It was my seventeenth appearance for my country and the side also contained the talents of such as Alex Hamilton, the very fine Dundee full-back, Paddy Crerand, his Manchester United team-mate, Denis Law, and John Greig and Willie Henderson of Rangers. But we didn't play particularly well and scraped a 2–1 victory in Helsinki.

With five points in the bag, Poland to be faced at Hampden and Italy home and away, we seemed to be heading for the 1966 World Cup finals. The prospect of taking on the Auld Enemy in their own back yard appealed greatly, but it wasn't to be. The chill winds of autumn brought with them a 2–1 home defeat by Poland. I captained the Scotland team and scored an early goal. A victory looked to be on the cards when we led going into the final phase of the game, but with just seven minutes remaining, it all went terribly pear-shaped. The Poles scored twice as a consequence of slack defending and, suddenly, our World Cup fate now rested on a double-header against Italy.

I had the misfortune to be excluded from the team for the home tie, highlighting the ruthless side to Jock's nature. I had been troubled by a niggling injury and Jock refused to take a chance on me lasting the ninety minutes. 'You aren't as fit as you should be,' he declared. Ronnie McKinnon was preferred to me and I was forced to spectate when the Rangers centre-half made his debut, on 9 November 1965, in front of a crowd exceeding 100,000. Scotland pounded the Italian defence for the most part, but the efforts of our strikers, Alan Gilzean and Neil Martin, proved fruitless and, with the referee poised to whistle for full time, our situation looked grim. But it's at times like these that great players invariably come into their own and Jim Baxter was no exception. For all that Jim lived life in the fast lane, preferring a hectic social life to training, he was nevertheless a truly outstanding footballer and loved pulling on the dark blue shirt of his country. With just seconds remaining, Jim played a perfect through ball for Greig to run on to and Greigy completed the match-winning move by driving the ball powerfully into the Italian net. The dream was still alive.

But in Naples, on 7 December, Jock and Scotland ran out of luck. A horrendous list of call-offs meant that almost an entire team was denied to the manager: goalkeeper Bill Brown, his Tottenham team-mates, Dave Mackay and Alan Gilzean, Rangers' flying winger, Henderson, Law, Ian St John and Baxter. I was also forced to miss out because of an injury. Jock's makeshift team, which included Liverpool centre-half, Ron Yeats, at centre-forward, never stood a chance. Scotland did well to deny the opposition until just before half-time, but once Italy had scored there was no way back. A 3–0 defeat meant Jock was free to concentrate fully on his duties at Celtic Park and, indeed, he decided to quit the part-time Scotland job to focus on being manager of Celtic.

By then it was mid-season and we were locked in a desperate struggle with Rangers for the title. Christmas Day was not an official public holiday in Scotland at that time. New Year was celebrated much more north of the border, so it was normal for teams to play on Christmas Day if it happened to fall on a Saturday. Obviously it was disruptive for players with young families, but, provided we were playing at home, we could spend time opening presents with the kids in the morning, before heading for the ground at lunch-time. I never found it a huge problem. Once the game had been played we still managed to have a family Christmas dinner in the evening when it was possible to let your hair down and have a few drinks, sometimes with team-mates, if we gathered together for a party. So, Christmas Day 1965 saw us hit eight goals past Morton at Celtic Park and we ended the year ahead of Rangers on goal average. When we whipped our arch rivals, 5–1, on 3 January 1966 the feeling grew that we were more than capable of adding the championship to the League Cup success we had enjoyed against Rangers the previous October.

That League Cup final win had been highly significant. We had proved to ourselves that we could beat Rangers in a final and, in doing so, dismantled a psychological barrier. Jock was often quoted as saying that playing Rangers was just another game, but that was nonsense. No game was more important to him, because he believed that Old Firm games were a continual proving ground. 'Don't mistake what you read for fact,' he would tell us. 'Those comments are for the benefit of the fans.'

As things turned out, winning the league proved a damn sight tougher than we had anticipated on the back of our Old Firm win at New Year. The championship went to the wire and only one minute remained of our match at Fir Park when Bobby Lennox scored to give us a 1–0 win over Motherwell and leave us two points clear of the opposition. However, I should point out that even if we had lost, Celtic would have been crowned champions for the first time for twelve years by virtue of our superior goal average.

There were nearly 127,000 at Hampden for the 1966 Scottish Cup final on 23 April, but they were short-changed in terms of entertainment. It was a dull affair with defences on top and the forwards lacking sufficient imagination to prise them open. The replay, the following Wednesday, was much livelier. We started favourites, but Rangers upset the odds, thanks largely to Jimmy Millar, who had an outstanding match. Jimmy Johnstone gave their left-back, Davie Provan, a bit of a roasting, but we missed two or three scoring chances and Kai Johansen won the trophy for Rangers with the only goal of the game in the seventieth minute.

Rangers may have had the satisfaction of beating us in the Scottish Cup final, but the championship was the one we all wanted most of all and we felt that we were entitled to celebrate our success. Most of us enjoyed a drink, but it tended to be a weekend thing. We weren't a bunch of Champagne Charlies, out on the town every night, and on those occasions when we did meet for a few drinks during the week we knew we could sweat off any excesses the following morning at training. To mark winning the championship, the team decamped to the Vesuvio restaurant in Glasgow's St Vincent Street. It had become our preferred watering hole because the owners, Mario Romano and Enzo Rippa, always ensured that we were left in peace. They protected us from the preying eyes of the press and public so we could let our hair down – and when the occasion demanded it we certainly knew how to do that.

Jock had also shown himself to be more than capable of rubbing shoulders with Europe's master tacticians in the Cup Winners' Cup, where we reached the last four. Having accounted for the Dutch side, Go Ahead, Aarhus, of Denmark, and Dinamo Kiev, our reward was a semi-final with Liverpool, which brought Stein and Bill Shankly into direct conflict. Jock was from Lanarkshire and Bill was an Ayrshireman, but those who are familiar with the traditional rivalries that exist between the two counties may be surprised to learn that they had the greatest respect for one another. Both were teetotal, non-smokers who placed great store in discipline. They also had the ability to lift their players by convincing them that they were superior to the opposition, no matter who they were up against.

They were also wonderful at manipulating the press for their own ends. Shanks's ability to talk up any player or situation meant that he was a journalist's dream. Some of his statements bordered on the outrageous, but he was great copy all the same. Jock, on the other hand, was brilliant at wiping Rangers off the back pages of the newspapers. Using his network of press contacts he would find out what news was coming out of Ibrox and then top it with a story of his own – even if it wasn't necessarily completely accurate. For example, if he was tipped off that Rangers had arranged a glamour friendly against Spurs, he would leak a story to his press contacts stating that Celtic were considering an offer to play Real Madrid. If he learned that Rangers were lining up a big-money bid for a player, he would respond by announcing that Celtic were in the market for two players! Because of his strong personality and Celtic's superiority over their Old Firm rivals at that time, Stein invariably commanded bigger headlines. If challenged later about the accuracy of a story he had leaked, he would simply respond by saying that his efforts had been unsuccessful and he would then issue a further story and keep Celtic on the back pages.

Jock was more subtle and, I guess, at the same time also more manipulative, but something had to give when he and Shankly went head-to-head in April 1966.

The first leg was played at Celtic Park and we emerged with a narrow advantage. Bobby Lennox's solitary strike six minutes into the second half separated the sides, but, if the truth be told, we missed two or three other scoring chances and our failure to build a bigger lead proved decisive in the return. We held out for an hour at Anfield, before caving in to goals from Tommy Smith and Geoff Strong, and Liverpool sneaked through to meet Borussia Dortmund in the final. The outcome might have been very different, though, because Bobby Lennox 'scored' what was a perfectly legitimate goal late in the game. He was adjudged to have been offside, but I swear blind to this day that the linesman called it wrong and the Liverpool players agreed afterwards that we had been 'robbed'. The fact that the final was being played at Hampden made defeat all the harder to take, because I believe, with our incredible support, we would have gone on to lift the trophy and become the first Scottish team to triumph in Europe a year ahead of schedule. However, it had still turned out to be a highly successful first full season for Celtic under Stein, who was also named British Manager of the Year.

Jock had already established a tradition of taking us away for a few days prior to big games. We breathed the bracing sea air on the coast at Largs or Seamill and the change of scenery did us the world of good, but that summer we swapped Ayrshire for Bermuda on the first leg of a five-week tour to the States and Canada. We were given a taste of the millionaire lifestyle, enjoying the splendid luxury of the five-star Princess Hotel. It was Jock's way of rewarding us for our efforts and highlighting the benefits of success.

The tour was funded by the American Football Federation and it was a mix of work and pleasure. In addition to a couple of games in Bermuda, we also played matches in New York, St Louis, San Francisco and Vancouver, against sides of the calibre of Tottenham and Bologna. In fact, we played Spurs three times, beating them twice and drawing the other game. The success we enjoyed against Spurs was particularly significant in building confidence and self-belief and, to this day, whenever I bump into Alan Mullery, the former England player, he always asks if Bobby Lennox still possesses the same blistering pace. I have painful memories of the game against Bologna, though, as my face came into contact with an Italian head and I ended up in a Manhattan hospital having several stitches put in an eye wound.

The week we spent in Bermuda had effectively been a holiday, though. Few of us had visited that part of the world previously and it was a fabulous adventure. It represented paradise compared to the greyness of Glasgow. I had never even seen a proper barbecue until we visited the local cricket club. Our hotel was also the last word in luxury and attracted big-name entertainers. Bruce Forsyth was booked as the cabaret act and we became friendly with him, but Brucie avoided the fate that befell the hotel's assistant manager, an Irishman by the name of Pat O'Reardon. On our last day we threw Pat into the swimming pool, but resisted the temptation to chuck Brucie in after him, when he complained that he was suffering from a bad back.

I believe that tour laid much of the groundwork for the success that was to follow under Stein. Living in such close proximity for an extended period of time enabled us to get to know one another better. It was a form of bonding and increased our understanding of each other's personalities. Relationships were consolidated and these remain strong to this day. It was part and parcel of our future successes. We were capable of being an aggressive, argumentative bunch at times, but we were also a squad who stood together when the chips were down. It was a masterstroke by Jock and what was to follow in the coming twelve months would surpass all previous achievements by the length of Sauchiehall Street.

# CHAPTER 5

# INTERNATIONAL AFFAIRS

I had the misfortune to make the international debut from hell when I pulled on a dark blue jersey for the first time as a member of the full Scotland team. It had always been my dream to play for my country and in those days Wembley was something of a Holy Grail for Scotland fans, who made the pilgrimage to the capital in their tens of thousands for the bi-annual skirmish with the English. But when the final whistle sounded at 4.40 pm on 15 April 1961, they and I wished we were anywhere but London.

England 9 Scotland 3 – I still wince at the memory of the most humiliating defeat a Scottish side has suffered. It was one of the lowest points of my career and my first painful lesson on just how cruel sport can be. More than forty years have passed since that day, but nothing will ever completely expunge the memory. What was essentially a proud moment, playing in my first international, turned out to be an absolute disaster.

I wasn't the only debutant that day. There were three other new-comers: Bobby Shearer, the Rangers full-back, Johnny MacLeod, a winger with Hibs, and Pat Quinn, of Motherwell. But were we really so bad? Probably not. It was just one of those days when everything

England attempted came off for them, while every mistake we made was magnified and punished in the most brutal fashion possible. It also has to be said that England had a host of very talented players and it seemed that every one of them struck top form on the day. Johnny Haynes orchestrated the moves, Jimmy Greaves was like greased lightning and Bobby Robson oozed class.

We were also handicapped within the first few minutes when MacLeod suffered an ankle injury. There were no substitutes in those days and MacLeod was a virtual passenger, hobbling his way through the game on the wing. Incredibly, there was a stage in the game when we hauled England back to 3–2 after Davie Wilson, the Rangers winger, scored early in the second-half. Maybe that just made them angry, but Bryan Douglas 'stole' a couple of yards for their fourth goal, when he moved the ball forward at a free kick, which shouldn't have been awarded in the first place, and restored England's two-goal advantage. We disintegrated after that and, with Haynes, scorer of two of their goals, and Greaves, who notched a hat-trick, in outstanding form, England took us apart. I got some idea of how Custer felt at the Little Big Horn as the England forwards bore down on us with ruthless efficiency.

Frank Haffey, my Celtic team-mate, was in goal and he, by his own admission, did not have the best of games. He could not be held solely responsible for what was a shocking display, but, inevitably, he became the butt of cruel humour. The ball was orange and it was said that Frank refused to touch it and that the Rangers full-backs, Shearer and Eric Caldow, refused to kick it! Those versed in the religious divisions of the West of Scotland will require no further explanation but, for the benefit of the uninitiated, in the eyes of some people, the Orange Order represents Protestantism. However, perhaps the cruellest trick played on Frank involved a newspaper photographer spotting that our train had arrived at Glasgow's Central Station the following day alongside platform nine. The sharp-eyed snapper duly persuaded Frank to pose for a picture with the number nine forming the backdrop.

Hardly surprisingly, Frank never played for Scotland again. The Wembley debacle was only his second, and last, international. Bert McCann, the Motherwell wing-half, also paid the ultimate price. It was Bert's fifth Scotland appearance and he must have known in his heart of hearts that there would not be a sixth. On the Saturday evening following the game Bert, Ian St John, Pat Quinn, scorer of our third goal (Dave Mackay and Wilson got the others), Dunky McKay and myself had sought refuge in a backstreet London pub in an effort to escape the attentions of the media and the fans. The intention was to drown our sorrows with pints of overpriced beer in the hope that the effects of the alcohol would dull the pain sufficiently to allow us to sleep free from nightmare images of Haynes and company scoring for fun.

We were in possession of visas for the forthcoming World Cup qualifying game against Czechoslovakia in Bratislava the following month and, as the evening wore on, Bert suggested that we should have a ritual burning of the documentation, as none of us would be making the trip behind the Iron Curtain. Bert duly set his visa alight and watched it turn to ashes, clearly suspecting that his international career had gone the same way. Thankfully, the rest of us resisted such temptation and it was as well that we did, for Bert was the only one of our group overlooked when the next squad was named. There was a third Celtic player in the squad, Dunky McKay. He, however, had the good fortune to be twelfth man – and never was any player more relieved.

My team-mates will not thank me for reminding them, but this is how the teams lined-up all those years ago: England: Springett, Armfield, McNeil, Robson, Swan, Flowers, Douglas, Greaves, Smith, Haynes, Charlton. Scotland: Haffey, Shearer, Caldow; Mackay, McNeill, McCann, MacLeod, Law, St John, Quinn, Wilson.

Just one week later, with my emotions still in turmoil, Celtic took the field against Dunfermline in the Scottish Cup final. Was it any wonder that we lost, albeit after a replay? The fates were clearly conspiring against poor Frank Haffey who was responsible for a howler in the closing stages of the replay. Frank eventually emigrated to Australia where he made a new life for himself far from Wembley's Twin Towers and Glasgow's Central Station!

Without wishing to make excuses, international football tended to be pretty disorganised back then. There was precious little advance planning and, as a first-timer, I didn't have time to get to know my team-mates properly. I had played against most of them, of course, but the squad met up three days before a game and, although Ian McColl was manager in name at least, the real power lay with the SFA International Committee. They were the selectors and, as the name suggests, they picked the players for international duty. There was never any doubt in my mind that politics played a big part in deciding who was chosen. The committee was made up of club directors and I am sure that it was often a case of, 'You select one of my players and I'll choose one of yours.' That seemed to be the sole function of the selectors and international trips were effectively an all-expenses paid junket for the officials. No great thought was given to establish continuity and international matches, other than World Cup qualifiers, tended to involve the home countries, with the occasional fixture against a foreign side thrown in to boost the SFA's coffers.

Of course, there were far fewer opportunities to play for your country forty years ago so it meant a lot to be chosen, perhaps more than it does to the modern day player. Because of the volume of games, the modern day player can amass a large number of caps in an incredibly short space of time, and the competition for places is probably less intense.

I have a host of happy memories of international football, but I think the highlight was our win over England at Hampden twelve months after the Wembley debacle. Scotland had not beaten England in Glasgow since 1937, so to end a twenty-five-year wait in the manner we did gave us all a wonderful feeling of pride and achievement. We effectively regained our self respect and restored the fans' pride in the international team.

Five of the team had suffered the humiliation of playing in the 9–3 defeat and that was probably the key to our success. We were fired up by the need for revenge and played like men possessed. Beating England had little to do with a game plan, but I think the England players were taken aback by the ferocity of our approach. We fought for every ball and were so energised that we could have run and chased all day long. One report suggested that we were Scotland's best team for twenty-five years and added that England were fortunate to hold us to two goals. Significantly, it was the first time for fifteen games that England had failed to score.

We completely dominated the play for the first hour and only a good deal of luck and some inspirational goalkeeping by Ron Springett kept us down to a single goal in the first half. Denis Law was the architect of the goal when, after thirteen minutes, he dribbled round Springett and presented Davie Wilson with the simplest of chances. Denis was outstanding and his darting runs and constant movement pressurised the England defence. John White was also immense in the way he created space for himself and provided team-mates with a target to aim at. Our second goal came from the penalty spot, when Eric Caldow converted after Peter Swan had handled. In truth, though, England escaped lightly on an afternoon when we completely out-classed our opponents, two of whom, Ray Wilson and Bobby Charlton, later played in the 1966 World Cup final victory.

Any win over England was the ultimate for a Scotsman in those days and I was fortunate enough to be on the winning side again in 1964. I also played in the 2–2 draw at Wembley in 1965 and the 1–1 draw in Glasgow three years later. I prefer to forget the other three clashes against the Auld Enemy, in which I featured as they resulted in defeats – and losing to England was the pits.

The manner of our 1961 thrashing did not bode well for the next match, at the start of May, against the Republic of Ireland at Hampden, in the first part of a World Cup qualifier double-header. But, perhaps surprisingly, six of us retained our place and at least the selectors' apparent faith in some players was fully vindicated when Scotland won, 4–1. One who was not forgiven quite so readily was Denis Law. There was no greater patriot than Denis and I recall him telling me years later that he had found it difficult to resist physical retaliation, when he was the victim of so many jibes by both English team-mates and opponents in the wake of the heaviest defeat ever suffered by a Scotland team.

Like the rest of us, Denis's performance at Wembley had not matched his true abilities, but he had certainly not lacked passion or commitment. Indeed, I am sure Sir Bobby Robson would testify to that, for he was on the receiving end of a challenge by Denis in front of the Royal Box that left a lasting impression. I felt it was especially unfair of the selectors to point a finger at Denis because, such was his loyalty to the national team that he angered his club by choosing to play for Scotland. The club game he missed was a league match between Manchester City and West Ham, which had a significant bearing on City's First Division survival prospects.

In the event of Denis's absence, David Herd of Arsenal, who had been overlooked for two years, and Ralph Brand, the Rangers striker, were recalled to spearhead the attack, and they scored two apiece. Brand also netted in the three-goal success we enjoyed in Dublin four days later. But if I imagined that being part of the international football scene wasn't so bad after all, I was in for a rude awakening when we travelled to Czechoslovakia the following week, bidding to secure a win that would take Scotland a significant step closer to the World Cup finals in Chile the following summer.

There were only two changes to the team that had beaten the Irish, with Herd returning in place of Alex Young, who had scored two of our goals in Dublin, and Rangers' talented midfield player, Ian McMillan, the man known as 'The Wee Prime Minister', coming in to replace Quinn. If the back-to-back wins over the Irish had lulled us into a false sense of security that the Wembley result had just been one of those days, the Czechs quickly disabused us of the notion. A four-goal defeat was the sort of wake-up call that makes you sit up with a start. But we somehow succeeded in repairing the damage in the return at Hampden the following September and a double from Law and another from St John earned us a 3–2 victory and set up a play-off against the Czechs for a place in the finals.

Denis was a revelation and he had few poor games for Scotland. His electrifying darts into the penalty box allied to his razor sharp reflexes were his strongest assets. He also had a wonderful sense of anticipation, which enabled him to snap up half-chances when the ball broke off a defender, but perhaps people were less aware of just how tough and durable Denis was. In spite of his lean frame, Denis was as hard as nails. He gave and took knocks without complaint. His incredible timing and his ability to appear to almost hang in the air meant he had to be brave when he jumped for the ball with a big, bruising central defender.

Having managed to score eight goals in total against Northern Ireland and Wales prior to the play-off against Czechoslovakia in Brussels in November, there was an air of quiet confidence about the team that lined up in the Heysel Stadium. I had the misfortune to be injured and Ian Ure, the Dundee centre-half, who was to go on to play with distinction for Arsenal and Manchester United, took my place, having made his debut the previous month in the 2–0 win over Wales. Scotland were very much underdogs but, inspired by two goals from St John, the team pushed the Czechs all the way. We led twice and there were only eight minutes remaining when the opposition equalised for a second time, but a combination of the marginally superior skills of the Czech players and Scotland's tiring legs during extra-time proved too much. Scotland's 4–2 defeat meant there would be no place for us at the World Cup finals the following summer, but it's worth pointing out that Czechoslovakia contested the final against Brazil.

I am not suggesting that Scotland would have matched that achievement had we succeeded in beating Czechoslovakia in the play-off, but it was a measure of how far the team had come in the seven months since the England game. A feature of the team at that time was the contributions made by Dave Mackay and Jim Baxter. Although very different types of players they complemented each other in many ways. Dave was a complete all-rounder. He tackled like a demon and when he won the ball, which was almost every time, he used it to great effect. Perhaps not as mobile or as cavalier as Jim, Dave was nevertheless blessed with great ball control and had the ability to play intelligent passes. Dave was the sort who you would want by your side in the trenches. Tough as old boots and imbued with a never-say-die spirit, Dave was also very supportive of the younger players and I was grateful for his help and advice.

Dave was one of three Spurs players who were regulars in the Scotland side. Goalkeeper Bill Brown and the late, great John White were the others, and the three of them were always up to some sort of mischief. I remember Dave turning up to join the squad at Heathrow Airport and going to collect his flight ticket, only to discover when he opened the envelope that it had been ripped up into a dozen pieces. He was forced to borrow a role of sticky tape and piece it back together before he was allowed to board the aircraft. The three of them were always issuing crazy challenges and, on another occasion, in Stavanger, prior to playing Norway, Dave's White Hart Lane team-mates dared him to jump fully clothed into the harbour. Without further ado he threw himself feet first into the water!

Jim Baxter saw it almost as a duty to entertain and few Scottish players have given as much pleasure as Jim did in April 1967 when he orchestrated Scotland's 3–2 win at Wembley against the then world champions, six years to the day since the boot had been on the other foot. Jim was a complete extrovert who was, at various times, irreverent, undisciplined and downright potty, but he was also great fun to be with and generous to a fault. Jim believed in pushing life to the limit. A Fifer from the quaintly named village of Hill O' Beath, he came from mining stock. He enjoyed a good drink and a bet on the horses and, having survived not one but two liver transplant operations in 1994, he continued to live in the fast lane. He died in 2001, at the age of sixty-one, insisting that he was really 183 because he had effectively lived three lifetimes in one!

His natural aversion to training meant that Jim's career was over by the age of thirty. A combination of wild living and a taste for Bacardi denied us the sight of Baxter strutting his stuff for another four or five years, but you also have to ask, would he have been the same player had he not been such a flamboyant character? Probably not. Jim was a one-off. I recall hearing the story of Jim sitting in the Wembley dressing room in 1967, ten minutes before Scotland went out to face the world champions, with his nose buried in a newspaper studying the horse racing section. Bobby Brown, the manager, approached him and suggested that it might be a good idea if he did some stretching exercises to ensure he was properly warmed-up. Jim responded by lifting each leg in turn and pushing it out to the side before resuming his examination of the current form.

Another time, when we were on Scotland duty in Norway, Jim suddenly announced that he was for the off. 'I've had it with this lot, Cesar,' Jim suddenly declared, late one evening after several drinks had been taken. Referring to the SFA hierarchy, he added, 'That lot couldn't run a p***-up in a brewery.' I eventually succeeded in talking Jim out of his one-man rebellion, on the grounds that there was absolutely nowhere for him to go at that time of night, and we headed back to the team's hotel, but I was powerless to prevent Jim venting his ire at Willie Allan, the autocratic SFA secretary. Allan got both barrels before Jim signalled his utter contempt by flicking a balled up piece of paper in the direction of the luckless official and hitting him on the head. Given the power that the secretary wielded, it was a measure of Jim's greatness that his international career survived the incident.

I am glad to say that I enjoyed Jim's friendship for many years and I will always remember him as a great footballer and a thoroughly decent individual. Jim never lost his Fife twang and the last time I saw him he was still the same devil-may-care individual as when he first walked through the front door at Ibrox forty years earlier.

It seems ridiculous that Jim won just thirty-four caps. In 1960, when he made his Scotland debut in a 5–2 win against Northern Ireland at Hampden, Jim had a natural athleticism and he lost none of his fitness during the next five years. Some critics accused Jim of being a lazy player, but that wasn't true. He may have managed to give the impression of being disinterested at times, but Jim covered a hell of a lot of ground in the course of a game, plus he didn't have to expend huge levels of energy to be effective. He was blessed with natural talent. He could read a game better than most and see situations developing, which he could exploit, quicker than others. When Jim had the ball at his feet he had few equals. He was able to deliver short or long passes with great precision. Jim had wonderful control and he could also dribble with the ball. But it was Jim's ability to dominate games that marked him out as special. Jim was forever demanding the ball and inviting passes, which gave the team an instant outlet under pressure. Pele paid Jim the ultimate compliment when he suggested that his rival should have been born a Brazilian. Lofty praise indeed, but richly deserved all the same.

Following the Hampden victory over England in April 1962, over the next two years I was forced to vie with Ian Ure for a place. Ronnie McKinnon of Rangers and Ron Yeats, the Liverpool captain, also offered competition, but after making my fourteenth Scotland appearance in April 1965, in the 2–2 draw at Wembley, I enjoyed a six-match run before injury sidelined me and I drifted off the international scene for a while. Bobby Brown recalled me to the team against Russia at Hampden in May 1967, incidentally, a match we lost, 2–0, and I featured in six of Scotland's next fourteen internationals, but I was resigned to having played my last game for my country when I was omitted from the squad following our 3–2 defeat by West Germany in Hamburg in October 1969. My Celtic Park team-mate, Tommy Gemmell, was ordered off and the defeat signalled the end of our hopes of qualifying for the Mexico World Cup finals.

So, it came as something of a surprise, nearly three years later, when I got the call from Tommy Docherty. I was by then thirty-two, but Doc obviously felt I was still capable of doing a job for him and my recall for the Home International Championship turned out to be one of the most enjoyable experiences of my career. The period the squad spent at Largs on the Ayrshire coast was a lot of fun. Doc's very charismatic and didn't mind us larking about at times, but he was serious in his desire to achieve success for Scotland and also encouraged us to indulge our natural talents and play a lot of things off the cuff. I found him a stimulating and exciting personality and his training methods centred on short, sharp exercises to avoid the risk of boredom. He's also a great raconteur and never tired of recounting stories of his own career. Doc isn't everyone's cup of tea, and he certainly isn't the sort to stand any nonsense, but I am a fan – and not just because he extended my Scotland career by three games against Northern Ireland, Wales and England. In the event, we won the first two games before suffering a 1–0 defeat by England in what turned out to be my twenty-ninth and final Scotland appearance. It was the only time I worked with Doc, but I will always feel eternally grateful to him.

In actual fact, I had the chance to bow out on one of the greatest football stages of all, when Doc invited me to accompany the squad to Brazil for a three-game tour, culminating in a showdown with the hosts in the fabulous Maracana Stadium in Rio. Rather stupidly, I allowed Jock Stein to talk me out of going. Jock pointed out that the trip was sandwiched between what had been a long, hard domestic season and the beginning of another one and added that I wasn't getting any younger. On reflection, I should have ignored Jock's advice and realised a dream, but I turned Doc down and, a short time later, also rejected the chance to join him at Old Trafford, when he became manager of Manchester United.

However, my only real regret from my time as a Scotland player was that I never had the opportunity to appear in the World Cup finals. We came desperately close in 1962, and again four years later. Had Scotland made it to the 1966 finals in England I think it would have been very interesting indeed, but it wasn't to be.

The 1970 qualifying campaign turned out to be my last chance, but the draw was again unkind to us when we came out of the hat with

West Germany. At least we ran them close, though, losing in the Hamburg game, and before that drawing 1–1 at Hampden.

Nearly four years separated my first Scotland goal – in the 2–1 defeat by Poland at Hampden in October 1965 – and my last – in our 8–0 defeat of Cyprus in a World Cup qualifying tie in May 1969. However, while I managed only three in total, only fifteen days separated the second and third after I scored in a 5–3 win against Wales at Wrexham. I didn't even come close to having my portrait hung in the SFA's Hall of Fame, but I am very proud of my tally of twenty-nine appearances. For me, there was no greater honour than pulling on the dark blue shirt of my country. Every time I did so I could feel my chest swell with pride.

There was a time when I harboured the ambition of becoming Scotland manager, and I felt that might happen immediately following the 1986 World Cup finals in Mexico, but Andy Roxburgh was appointed instead, after Sir Alex Ferguson had taken over on a part-time basis following the sudden death of Jock Stein the previous September. My optimism proved unfounded and I knew then that I was highly unlikely ever to receive a call from SFA headquarters offering me the job that would have been second only to being manager of Celtic.

Ironically, I was given the opportunity to become a manager at international level when I was offered the Republic of Ireland job, prior to Jack Charlton taking over in 1986. I was with Manchester City at the time and the chairman, Peter Swales, granted me permission to talk with Irish FA officials. Their feeling was that I would be able to fill the role on a part-time basis as most of the players were based in England and, of course, I would be on hand to assess their current form. But after talking the matter through with Swales, I quickly came to the conclusion that it would not be practical to try to divide my time between City and the Republic. Frankly, I would have been in danger of short-changing both employers as I have always held the view that you must give total commitment to the job of being a club manager.

The Irish FA then offered me the job on a full-time basis and, while I was flattered to be held in such high esteem, I still hoped that Scotland would seek my services once Fergie had relinquished the post. I even went as far as to enquire of a high-ranking SFA official, who had sounded me out, whether, by agreeing to become manager of Ireland, I would prejudice my chances. I was advised that it might well do, so I said 'thanks, but no thanks' to the Irish – only to be snubbed by the SFA.

# CHAPTER 6

# THE GLORY ROAD

I am often asked at what point did I begin to believe that Celtic could win the European Cup? To be honest, I never thought about the prospect of us actually winning the trophy on the road to Lisbon. We simply viewed it as a great adventure, from the moment we launched our campaign against Swiss champions FC Zurich on the evening of 28 September 1966 at Celtic Park until our arrival in the Portuguese capital eight months later.

Zurich were a decent side, but they tended to put the emphasis on physical contact and I remember wee Jimmy Johnstone being singled out for special attention. Jinky took a lot of stick and ended the game black and blue, but we won comfortably all the same. For most of the time we were on the offensive, but it took us until midway through the second-half to turn our superiority into a goal, when Tommy Gemmell scored after sixty-four minutes. Joe McBride claimed a second five minutes later to put us in the driving seat for the return in Zurich a week later.

Jock Stein had chosen to ignore the maxim of teams defending a lead away from home in Europe and we were given full reign to attack in Switzerland. Jock recognised that it was alien to our nature to be defensive and invariably encouraged our attacking flair. Zurich put us under pressure during the opening period of the game, but when Tommy Gemmell scored somewhat against the run of play, the tie was dead. He scored a second – with a penalty – early in the second second-half and Stevie Chalmers completed a satisfactory night's work by notching a third to give us a 5–0 aggregate victory.

In the second round we were drawn against Nantes, with the first leg away from home. French football was not of the standard we came to expect after the national team won both the World Cup and European Championship, but Nantes could not be dismissed lightly. Nantes, in fact, opened the scoring, but Jock stuck to his pledge that we would carry on playing attacking football. Indeed, the French side were probably taken aback by the fact that we continued to look to exploit openings, rather than try to contain them and settle for a narrow defeat. Consequently, we quickly clawed our way back into the game and Joe McBride equalised after twenty-four minutes. The goal settled us and two more from Bobby Lennox and Stevie Chalmers in the second-half ensured that we had a healthy lead for the return.

We won by an identical score at Celtic Park at the start of December and the margin of our success, against substantial opposition, began to make others sit up and take notice. On reflection, there was probably greater conviction about our win in France, but any team scoring six for the loss of only two goals is worthy of respect and we had clearly earned our stripes in our first venture in the European Cup.

Following the Nantes tie, there was a break of three months when the tournament entered a winter recess, but we had plenty of time to relish the prospect of a quarter-final against the Yugoslav side, Vojvodina, the following March. The first leg was to be played away and I sensed that Vojvodina would almost certainly be a much tougher nut to crack than either Zurich or Nantes. My judgement proved correct. Jock Stein also recognised the strength of Yugoslav football and cleverly arranged for us to play a friendly against another Slav team, Dinamo Zagreb, early in February, to get a firm indication of what we could expect from Vojvodina. In the event, we lost to a late goal, but Jock was able to experiment and gain valuable knowledge.

Vojvodina had a powerful physical presence with big and strong players. For forty-five minutes in Novi Sad we had to defend brilliantly to keep them out and we were relieved to go in at the interval with a blank score sheet. Having weathered the storm, we felt that the Vojvodina players might be feeling just a little dispirited at not having managed to turn their pressure into at least one goal and the second-half proved to be a little less frenetic. However, Vojvodina were the most difficult opponents we had to beat that season. They had both power and skill and a mistake by Tommy Gemmell allowed them to secure a slender lead. He attempted to play a pass back to John Clark and mishit the ball. Clark was taken by surprise and allowed the ball to run to Stanic, who had the easiest of finishes. I must confess that I missed a good chance to level the match but, by then, we felt that we could give any team a goal start and beat them at home. Vojvodina, though, had other ideas.

With a 75,000 crowd packed into Celtic Park, the atmosphere was electric, but the Vojvodina players appeared to be unaffected by their hostile surroundings. Indeed, they created an early chance and if they had scored then I question whether we would have been able to come back, but we got the break we needed and eventually scored thirteen minutes into the second-half. Stevie Chalmers cashed-in on a mistake by the goalkeeper and levelled the tie. There was a palpable sense of relief among our players that we were going to get a replay at least.

The tension had reached breaking point as the game entered the final minute, but we were determined to mount one last desperate assault and Jinky burst down the right side to force a corner. Charlie Gallagher elected to take the kick and flighted a perfect cross on to my head. I timed my jump to perfection and I can still see in my mind's eye the ball going into the net, but if Vojvodina had not chosen to position the smallest player in their team on the line, it might not have gone in. There have been few more dramatic climaxes to any game at Celtic Park and I suspect they heard the roars of the Celtic fans four miles away at Ibrox.

Having had experience of the Czechoslovak international team, I realised that our semi-final opponents, Dukla Prague, were deserving of the utmost respect and we treated them accordingly in the first leg at Celtic Park on 12 April. Dukla counted among their number the legendary Josef Masopust, who had captained his country in the 1962 World Cup final against Brazil, and were vastly experienced, but we were by now brimful of confidence, having accounted for Vojvodina.

That confidence appeared to be fully justified when Jinky gave us the lead, but the first half didn't quite go to script. Strunc equalised seconds from the interval and it was game on for a second time. However, Willie Wallace, who had been purchased from Hearts just the previous December, paid off his £30,000 transfer fee at one fell swoop with two goals in the space of six minutes, and the odds swung dramatically in our favour for the return in Prague thirteen days later.

For once, Jock decided that we should abandon our attacking philosophy and prepare for a siege. I don't recall him actually saying that we should expect to have our backs to the wall for ninety minutes, but it certainly seemed that way for much of the game. I don't think we made it beyond our 18-yard line for the first twenty-five minutes. Whether by design or through necessity, the plan worked to perfection and the frustrations of the Dukla players became increasingly evident the longer the game went without them scoring. I had a half chance with a shot in the first-half, but it hardly mattered when we secured the 0–0 draw that took us into the final, the first British team to achieve such a distinction.

The bitter disappointment of the Dukla players was evident and none was more emotionally scarred than Masopust. He, in fact, refused to shake hands at full time. His reaction was wholly understandable, given the depth of his emotion when he realised that he would probably not have another chance to reach the final, and later he came to our dressing room to offer a sincere apology. We appreciated the gesture, but even if he had simply faded into the night without bothering to explain himself it would not have mattered, for Masopust was a truly great player. Life behind the Iron Curtain could not have been much fun, even for the leading sportsmen, and success on the sports field probably meant a little more to them than it did to those of us fortunate enough to live in a free society.

The drabness of Dukla's strip typified our bleak surroundings. It was a mixture of khaki and grey and highlighted the fact that Dukla was the army team. Prague is a beautiful capital, but what was effectively Soviet rule cast a dark pall over the city. Little did we realise then that just one year later the Russian tanks would roll in and bring further repression. Thankfully, Prague is once again blooming and has clearly recaptured much of its old magic, but some things don't change. When I visited the city again in February 2004 for Celtic's UEFA Cup-tie against FK Teplice, I realised that I was staying at the same hotel where the team had resided in 1967. The place was built during the period of Soviet influence in that part of the world and is typically Russian in scale – large and imposing with a magnificent staircase and spacious bedrooms. Minor changes had been made to the décor but, in the main, the ornate design remains largely untouched. It has a certain opulence that exemplifies the character of East European cities. The hotel is also just a stone's throw from the stadium and the ground was so close that we actually walked there. Somehow, I can't imagine the Real Madrid players hoofing it to a European Cup semi-final!

Masopust wasn't the only one who felt a need to say sorry. Jock was also apologetic. He vowed to never again adopt such defensive tactics, but there was no need for him to explain himself. The ends fully justified the means as far as our fans were concerned, but Jock's concern was indicative of the man and his philosophy about how the game should be played. He was rarely negative in his thinking and believed that football is part of the entertainment industry. Having said that, results determine the fate of managers and I can understand those fighting for survival who adopt the view that it's more important to avoid defeat than it is to satisfy the demands of the purists. They, like the rest of us, have a duty to provide for their families and there aren't many more precarious professions.

However, there was no time to celebrate our achievement in reaching the final. Just four days later we had another big game to contend with when we met Aberdeen in the Scottish Cup final at Hampden Park. Willie Wallace, who had been the hero of the hour in the first leg against Dukla, again emerged as our match-winner, with goals either side of half-time, and Aberdeen were beaten, 2–0, by the same eleven who had held out in Prague.

With the League Cup, which had been won by dint of a 1–0 victory over Rangers the previous October, and the Scottish Cup also secured, that left only the league championship to be won to complete the grand slam of domestic honours. And on 6 May, nearly three weeks before the European Cup final, we attained the one point we needed to take the title when we drew, 2–2, with Rangers at Ibrox. The game, incidentally, was watched by Helenio Herrera, manager of Inter Milan, who we had learned would be our opponents in Lisbon.

Inter had booked their place in the final via a play-off against CSKA Sofia and I suspect that most observers, with the exception of those with Celtic leanings, imagined that the outcome of the final was already a foregone conclusion. We were clearly highly regarded at home, though, as four of the Celtic team – Ronnie Simpson, Tommy Gemmell, Willie Wallace and Bobby Lennox – had been included in the Scotland side which beat England, 3–2, at Wembley on 15 April, with Bobby scoring one of the goals in an historic victory. And on 10 May no fewer than seven Celtic players faced Russia at Hampden. Simpson, Gemmell and Lennox were joined by John Clark, Jimmy Johstone and me, with Willie Wallace coming on as a substitute for Denis Law. Unfortunately, Tommy Gemmell had the misfortune to score an own goal and we lost, 2–0.

When I hear modern day players complaining about having to play too many games I allow myself a wry smile at the thought of how some of us faced the exigencies of a sixty-match programme, excluding internationals, but we never seemed to feel tired or jaded. There was too much happening for us to have time to dwell on the demands placed on a successful team.

A week before going to Lisbon, Jock took the squad to Seamill, on the Ayrshire coast, to complete our preparations for the biggest game in the club's history and I think it was at that point that we realised our newfound standing in the game. We suddenly became aware of our importance. The Italian media were everywhere. We couldn't escape their TV cameras, even on the golf course, and it seemed to be one long round of interviews, but I wouldn't have swapped that period of my career for anything, though little did I know then that life would never be the same again following the events of 25 May 1967.

# A PRIDE
# OF LIONS

I ndividually the Lisbon Lions were not the most accomplished players in Europe, but collectively, for one season at least, we were the best team.

There were times when we were at each other's throats and nowhere was the rivalry greater than on the training pitch. Jock Stein used to pick two teams to play practice games, one wearing training bibs, the other without. Depending on his mood, the teams might not change for a fortnight, by which time the competitive element had grown to the point where we were really laying into each other. Physical confrontation becomes almost inevitable in these circumstances and there were quite a few incidents. Most of these 'punch-ups' lasted no more than a few seconds, before the other players rushed in and pulled the protagonists apart. That's the way it is on the training ground, and blows are rarely struck, but I recall one period lasting several weeks when the bibs hadn't managed to beat the non-bibs once and tempers had become positively explosive. Jock sensed that the situation was in danger of getting completely out of hand and wisely decided to shuffle the teams around before someone got hurt. However, to the world at large, we displayed a united front and any disputes and differences were kept in-house.

Much has been made of the fact that Jock Stein assembled a squad from within a twenty-five mile radius of Glasgow, something that could never happen in the modern game, and I believe that was a significant factor, although perhaps not the key to our success. Certainly, there was never any shortage of aggression. That was an essential ingredient in our make-up and it formed an integral part of our very determined attitude. But we won, and occasionally lost, as a team and we celebrated together just as hard as we played. Jock regularly took us away for a couple of days' rest and relaxation and he turned a blind eye to us letting our hair down and having a few drinks. He was clever that way. Jock didn't approve of alcohol, but he realised that we needed a safety valve to let off steam.

I think, too, that was why we rarely flew home from Europe directly after a game. He gave us our heads, because he realised that we would simply go out and enjoy ourselves in Glasgow where the potential for problems was probably greater, but while we certainly knew how to party, we never allowed our social activities to impinge on the football side of the business.

Being able to laugh was another important aspect. There were times when we behaved like a bunch of kids, but it was good for morale. Jimmy Johnstone and Bobby Lennox, two of the youngest members of the squad, were the principal pranksters and they rarely missed an opportunity to get up to mischief. For example, at that time neither of them played golf and they thought it was hilarious when they stood on the ball and pressed it into the ground or threw it into a bunker or the thick rough. Whenever they were quizzed as to the ball's whereabouts they managed to appear entirely innocent and just shrugged their shoulders. Given that Bobby never played the game during his career, it's interesting to note that he has since developed into an enthusiast who spends a large part of his life on the golf course.

However, the Lisbon Lions might never have been heard of but for the intervention of our chairman, Sir Bob Kelly, and his prompt action sixteen months before we made history. He prevented a potential tragedy on a par with the Munich air disaster that wiped out the bulk of the Manchester United team in February 1958. We were returning from a European Cup Winners' Cup tie against Dinamo Kiev in Tbilisi in January 1966 when the drama unfolded. The temperature had plummeted to well below zero when, because of a technical fault, our Aer Lingus flight landed at Stockholm and the aircraft quickly began to ice up. After two failed attempts at take off, the pilot was set to try again when Sir Bob suddenly leapt to his feet and ordered him to abort the take-off, convinced that the pilot was tempting fate.

We spent the night at the Swedish capital's world-famous Grand Hotel, which was the setting for the movie *The Prize*, starring Paul Newman and Edward G Robinson, and eventually arrived back in Glasgow twenty-four hours later. But despite stepping off the plane at 12.15 a.m. on Saturday, Jock took us straight to Celtic Park for a training session under the floodlights, as we were due to play Hearts at Tynecastle the following afternoon, the Scottish League having turned down a request to postpone the match. Incidentally, we won the match, 2–1, but so much for the administrators assisting the efforts of Scottish clubs in Europe. However, at least we survived the moment and eight of the side who drew 1–1 in the Ukraine went on to play in Lisbon.

Incredibly, the Lisbon Lions only ever won one European match – the final itself. We were, in fact, together for only three games against Continental opposition: the semi-final second leg against Dukla

Prague in Czechoslovakia and the opening game of our defence on 20 September 1967. The holders were not normally included in the following season's first round draw, but the Albanian champions withdrew, leaving thirty-two teams, and we went into the hat along with the rest. When we were drawn against Dinamo Kiev we knew we faced a stiff test. However, we could not have imagined that we would produce one of our poorest European displays for years when we entertained the Russians at Celtic Park.

For reasons I cannot explain we were completely out of sorts and our shakiness in defence enabled Kiev to take a two-goal lead. Bobby Lennox pulled a goal back in the second-half, but a 2–1 defeat meant that we were faced with having to do what no other team had managed in the Ukraine – win a tie after losing at home. When Bobby Murdoch, who had been cautioned earlier, was sent off after fifty-nine minutes, for throwing the ball away in frustration, the improbable looked impossible. We were required to score twice to go through and Lennox gave us renewed hope when he struck just two minutes after Murdoch's dismissal. But we simply could not find a second goal and when Kiev scored on the stroke of full-time our reign as European Champions ended as spectacularly as it had begun.

Of my team-mates from thirty-seven years ago, sadly, two are no longer with us and Bobby Murdoch's passing in 2001 and our goalkeeper Ronnie Simpson's sudden death in 2004 had a profound effect on the surviving members of the team. However, those of us who remain enjoy a close bond and enjoy each other's company and friendship as much now as we did all those years ago.

We had what we called a 'snifter box' in the dressing room at Celtic Park and Ronnie Simpson was in the habit of having a quick whisky to relax before a game. Heaven knows why, because he gave the impression of being calmness personified. Those who are old enough to remember watching the European Cup final will recall that Ronnie actually back-heeled the ball across the penalty area to John Clark at one stage.

Having someone as our last line of defence who was so cool was vital and Ronnie was an important cog in the wheel. Yet, when Jock Stein returned to Celtic Park as manager, Ronnie was convinced that his career was about to come to an inglorious end. He had previously been let go by Jock, when the pair of them were at Hibs, and Ronnie imagined that he was effectively being kicked into touch, but, amazingly, Jock's return coincided with the most successful period of Ronnie's career and at the age of thirty-six he became a hero all over again, also winning five Scotland caps.

Ronnie had played in two winning FA Cup finals for Newcastle, in 1952 and 1955, and was so highly thought off on Tyneside that he has a function suite named after him at St James' Park. He wasn't a stylist as such, but he was quick thinking and agile and could make the most difficult shot appear almost easy. His concentration was also quite remarkable and he was able to spring into action after lengthy periods of inactivity. Because of the way we liked to play, pushing forward all the time, there were occasions when we were caught on the break, but Ronnie had this wonderful knack of being able to make saves with just about any part of his anatomy – knees, elbows, at times anything but his hands.

Ronnie was given the nickname 'Faither' for the obvious reason that he was older than the rest of us. But that also gave him the benefit of experience. We had a tendency to blame Ronnie whenever we lost a goal, but he invariably reacted by pointing a finger at a fellow defender before throwing his arms in the air and accepting his fate. I cannot recall ever seeing him lose his temper, though, and I always found him an easy guy to talk to. He was able to converse on a variety of subjects and his sense of humour and ability to tell tales against himself made him enjoyable company.

Jim Craig was known variously as the 'Happy Amateur' or 'Cairney'. I suspect that he prefers the latter. The Happy Amateur tag arose from the fact that Jim graduated as a dentist from Glasgow University and gave the distinct impression at times that he regarded football almost as a side issue in his life. Indeed, I remember reading an article a few years ago in which Jim was quoted as saying he would rather watch an athletics meeting than a football match. The moniker Cairney derived from the TV programme, *This Man Craig*, starring John Cairney.

My earliest recollection of Jim was of him arriving at Celtic Park during Student Rag Week, dressed like a tramp. We, in fact, threw him straight into the bath, but Jim's studious nature meant that he was great when it came to the popular TV programme, *Quiz Ball*, which featured teams of three players and a celebrity answering sports questions. His vast knowledge meant that Celtic usually came out on top, but he was very much more than just a clever bugger. He was also a very quick and thoughtful player and possessed great stamina.

On the pitch, Jim and Tommy Gemmell were expected to overlap and Jim was able to get up and down the pitch all day long because he was so fit. He was conscientious in everything he did and he was an assured tackler, although he rarely dived in. In the final in Lisbon it was Jim's pass to Tommy Gemmell that set up our equaliser and underlined his ability to time his runs to perfection, but Jim should stick to dentistry rather than telling jokes, because most of them are as painful as having a tooth pulled!

Tommy Gemmell is an extravagant character in just about everything he does. To this day he lives life to the full. In his youth, he had a tendency to get up to the most outrageous exploits and when you were in his company you could never be sure what was going to happen next. Football gave big Tom the opportunity to express himself in a manner that suited his exuberant personality and he always gave the impression that he was enjoying what he was doing.

On the close-season tour to America in 1970, after we had lost in the European Cup final, Tommy and Bertie Auld ended up being sent home following an incident. We were guests of the Kearny Celtic Supporters' Club in New Jersey and we had enjoyed rather too much hospitality. A few of us ended up sozzled and the situation got a little out of hand when a waitress dropped a tray of drinks. I have never been exactly sure how that happened, but Tommy and Bertie had a hand in it. In truth, after our defeat in Milan, none of us had wanted to go on the trip in the first place and it was an accident waiting to happen. Jock had returned home by then, to discuss a possible move to Manchester United, and Sean Fallon was in charge, but we thought we could keep the matter under wraps because of the close relationship that existed between the players and the travelling Scottish press corps. However, one of their number tipped off his news desk in Glasgow and the story hit the front pages. The upshot was that Tommy and Bertie were sent packing, but I suspect they weren't too unhappy in the circumstances.

Like Cairney, Tommy was blessed with an exceptionally high level of fitness and managed to get himself up and down the park for ninety minutes. He had an explosive shot, as his remarkable record of having scored in two European Cup finals and the World Club Championship highlights. Tom powered in our equaliser in Lisbon and he was also our penalty-taker for a while. He had a habit of taking a long run up and half the time he seemed to miskick the ball into the net, but his style was effective. For a big man, Tom was skilful and he must have been a nightmare to play against, because he was prepared to take people on and run at them. He had pace and joined in the attack with a relish. He was never afraid to clatter an opponent either.

Tom bore a facial resemblance to the American comedy actor, Danny Kaye, and I remember on a trip to the States, when he entered a talent competition in a Miami hotel, one Yank shouted, 'Gee, it's Danny Kaye.' That was all the encouragement Tom needed. He refused to sit down after that and proceeded to put on a show for the audience. Tommy is great company and there's never a dull moment when he's around.

Bobby Murdoch's death at the age of just fifty-six hit us all very hard. Being the second youngest Lion, we had naturally assumed he would be around for longer than some of the older members of the team. The rest of us were aware that he had not enjoyed the best of health for some years, but it was nonetheless a huge shock when he passed away. I think I had begun to imagine that we would all go on forever.

Bobby was the vice-captain and a real Jekyll and Hyde character. Off the pitch he was quiet and inoffensive. On it he was aggressive, argumentative and prepared to win at any cost. His Chopper nickname derived from his willingness to chop down an opponent if necessary. He was fierce as hell, but it would be a disservice to Bobby's memory to suggest that he was just a hard man. The first time I saw Bobby play he was starring in Celtic's junior team and he stood out like a sore thumb. The half-back line was Murdoch, John Cushley and Benny Rooney. All three went on to play for the first team, but few players could match Bobby. He was blessed with wonderful ability and great vision. He could see situations developing more quickly than most and rarely wasted a pass. Bobby's control and touch coupled to his self-assurance was such that he was able to dictate games and dominate the play. A truly superb player, Bobby was the playmaker and he had the added gift of being able to score spectacular goals with either foot.

I must confess I was responsible for John Clark acquiring the nickname 'Luggy', when he was playing in goal one day during training and dived for the ball. Unfortunately, his head made contact with my shin and he split his ear wide open. Despite this, I was probably closer to John than to the other members of the team, because we had known each other longer. He arrived at Celtic Park shortly after me and, as we came from roughly the same part of Lanarkshire, we travelled to training together. The fact that we came through the reserve team together enabled us to develop an almost telepathic understanding, despite having somewhat different personalities. Later, he became my assistant at Aberdeen and the first time round at Celtic and I knew I could always rely on him as a steadying influence.

John was certainly fairly quiet and sensible and, I suspect, a little shy. He was also a complete football nut, who had no other interests or pastimes than the game itself. While the rest of us read novels when we were on trips abroad, John invariably had his nose buried in a football magazine and he developed an extensive knowledge of the game and its personalities. He is still the same today. John, now Celtic's kit man, has instant recall of games and places and if any of us needs to check a particular detail he is the man we turn to.

But it would be wrong to paint a picture of John as a football anorak. He was always good company, particularly with a couple of drinks inside him. We roomed together on trips and there was never a shortage of Mars bars in the bedside cabinet, for the pair of us are very sweet-toothed – not that it appears to have done us any great harm. As a player, John was positive, determined and hard as nails, and for someone who isn't the biggest guy in the world, incredibly powerful.

There were few more exciting players in the world at that time than Jimmy Johnstone. Jinky had great difficulty conforming to a set pattern of play, but he was an entertainer and was adored by the fans. He told me that as a kid he developed his God-given talents by dribbling round milk bottles in his back garden and he loved people making a fuss and telling him how skilful he was. It had nothing to do with egotism, though. He genuinely enjoyed mixing with the fans and they considered him to be one of them.

On the pitch, Jimmy jinked this way and that, turning defenders inside out. He had wonderful balance, skill and flair and was as sharp as a tack. I used to think that if Jimmy had been a boxer he would have been a huge success in the ring, because he had such powerful shoulders for a wee man and was incredibly fit and aggressive. In addition to his power, Jimmy was proud and determined and as brave as a lion. That bravery is still there for all to see in the way Jimmy, since being diagnosed with motor neurone disease, has gritted his teeth and refused to give in. You'll never hear him bemoaning his grave misfortune. It's an attitude of mind that you have to admire.

But the wee man was never conventional in thought or deed. When he was employed as a ball boy at Celtic Park, Jimmy wasn't content to just retrieve the ball and throw it back. He had to juggle with it first. Anything could happen when Jimmy was about but there was nothing malicious in his behaviour. He did daft things, but the only person Jimmy harmed was himself. I recall Jimmy buying a silver Jaguar motor car and within weeks it was full of dents and scrapes. He didn't care.

I also remember us being at Seamill Hydro, for what Jock described as a spot of rest and relaxation. A dance was being held in the function suite and we joined in and had a few drinks, but when it was time to leave, Jimmy was nowhere to be seen. 'Where's Jinky disappeared to?' asked Sean Fallon. Bobby Lennox explained to the rest of us that he had seen him disappear into the cloakroom, where he was hiding behind a pile of coats. Jimmy's cover was blown, though, when guests began collecting their coats and the sight of him crouching in a corner with a cheeky grin on his face had us in stitches. Jimmy regularly got up to mischief, especially after he'd had a couple of drinks. He had clearly hoped he wouldn't be missed and that he would be able to sneak back into the dance after the rest of us had gone, and carry on partying.

He gave Jock Stein plenty of headaches, because he proved difficult at times and also had a fear of flying. He was a nightmare to sit beside on a flight, because whenever the engine noise changed or the plane made a sudden movement, he grabbed the person next to him and his panic transferred itself to those around him. He just had to learn to live with what was a real problem for him, but Jock treated Jimmy differently from the rest of us and handled him superbly. Although that still didn't stop Jimmy from making headlines for the wrong reasons from time to time, once he had escaped from Jock's clutches. One of his most talked about exploits concerned the rowing boat incident while he was with the Scotland squad at Largs. Encouraged by a few of his teammates, Jimmy decided to go boating in the Firth of Clyde and had to be rescued when he lost his oars, but without him the Lisbon Lions might have found themselves up a creek without a paddle.

Quietly spoken with a throat whisper, Willie Wallace inevitably became known as 'Whispy'. Willie had a wicked sense of humour and kept us all going with a string of jokes. Liz and I socialised with Willie and his missus, Olive, from time to time and in 1970, when Celtic played Ajax, we decided to take our wives to Amsterdam with us. We arranged to meet up with them after the game, but instead of taking a taxi we jumped on a tramcar, still wearing our club blazers. Our fellow passengers recognised the pair of us straightaway and every time the tram reached a junction the driver played one of the football chants of the time on his horn.

In many ways, Willie was the final piece in Jock's jigsaw. He had been about a bit at Raith Rovers, where he began his career, and Hearts, and was experienced, and although bought to score goals, he was adaptable and could slot into midfield when required and would do a decent job. He maybe didn't look it, but Willie was also a bit of a hard man on the pitch. He was quick, sharp and kept defenders on their toes, but if one took liberties with him, Willie would never make a fuss or complain. He simply bided his time and when the moment came he quietly extracted revenge in full. His finest hour came in the semi-final first leg against Dukla Prague, when he scored twice in a 3–1 win at Celtic Park to set us up nicely for the return.

Steve Chalmers was the gentlemen of the team, to the extent that when we came back from a European trip most of us told our wives we had been out socialising with him to allay any suspicions of misbehaviour. Stevie always conducted himself properly and whenever there was a risk of something controversial happening he would walk away. I don't mean to infer that Stevie was one of those goodie-goodie types who disapproved of his team-mates enjoying themselves. He wasn't. But he was dedicated to making the most of his career and, while he enjoyed a laugh and a joke, he was more serious and quieter than the rest.

For all that he is a lovely guy, though, Stevie had an explosive temper and was capable of being naughty on the pitch if he fell victim to any underhand tactics. Like Whispy, he never complained, but if an opponent had a dig at him, Stevie would have one back and he could look after himself. I think because he had been at Celtic Park longer than most of us, he appreciated being successful more than some and could always be relied on to give it his best shot. He was the persistent sort, who would keep nipping away at the centre-half and be on the heels of defenders, trying to pressurise them. That persistence, sharpness and work ethic all contributed to him scoring the winner against Inter and ensuring himself of a permanent place in the hearts of the Celtic fans.

Bertie Auld is a remarkable character and a typical Glaswegian; gallus and as sharp as a tack when it comes to delivering one-liners. He has always had a wee swagger in his step and can best be described as a loveable rascal with a sharp mind and an even sharper tongue. To this day, when you hear one of his apparent off-the-cuff quips you wish you had thought of it first. Such is his personality that he can walk into a roomful of people and take over, and his personality carried over into his play.

Bertie began his career as a flying left winger, but developed into an astute and accomplished midfielder and formed an ideal combination with Bobby Murdoch. He was a superb passer of the ball and was capable of making things happen quickly. Skilful, flash and a bit of a showman, he was always liable to do the unexpected. During a match against Fiorentina in Italy, Bertie was time-wasting while preparing to take a corner kick and was warned by the referee to get on with it. He reacted by turning and booting the ball into the crowd.

Bertie had a great left foot, posed a threat at corners and free kicks and scored good goals. But he had a bad temper and could be downright nasty at times. He liked to be thought of as a bit of a hard man, but he wasn't really, although he could look after himself and was never intimidated. He was certainly never afraid to speak his mind if something was bothering him, but there was a compassionate and caring side to his nature as well. Whenever one of his pals was unwell or had a problem, Bertie was first on the scene with an offer of assistance.

Bobby Lennox is a candidate for the nicest bloke I have ever met and you'd have to travel far to find someone with a bad word to say against him. You always find Bobby the same way, with a beaming smile on his face and a new joke to tell. He is blessed with a wonderfully friendly, cheerful and open disposition. Shortly after I had undergone open heart surgery in 1997, Bobby and Stevie Chalmers were the first of the Lions to visit me in hospital, but within minutes I was in agony. Having just had my breast plate opened up I was feeling extremely tender and in no condition to be laughing non-stop as Bobby told one joke after another. I begged him to stop, but Bobby turned to Liz with an impish grin and asked, 'Is it okay if I tell just one more?'

Bobby's nickname is 'Lemon'. Apparently his name was once misspelled in a newspaper report and it stuck, thanks to Willie Wallace spotting the error, but he was no lemon on the pitch. Bobby must have been a nightmare to play against because he was probably the fittest player in the team and he had fabulous pace and never stopped grafting. He timed his runs to perfection and provided a great release, because he was willing to chase every ball, irrespective of whether it was a measured pass or a high punt over the heads of defenders. Bobby was also a superb finisher, as his achievement in winning the European Bronze Boot award the season after our triumph in Lisbon testified to. In fact, his total was thirty-two.

When I became manager of Aberdeen I was keen to take Bobby to Pittodrie, but Jock persuaded him to take up an offer to play in the States instead. I'm convinced that he did so because he feared Bobby would return to haunt him if he moved to another Scottish club. However, when I returned to Celtic in 1978 I brought Bobby back in the knowledge that he would set a great example to the younger players and also add a bit of vibrancy to the team. I had no reason to regret my decision. Bobby did a first-rate job for me and, while it was still 'Billy' in private, he never had a problem calling me 'boss' in front of the players.

Others played their part in bringing the European Cup to Celtic Park – a total of fifteen players featured in at least two of the games on the road to Lisbon – and their contributions must never be forgotten.

RIGHT *The earliest snapshot of me, aged four. I guess someone must have stolen my scone!*

FAR RIGHT *A picture of innocence. My first communion at the age of eight.*

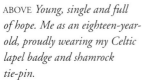

ABOVE *Young, single and full of hope. Me as an eighteen-year-old, proudly wearing my Celtic lapel badge and shamrock tie-pin.*

RIGHT *The biggest match of all and a contract for life. Liz and I proudly pose as a married couple following our wedding at the Sacred Heart Church, Bellshill, on 22 June 1963.*

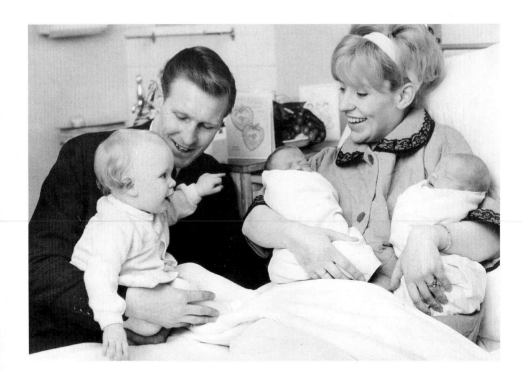

LEFT ABOVE *The proud father and daughter Susan are introduced to newly born twins Carol and Libby in 1966.*

LEFT *Liz and I soak up the sunshine in the garden of our first house in Simshill, Glasgow in 1969. However, there's no chance of any peace and quiet with this trio about – a very young Susan, Carol and Libby.*

ABOVE *Up before the beaks. From left: Ian Gordon, Mike Jackson, Me and John Ward, about to enter SFA headquarters in Glasgow to attend a hearing after taking part in a game in Spain. We were each fined for our 'crime'.*

RIGHT *Bring on the English! Not a hint of pre-match nerves as I get ready to face England at Hampden in April 1962. I loved playing for Scotland, especially on this occasion when we beat the Auld Enemy 2-0.*

ABOVE. *Probably the most important goal of my career. Heading the winner against Dunfermline in the 1965 Scottish Cup final to kick-start Jock Stein's incredible haul of 25 trophies and end Celtic's seven-year famine.*

LEFT *Last one back is a sissy! Jimmy Steele appears to find it easier than me to keep his feet on the sand dunes at Seamill during a visit to Ayrshire in the 1960s.*

RIGHT *The expression of panic on this lady's face as she makes her getaway suggests that she's just spotted a pride of lions on the prowl near Celtic Park. John Hughes leads the way to training at Barrowfield in 1967.*

BELOW *Scottish Cup winners again! Celebrating in the Hampden dressing room after beating Aberdeen in 1967. From left to right, back row: physiotherapist Bob Rooney, Jim Craig and Ronnie Simpson. Middle row: Willie Wallace, Stevie Chalmers, Bertie Auld, Jimmy Johnstone, Me, John Clark and Tommy Gemmell. Front row: Bobby Lennox, Bobby Murdoch, trainer Neil Mochan and assistant manager Sean Fallon.*

ABOVE *Timed to perfection. My last-gasp winner against Vojvodina Novi Sad at Celtic Park in March 1967 took us through to the European Cup semi-final. The aggregate score stood at 1-1 when I rose to head the ball with just seconds remaining.*

LEFT *Lisbon here we come. Jock Stein and I embrace at full time, following the draw with Dukla Prague in Czechoslovakia in April 1967.*

ABOVE *A joyous dressing room following the Dukla game as we realise that we have made history by becoming the first British team to reach the European Cup final. From left to right, back row: Jimmy Steele, me, Stevie Chalmers and Tommy Gemmell. Front row: Willie Wallace, Bobby Murdoch, Bertie Auld, Bobby Lennox and John Clark.*

RIGHT *From top to bottom: John Clark, Me, Bertie Auld, Willie Wallace and Stevie Chalmers at our hotel in Estoril prior to the 1967 European Cup final.*

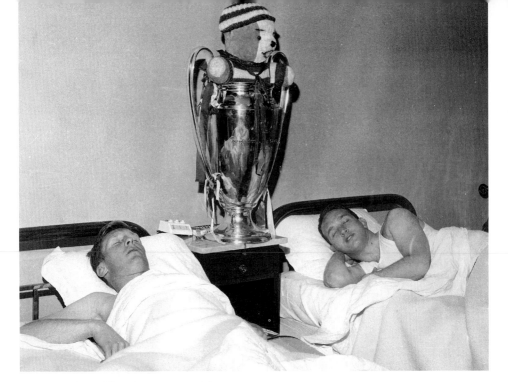

ABOVE *John Clark and I sleeping on guard duty. No need to worry – the European Cup remains in safe hands! But what about the ham acting?*

LEFT *The smiles say it all. Arriving back at Celtic Park with the Cup. Bobby Murdoch and I lead the way, closely followed by Jimmy Johnstone and Bobby Lennox, with John Clark bringing up the rear.*

John Hughes, known as 'Yogi' because of his substantial build and intimidating appearance, actually featured in more than half the nine matches we played, including the semi-final first leg against Dukla. For such a big and powerful man, Yogi was remarkably quick and skilful and was hard for defenders to handle. Strangely, he was not the best in the air, but he could play through the middle or wide left and possessed good ball control.

Willie O'Neill actually began the campaign at right-back, before Jock decided to introduce Jim Craig at left-back and switch Tommy Gemmell to the opposite side. I think Jock did so because Willie was not the quickest and he felt he needed Jim's pace as, given the way we played, we required two quick full-backs overlapping to support the attack. Willie was a fine player, nonetheless, blessed with a superb left foot and passed the ball with great accuracy.

Possibly the unluckiest of those who missed out was Joe McBride. His season was wrecked by injury and, but for that, Joe would very probably have featured in the final. Jock liked to freshen the team up from time to time and it was invariably the forwards who suffered. He rarely tinkered with the defence. Joe was an explosive character on the pitch and was never afraid to get involved in risky challenges. He regularly came deep, looking for the ball, and had a magnificent record as a goal-scorer.

Charlie Gallagher, who was a bit of a quiet man, was another with strong claims. He vied with Bertie Auld and had wonderful distribution skills and a powerful shot, but Bertie was probably more of an all-round performer.

John Fallon supplied the back-up for Ronnie Simpson and probably considers himself unlucky not to have featured at some stage during our run. To be fair, though, Ronnie was more suited to the task because of his remarkable levels of concentration and his ability to venture off his goal line and make last-gasp saves. I had the responsibility of coming for the high balls into our box, because that was not Ronnie's forte, but in every other sense he was the ideal goalkeeper.

While the players made it happen on the pitch, Celtic were fortunate to have a strong backroom team assisting Big Jock. His number two, Sean Fallon, was the ideal foil for the manager. While Jock tended to be abrasive and aggressive in his approach, Sean was much more measured and liked to talk through situations, using his Irish charm and outgoing personality to good effect, but the same man could turn fierce when it came to a confrontational situation, as evidenced by the way he wanted to set about the Inter Milan management team when they tried to commandeer the Celtic bench prior to the kick-off in Lisbon. Likewise, when a fight broke out in the tunnel at the end of our European Cup semi-final first leg against Atletico Madrid at Celtic Park in April 1970, Sean was at the heart of the battle, trading punches with the Spaniards and laying them out good style.

Our trainer, or coach, was Neil Mochan and he was a good-natured individual with a keen sense of humour. Neilly could always be relied on to offer words of comfort and advice and I was especially fond of him. He was also famous for his walks last thing at night, when he would take us on what could best be described as route marches, maintaining a blistering pace. He also led us into several scrapes, including on the evening before the final, after we had gone to the home of an exiled Scot, Brodie Lennox, to watch England playing Spain at Wembley on TV. Neilly actually managed to lead us down a dangerous hillside overlooking our hotel, where we risked injury as we slipped and slithered our way down a near vertical slope.

On another occasion, in Israel, shortly after the Six Day War, we ended up trapped on an exposed beach after Neilly omitted to check what time the hotel security came into force and we found the back entrance to our hotel padlocked. A couple of us had to clamber over a fence to get help and eventually gain entry. There was also the time when we were chased by a couple of Alsatians, on the eve of the European Cup semi-final in April 1967. Neilly had taken us on another of his legendary route marches when, as we walked across a public park, we were confronted by the sight of these ferocious beasts with their teeth barred. I think the dogs were accompanied by their owner, but we didn't bother to hang around to find out and took to our heels to escape a potential savaging. Neilly also loved to remind us of his goal in the 1953 Coronation Cup final, when Celtic beat Hibs, 2–0, every time we went to Hampden. Each passing year he seemed to manage to add an extra yard to the distance.

Unlike today's physiotherapists, Bob Rooney had to make do with the most basic equipment. I think Bob's consisted of a lamp and another couple of bits and pieces. Bob, who also involved himself a lot in our training sessions, was a big, aggressive man, who was quick to react, and we enjoyed winding him up whenever the chance arose. It was easy to do because Bob had an explosive temper, and the players went out of their way to trigger it. If Bob told us to do one thing, we invariably did the opposite in the knowledge that he would react. Bob didn't approve, either, of us jumping, fully clothed, into the Seamill Hydro swimming pool after completing a pre-season training run of several miles from Dalry. So we threw him into the water as well. It was only when he started to go under for the third time that we realised he couldn't swim and he had to be saved from drowning. We kept out of his way for a while after that. The thunderous expression on Bob's face suggested that he hadn't appreciated our idea of fun.

The fourth member of the team was Jim Steele, or 'Steely', who was universally popular and worked unpaid for Celtic for more than forty years. A wealthy man in his own right, Steely just loved being about the place in his role as masseur. He had been a PT instructor in the RAF and had also trained Freddie Mills, the former world light-heavyweight champion. Steely had come to Celtic through his friendship with the chairman and he had this marvellous ability to bridge the generation gap. He was loud, noisy and full of fun. Sometimes he acted just plain daft and the players were very fond of him, especially as he kept a large supply of chocolate and sweets in his room and he always made us welcome. Like the others, Steely was an essential part of the backroom team, although, sadly, he, Bob and Neilly are no longer with us.

# JOCK

**J**ock Stein was the biggest single influence on my career and the most successful manager in the history of Scottish football. Only one man even runs Jock close, but whereas much of Sir Alex Ferguson's success has been achieved south of the border, Jock won twenty-five major trophies in Scotland. It perhaps doesn't sound much if you say it quickly, but I doubt very much that Jock's record will ever be matched.

When Jock became manager in 1965, Celtic was a club stuck in a time warp. But when he quit thirteen years later, Celtic was a name known and revered throughout world football. I was closer to Jock than most, but few people ever got really close to him. Jock kept most at arm's length and dictated the depth of his relationships.

Jock was a complex man, full of contradictions, and sometimes he wasn't easy to love in the traditional sense of the word. Jock was capable of sympathy and understanding, yet he could also appear extremely hard-hearted, but I felt genuine warmth and respect for him, because he was my dream-maker.

I would very probably not have ended up at Celtic Park but for Jock's influence, and I would certainly not have reached the heights I did had it not been for him. Even if my career had panned out differently, though, I would always have appreciated the fact that he took me to Celtic in the first place.

We always knew who was boss. Jock kept a respectable distance between himself and his players, but, such was our devotion, that there was not one Lisbon Lion who would have refused to have walked across hot coals for him.

Reputations did not stand in Jock's way if he felt a change to the team was necessary and he regularly 'freshened up' the side to guard against complacency. However, we appreciated the fact that Jock rarely criticised any of us in public, unless he felt it would benefit both the individual concerned and the team.

If Jock told you to do something and you failed to carry out his instruction, the consequences were dire. Retribution was swift and costly. Every one of us fell foul of his explosive temperament at some stage, but Jock rarely had to discipline us, because we never let him down when it came to displaying a will to win and an appetite for success.

As I've said, Jock regularly took the squad to Seamill or Largs, on the Ayrshire coast, for what he described as a 'wee rest' and he allowed us a reasonable degree of freedom during these trips. We usually travelled down on a Monday morning, returning two days later. In between, we were capable of enjoying ourselves!

Mind you, Jock's idea of players enjoying the freedom to let off steam differed from the normal – and certainly from what we took it to mean. I don't think he ever fully understood or recognised the need for fit young athletes to let their hair down from time to time or was comfortable with the idea of football players consuming alcohol.

We seldom trained on these occasions. Instead, we relaxed by playing a couple of rounds of golf and going for walks along the beach. In the evenings, after dinner, we played various board games and took part in quizzes.

To an extent, Jock allowed us to set our own agenda and for us that involved card schools and a few drinks. Once the cards came out, we would phone down to the bar and request a drinks order be sent to the room, much to the horror of the barman at Seamill, a somewhat effeminate chap who was terrified of Big Jock. However, he was even more scared of the players and we used to threaten him with all sorts of repercussions if he didn't deliver, so we usually got our way in the end.

Occasionally, we were involved in nocturnal manoeuvres, sneaking into each other's rooms for a game of cards and a bevvy when we imagined that the coast was clear, but Jock was not a great sleeper and he was invariably still wide awake and on the prowl in the early hours of the morning.

Most times, he would be sitting with his assistant, Sean Fallon, and the trainer, Neilly Mochan, drinking endless cups of tea. What we didn't realise at the time was that Jock had a habit of casting his gaze towards the ceiling, to try to spot any movement, and as soon as he saw a lamp shade sway even slightly he sprang into action. 'Right, Neilly, up you go and see what they're up to,' he would say and off Neilly would go to check up on us.

On one occasion, this happened three times and each time Neilly reported back to Jock, insisting that he had not spotted any signs of life, but Jock had a highly suspicious nature and on the fourth occasion he accompanied Neilly. As luck would have it, the door to the bedroom we were crammed into was ever so slightly ajar and Jock spotted a chink of light.

Next thing we knew the door burst open and there was the burly figure of the manager, face like thunder, as he took in the sight of a selection of bottles containing vodka, rum and whisky. Jock flew into a rage and, scooping up every bottle up, marched straight into the bathroom and hurled the lot into the bath. As it happened, only two smashed – an empty vodka bottle and a Guinness bottle. To this day, none of us knows where the Guinness bottle came from!

It was like being handed an instant sober pill. We were supposedly grown men, but we scattered in every direction to escape Jock's wrath, made worse by the fact that only two of the bottles had smashed. 'Get to your beds,' he bellowed. We didn't need to be told twice, for Jock had hands the size of shovels and you wouldn't have wanted to risk a clip round the ear.

Jock hated alcohol. Some people have tried to suggest that he took a drink in private, but I have never believed that and I certainly never saw any evidence of it. Jock said that if we won the European Cup he would have a drink with us to celebrate, but he never did. Yet, Jock's closest pals, Tony Queen and Jack Flynn, were seasoned drinkers. Tony, a bookmaker, and Jack, an hotelier and publican, could sink them in good style. Jock himself was good company and I guess he just enjoyed being with them because he found them exciting people.

As I've indicated, little got past Big Jock. On our American tour in 1966, for example, I recall him coming up to the bar of our hotel, where we were having refreshments, and asking one of the lads for a drink of his Coca-Cola. 'We'll get you one,' said a chorus of voices. 'Naw,' replied Jock. 'I just want a mouthful to slake my thirst.' Naturally, the glass contained more than just Coke and as soon as he tasted it Jock was aware of the fact, but he had known all along anyway. In a sense, he was checking up on us but he was also just letting us know that he was fully aware of what we were up to. Jock liked doing that sort of thing, because it gave him the opportunity to demonstrate to us that he was on top of the job. It was a game he played with us in the knowledge that both he and his players knew what to expect. It also kept us on our toes.

It would be wrong, though, to give the impression that we were a bunch of boozers who jumped at the chance to have a drink whenever the manager's back was turned. We knew how to enjoy ourselves alright, but when it came to the serious business of preparing for games we were very professional in our approach.

That trip to the States lasted five and a half weeks, during which time we played something like eleven games, and it was a masterstroke by Jock, because it formed a huge part of our bonding and laid important groundwork for what was to follow.

However, no player gave Jock more headaches than Jimmy Johnstone. Jinky was the bane of Jock's life at times and the wee man fell foul of the manager on countless occasions. Jock was fond of Jimmy, though, and did everything in his power to protect Jinky from himself, often placing a protective arm round his shoulder and assuming the role of father figure.

One example was the time Jinky was suspended and sent home for a breach of club discipline. In those days, when a player was suspended by his club, his wages immediately stopped. A couple of days later Jock approached me and revealed that Jinky had telephoned him several times, begging to be allowed to return. 'What are you going to do?' I asked. 'I've already sent him his wages,' said Jock. 'Fine, can I be suspended, too?' I retorted, tongue in cheek, but that incident demonstrated that there was a softer side to Jock that not a lot of people were aware of.

It was suggested that Jock had a spy network, operating to keep an eye on the players, in particular Jinky, but that wasn't quite true. Jock was well informed, because he knew so many people and others were only too willing to phone Celtic Park and report any incidents – real or imagined.

A lot of the time Jock reacted for effect, but anyone seeing him in an apparent rage for the first time would have been shocked all the same. I don't recall any acts of physical violence. Mind you, there were times when it was a close call, especially if you tried to argue with him when he was in full flow. When you were the victim of a blast, it was as well to keep your mouth shut, in the knowledge that it would be over and done with in five minutes and not mentioned again.

Most of us learned our lesson early, but Tommy Gemmell had a habit of answering Jock back. On one occasion, he made the mistake of doing so when he and I were on the receiving end of a Stein dressing down in a hotel room in Malta, in November 1971. Having beaten Sliema Wanderers, 5–0, in the first leg of our European Cup second round tie, Jock, for once, allowed us to let our hair down prior to the return leg on the Wednesday and we travelled to Malta on the Sunday for what was effectively a bit of a holiday.

We didn't require any prompting and after a night on the town in Valetta, drinking various local concoctions, we returned to our hotel slightly the worse for wear. As we approached the front door of the hotel, I spotted Big Jock standing guard, so I immediately steered Tom Callaghan, who was in a somewhat more advanced state of inebriation than the rest of us, in the opposite direction.

In an effort to sneak Tom into the hotel without Jock knowing, I suggested to Tommy Gemmell that he and I try to divert the manager's attention, so I told Tom to sneak in behind Jock's back while Tommy and I engaged Jock in conversation. The plan might have worked, but for the fact that Tom could hardly stand unaided and a combination of him swaying violently before throwing up alerted Jock as to what the two of us were up to.

Jock blew his top and we decided that the safest course of action was to make a run for it and lock ourselves in our room, but seconds later the door burst open and Jock launched a tirade, accusing the pair of us of leading a younger player astray and adding that we were a disgrace.

I knew better than to argue, so I just stood there and let Jock rip, but Tommy refused to remain silent. 'I don't believe you,' he declared. 'What's the big deal? You were the one who said we could have a drink.' Jock dived at Tommy and, fearing the worst, I tried to come between the pair of them. What a mistake. Next thing I knew I had been hurled aside and landed on my back, stuck between two single beds. As things turned out, we probably had overdone things. But as the game was still three days away we had plenty of time to recover, even though Sliema shocked us by scoring after just sixty seconds.

Jock could be impetuous and he was a fearsome sight when he was in full flow at half-time in the dressing room. It must have terrified the life out of any newcomer, although you eventually got used to it. Forget about Fergie and flying boots. Jock was capable of picking up the nearest object he could get his hands on and hurling it at some luckless individual who had incurred his displeasure. Cups, saucers, bottles, articles of kit – all went flying at some time or other – but he also had a lovely smile and when we achieved a notable result he expressed his delight.

Jock was a great coach and knowledgeable about the art of coaching. As a youngster, I remember going to his home and listening to him talk about the game in great detail. Nobody else at Celtic did that at the time and it was a marvellous learning experience for young players.

He also made training interesting. He was a great innovator and encouraged us to experiment on the football field. He believed that there was nothing that couldn't be changed on the park, but he also placed great store by extreme hard work and fitness. The training ground was not a place for the faint-hearted and Jock worked you extremely hard, particularly in pre-season training, but he never asked a player to do more than he knew he was capable of. He was also flexible and allowed players to express their talents, because he wanted us to enjoy ourselves on the football field.

Few players could claim that Jock didn't have their best interest at heart, yet, Jock didn't fight our corner when it came to wage increases and the rewards our achievements deserved. I suspect that it had something to do with his working-class background. Jock was a miner and I think he had a degree of subservience, in the sense that you didn't challenge the authority of your employers. Ian St John told me that Bill Shankly was the same and, of course, Shanks came from a similar background to Jock.

Neither was Jock rewarded in the way he should have been, both in terms of his own remuneration and financial backing from the directors to enhance the squad when it was needed. Had he been given more support by the board, I am convinced he would have gone on to achieve even more.

I have always felt that Jock began to change after the 1970 European Cup final, in the same way that football began to change, with the young breed of superstars demanding a higher rate for the job. I imagine that he eventually became disillusioned by his treatment at Celtic and he was no doubt listening to counterparts in England, telling him what they were earning, while he wasn't on even half as much. Money was clearly never a great motivator for Jock, but it must have been galling to discover that men with half his ability were picking up twice as much in wages.

At the time of Jock's death, in September 1985, he had drifted apart from the Lions. We were rarely in his company and saw him only on the odd occasion, but Jock's passing hit us all very hard. I was sitting at home in Manchester, watching the game on TV, when the news came through and my reaction was a mixture of sadness and utter disbelief. However, when I reflected on the events of the evening of 10 September 1985 at Ninian Park, Cardiff, I realised that it had perhaps not been completely unexpected.

Jock had not enjoyed the best of health for a number of years and, following his heart attack in 1973, I remember visiting him in the intensive care unit at Glasgow's Victoria Infirmary. His near fatal car crash in July 1975 had also taken a hell of a lot out of him. It was nothing short of miraculous none of the occupants of the car was killed. Jock, who invariably drove at high speed, was behind the wheel of a Mercedes when his vehicle collided head on with a Peugeot, on the notorious A74 near Lockerbie in Dumfriesshire. There were four others in the car, Jock's wife, Jean, Bob Shankly, who had succeeded him as manager of Hibs, along with his wife, Margaret, and a friend of long-standing, Tony Queen. The party was returning from a holiday in Minorca, where they had stayed at Tony's villa. Amazingly, the two women and Bob Shankly escaped comparatively unscathed, but Jock and Tony sustained serious injuries.

They were rushed to Dumfries Royal Infirmary, where Jock underwent an immediate operation to relieve his breathing, but, remarkably, Jock apparently still managed to joke with the nurses by means of scribbled notes. Jock remained on the danger list for several days, but he pulled through, largely I suspect, because of his natural strength and determined personality. The other car had been travelling on the wrong side of the duel carriageway when the accident happened and the other driver was eventually convicted of reckless driving, fined and disqualified.

Jock carried the scars of the accident, but he never lost his desire or his need to be involved in every aspect of the team and the club, and when he went on to manage Scotland his commitment was no less. He was desperate to take the international team to new heights and the pressures on him that evening in Wales must have been enormous. As a consequence of having lost to the Welsh at Hampden the previous March, Scotland had to at least draw the match with Wales to earn a play-off against Australia for the right to a place in the 1986 World Cup finals in Mexico. The stakes could hardly have been higher.

The drama was heightened by the fact that Jim Leighton, the Scotland goalkeeper, had lost a contact lens and had to be replaced by Alan Rough at half-time. This apparently led to a verbal altercation between Jock and Leighton, who had not even made his manager aware that he wore contact lenses. Clearly there was a combination of factors adding to the stress Jock was under, including an incident with a photographer whom Jock was forced to physically push away from the dug-out area, and I recall that he looked ashen every time the TV cameras panned to the Scotland bench.

But what was tragically Jock's last tactical move turned out to be an inspired one, when he sent on Davie Cooper, the Rangers winger, in place of Gordon Strachan of Manchester United. There were less than ten minutes remaining when Scotland were awarded a penalty kick and it was to the recently introduced Cooper that the daunting task fell. But Cooper, who died of a brain haemorrhage in 1995, at the tragically young age of thirty-nine, converted the kick with the calmness of someone taking part in a practice game.

So, Scotland booked their place in the play-off, but at a terrible cost. Jock's heart could not withstand the stress of the situation and he collapsed and died in what should have been one of his finest hours. However, Jock lived for football and such was his passion for the game that I am sure that if he could have picked his moment he would have settled for it being that evening in Cardiff.

It's almost impossible to sum Jock Stein up, but for me he was the single most influential figure in the history of Scottish football. When you consider that we are a country of approximately five million people, Scotland has no divine right to expect one of its football teams to become champions of Europe. None of us goes on forever, but perhaps the most fitting epitaph to Big Jock was delivered on the evening of our triumph in Lisbon, when Bill Shankly declared, 'Jock, you're immortal.'

# MUGGED IN MILAN

J ock Stein didn't make many mistakes, but not even Jock was infallible and his costliest misjudgement contributed to our failure to win the European Cup for a second time. Whereas in 1967 we had been underdogs against Inter Milan, we were strongly fancied to beat Feyenoord three years later. Dutch football was not at the level it later reached, but no one seemed to have noticed that a team called Ajax had made it to the final twelve months earlier. Ajax had been trounced, 4–1, by AC Milan in Madrid, as it happened, and that probably added to the conviction that they had overachieved even getting that far. However, on reflection, Milan's success said more about their strengths, rather than illustrating the opposition's weaknesses, for Ajax were soon to win the trophy three years in succession, immediately following Feyenoord's triumph.

In the wake of our defeat I heard ridiculous stories about how we had only been interested in the financial rewards to be gained from reaching the final and that our attitude had contributed to our downfall. According to the rumour-mongers, the Celtic players had not been able to agree a share-out of the cash and we had allegedly squabbled amongst ourselves right up to the kick-off. The only flaw in that particular theory was that there had been no cash to share out. By my calculations, one per cent of nothing is zero, but I could understand how such a rumour had arisen in the first place. For reasons best known to himself, Jock astonished us by employing the services of a Glasgow journalist, Ian Peebles, to act as an agent on the squad's behalf. I'm sure that Jock was well intentioned, but, be assured, we got bugger all out of the deal and it still rankles with me that some people continue to labour under the misapprehension that the players made bundles of cash.

Even if Ian Peebles had managed to generate a bit of cash, money would never have become more important than winning, and the explanation for our defeat on 6 May 1970 was much more straightforward – Feyenoord was a game too far! Our final was effectively the semi-final against Leeds United the previous month. For the best part of three weeks afterwards we were forced to twiddle our thumbs waiting for the big one. The league had finished on 18 April and the Scottish Cup final had been played on 11 April. It also hadn't helped that we had been beaten, 3–1, by Aberdeen at Hampden. Our preparations involved games against Stenhousemuir, Fraserburgh and Gateshead. Feyenoord, meanwhile, were still involved in competitive action.

Jock and Sean Fallon had gone to see Feyenoord play and I believe that the pair of them underestimated the quality of the opposition. The message we got from the manager was that Feyenoord weren't anything special. The Scottish press corps joined in the chorus. What I didn't realise until much later, when I spoke with Feyenoord midfielder, Wim Van Hanegem, was that the reports in the Scottish newspapers found their way to Holland and created an instant backlash. Wim told me, 'Billy, every time we read a report from Glasgow we became more inflamed and determined to ram the words down the throats of the Celtic players. By the time we reached Milan we almost had to be restrained with chains such was our desire.'

It would have been much better had we been drawn against Feyenoord in the semis and Leeds had been kept for the final itself, because that way there would have been no danger of us underestimating our opponents. Leeds were seen as clear favourites to beat Celtic, the same as Milan three years earlier, but we travelled to Elland Road for the first leg believing that we could upset the odds. And when George Connelly scored after only forty-five seconds our confidence soared. Even though I say so myself, we were brilliant that night and the 1–0 scoreline flattered Leeds. Jimmy Johnstone, in particular, was outstanding. Jinky roasted the Leeds full-backs to the extent that Terry Cooper, the England defender, was still recalling the wee man's brilliance years later when I met him on holiday. 'I still have nightmares,' confessed Cooper. 'I reckon I had good anticipation, but I could do nothing to take the ball off Johnstone.'

The Scottish Cup final was played between the two legs against Leeds and I had the misfortune to damage my right ankle. I saw the game out, but my ankle was so badly swollen that it looked as though I didn't have a hope in hell of being fit for the return at Celtic Park. However, physio Bob Rooney went to work on me with his hot and cold treatment and performed a minor miracle, albeit that I went through agony. Bob's therapy involved me placing my ankle in a basin of scalding hot water and then quickly removing it so he could hose my limb with a powerful jet of ice cold water, the idea being to stimulate the blood flow. This medieval form of torture had the desired effect, but my ankle was still heavily strapped when I took the field against Leeds. Consequently, it was one of the few occasions when Jock Stein encouraged us to wear tracksuit bottoms during the pre-match warm-up. Normally, such a request from the players, even on the coldest winter evenings, was met with a growl of derision and questions about our manhood, but Jock was keen to ensure that the Leeds players didn't twig that I had a problem.

In the event, I got through the game as much on adrenaline as anything and we beat Leeds, 2–1. Billy Bremner had squared the tie with a first-half goal, but John Hughes and Bobby Murdoch hit back in quick succession early in the second to earn us a 3–1 aggregate success in front of a record European Cup crowd of 136,505. Was it any wonder that the bookmakers now installed us as firm favourites to lift the trophy?

I don't think being strongly fancied suits the Scottish psyche too well, though. As a nation, we invariably respond better to challenges when we are written off, because of our bloody-minded approach to situations. Not that there was a shortage of bloody-minded individuals in the Celtic team that lined up for the final. Jock picked: Williams, Hay, Gemmell, Murdoch, McNeill, Brogan, Johnstone, Lennox, Wallace, Auld, Hughes. Substitute: Connelly. Feyenoord chose: Graafland, Romeijn, Laserons, Israel, Van Duivenbode, Hasil, Jansen, Van Hanegem, Wery, Kindvall, Moulijn.

Our side included seven of the Lisbon Lions, so we couldn't claim lack of experience of such a high-profile occasion, but, looking back, Van Hanegem's suggestion that the Feyenoord players were champing at the bit to get at us was very probably true, because they approached the game like men who had just been unchained and set free. When we beat Inter, 2–1, the margin of our victory could have been considerably greater, given our overall superiority and the number of chances we created. The result flattered the Italians. The reverse was the case in Milan. Feyenoord's 2–1 victory in extra-time flattered us. In truth, they slaughtered us on the night. Feyenoord were by far the better team. Perhaps if we had still been involved in competitive games right up to the final the outcome might have been different, but I am honestly not sure that we could have beaten Feyenoord. My feeling is that they were maybe a better side than us, even if we had performed at our best.

Feyenoord were terrifically strong and pacey and they had the added ingredient that we had displayed in Lisbon – a real desire to win. Although we never had command of the game, Tommy Gemmell gave us the lead after half an hour. But a player by the name of Israel equalised just two minutes later and the writing was on the wall for us. What made it worse for me, personally, was that I had deliberately handled in the penalty box in extra-time, something that I couldn't recall having done before. Kindvall had got on my wrong side and that caused me to react the way I did, but, even though I didn't concede a penalty, to have that happen in a European Cup final was especially galling. I got away with it in a sense, but Ove Kindvall swept round me and lobbed the ball into the net for what ultimately proved to be the winner, four minutes from the end.

Our despondency was all the greater because so few of the team had played well, but I felt for the younger element even more, because at least the more experienced of us had enjoyed the experience of winning the European Cup. Jock had left out several of the younger players – notably George Connelly, who was on the bench – in the belief that they would have other chances to play in a European Cup final, whereas it would almost certainly be the last for the majority of us. On reflection, there was maybe a wee touch of arrogance about us. After all, our win three years earlier had been a statement of fact that we were a top European side, while Feyenoord were newcomers to the scene, but I do believe that if Jock Stein had been given the necessary financial backing by the club, Celtic would not have had to wait until 2003 to contest a third European final.

As you might imagine the atmosphere in our dressing room was similar to that of a morgue. We returned to Glasgow with our heads down, because we were a proud bunch and we found it very difficult to face up to defeat. Mind you, I had to laugh when I read one newspaper headline that declared, 'End To A Disastrous Season For Celtic'. Right enough. We had only won the league championship and the League Cup and played in the Scottish Cup and European Cup finals. Some disaster, eh? But maybe it was more of a back-handed compliment than a slur, and indicated just how highly we were rated.

The defeat in Milan hit us all very hard. It was the nearest we ever came to falling out with one another and it took months to recover from the disappointment. The emotional pain was certainly far greater than the physical variety I had suffered at the very start of our run, the previous September. In our very first match, in Basle, when we drew 0–0 before winning the return by a couple of goals, I had received a blow in the face. The upshot was a fractured cheek bone and I remember the doctor, John Fitzsimmons, warning me at half-time not to blow my nose as that would create a vacuum and my face would immediately swell up. I knew better, of course, and the doc was proved right, but I somehow managed to get through the ninety minutes.

On returning to Glasgow, I was told by the specialist that I had the choice of an operation or I could allow nature to take its course and the break would heal naturally. I chose the latter course of action and I was left with a small indentation in my face, just above the cheek bone. I was also advised not to play for five or six weeks, but, Jock being Jock, my recovery period lasted just one game, after which he somehow managed to talk me into soldiering on regardless. He was good at that sort of thing.

Unfortunately, after we had swept aside the challenges posed by Basle, Benfica, Fiorentina and Leeds, to reach our second European

Cup final, just for once he misread the situation. Mind you, I also have to say that we rode our luck in the second round tie against Benfica, when it finished all-square after extra-time. The Portuguese had reversed our 3–0 first leg win led by the great Eusebio, scorer of the first goal, to force a situation where the tie was to be decided on the toss of a coin.

I had the honour – if you can call it that when your insides are churning and you'd rather be anywhere else than the referee's room at that moment – to call first, after winning the initial toss of the coin. Having called 'heads' to earn that right, I stuck with my hunch and shouted 'heads' again as the coin was about to land. Thankfully, my luck held. However, when I asked Jock what he would have done had the coin landed in favour of Benfica, he replied, 'I would have kicked the coin before it had even stopped rolling!' I am sure he wasn't joking either.

# NINE IN
# A ROW

By any standard, Celtic's achievement in winning nine successive league championships between 1966 and 1974 was remarkable. It also underpinned Jock Stein's status as a legend of the game. To have maintained such an incredible level of consistency for the best part of a decade was truly astonishing. Jock was, without any shadow of doubt, the most influential figure in the history of the club, transforming Celtic from a mediocre Scottish team into European champions, so, it will no doubt surprise many people when I say that Jock stayed too long. In my opinion he should have left after the second European final in 1970 and become manager of Scotland.

Jock visibly wilted after our defeat in Milan and was never again the same vibrant personality. Part of the reason, I believe, was his continual struggle with the board to loosen the purse strings to allow him to strengthen the squad. However, perhaps Jock allowed himself to be conned into carrying on beyond 1970 because of the emergence of the band of hugely gifted youngsters who became known as the 'Quality Street Kids'.

The team was at a crossroads when along came the most exciting batch of young players in the history of the club. Almost an entire team emerged at roughly the same time: Davie Hay, George Connelly, Jimmy Quinn, David Cattenach, Victor Davidson, Lou Macari, Paul Wilson, Danny McGrain and, of course, Kenny Dalglish. Jock saw them as the future of the club, and no one could blame him for that, but I feel he allowed the Lions to break up prematurely.

Maybe that had something to do with the fact that Jock never wanted to see the 1967 team upstaged. We were precious to him and he could have been accused of being overprotective of us. An example of that was his decision to leave Ronnie Simpson out of the team that faced Real Madrid at the Bernabeu in Alfredo di Stefano's testimonial match a fortnight after we had won the European Cup. Jock's reasoning was that if we lost no one would be able to claim that Real had beaten the European champions! In the event, we won, 1–0, when Bobby Lennox scored midway through the second half of what was a testimonial in name only. Bertie Auld was sent off, along with Amancio, for trading blows in front of a crowd of 120,000. Incredibly, Lennox's goal was our 201st of a season spanning sixty-five games!

By the time the Quality Street Kids emerged on the scene, attitudes were rapidly changing and, unfortunately as far as Jock was concerned, the new breed of players had been brought up in a different world. They knew their worth and when they didn't receive the rewards they believed they were entitled to they took steps to remedy the situation. Consequently, Macari left for Manchester United in January 1973 for a fee of £200,000 and Hay followed eighteen months later, when he joined Chelsea in a £250,000 deal. Dalglish later became a Liverpool player in a record transfer, but in the case of Quinn, Cattenach, Davidson and Wilson, the quartet never quite lived up to their potential. Of the four, Wilson enjoyed most success, but Cattenach was allowed to move to Falkirk, while Quinn and Davidson were eventually released.

The break-up of the Lions began with Ronnie Simpson announcing his retirement immediately following the 1970 European Cup final and, by the end of the 1972–73 season, there were only four of us left at Celtic Park: Bobby Murdoch, Jimmy Johnstone, Bobby Lennox and yours truly. Murdoch left soon afterwards, on a free transfer to Middlesbrough, whom he later managed, and his place in the team was taken by Steve Murray, a £50,000 signing from Aberdeen.

The Lions could not go on forever, of course, and Celtic made a dreadful mistake in not trying to do more to hold on to players of the calibre of Macari and Hay. However, there was nothing anyone could have done to prevent the tragedy that was George Connelly, perhaps the most gifted of the new generation. George had the potential to become a world class player, but he was also blighted by an inability to handle being in the spotlight, which left his career unfulfilled. In truth, while George wanted to be a footballer, he had no desire to be a high-profile personality and the constant public scrutiny that goes with that.

However, there was no hint of the storm clouds slowly gathering over George when, still a teenager, he gave the fans their first glimpse of his burgeoning talents. When we played Dinamo Kiev in a Cup Winners' Cup tie in 1966, George entertained the fans with a spectacular display of his ball-control in the form of an impromptu performance of keepie-up during the half-time interval. Apparently his average was an astonishing 2,000, non-stop. But when he broke into the first team at the start of the 1968–69 season, at the age of 19, it soon became evident that he was more than just a showman. George had everything: a powerful physique and the ability to adapt and play several different roles in central defence or midfield. The only thing he lacked was pace.

George's best position was probably sweeper, because of his control and intelligent use of the ball. His elegant style drew comparisons with

Franz Beckenbauer and that wasn't an extravagant compliment. He was blessed with great vision and a lovely touch on the ball. He rarely wasted a pass and it was a mark of the impact he had on the game in the six years that he graced the stage that he was named Scotland's Player of the Year by the Football Writers' Association in 1973.

By the following February, George had made a transfer request which the club granted and he was made available at £200,000. Jock Stein had no wish to see him leave and did everything in his power to persuade George to have a re-think, but George was an introvert and was never comfortable trying to deal with stardom. A quiet and withdrawn individual, he had a tendency to brood. A native of the small Fife town of Kincardine, he was happiest among his ain folk.

So, when George announced in September 1974 that he was quitting football, while still in his mid-twenties, I can't say I was all that surprised. By then he had walked out on the club several times and had once quit the Scotland squad at the airport en route to play Switzerland in Berne in 1973. George left the game having played in a European Cup final, four championship-winning teams and three successful Scottish Cup finals. It was ridiculous that such a talented player won only two Scotland caps.

After Celtic, he had a brief spell with Falkirk, before being reinstated to play junior football, but he apparently once confided to a close friend that he preferred being a long-distance lorry driver to being a footballer. What an appalling waste of what should have been a truly great career.

George Connelly was beyond help. Lou Macari and David Hay ultimately proved to be beyond Celtic's budget. For a small man, Lou was brilliant in the air. He kidded defenders into thinking that he didn't pose a threat in aerial duels, but by the time they twigged it was invariably too late. Lou had an aggressive attitude on the field and he was as brave as a lion. He was also sharp, quick-witted, powerful and oozed confidence. The combination made for a potent force.

In the case of Davie Hay, I never played with anyone who was tougher. People talk about the game's hard men, the Roy Keanes and such like, but Davie was harder and more talented than Keane. He wasn't dubbed the 'Silent Assassin' for nothing, but there was much more to Davie's game than the physical side. He could play as well. Davie was equally at home at right-back, alongside the centre-half, or in midfield. His fitness also meant that he could run all day long. It was a great pity that his career was cut short by the eye injury he suffered playing for Chelsea.

I have often wondered what impact players of the calibre of Macari and Hay would have had on Celtic in the longer term, but we never found out. Neither player desired to leave Celtic to better themselves in a playing sense, but Macari and Hay felt they had done their bit and deserved much greater financial reward for their efforts. Had those running the club at the time looked at the bigger picture, they would have realised how important it was to retain the services of the top players at such a crucial period in the club's history. But Celtic were a selling club.

The rewards elsewhere for players were far greater. Years later, when I became manager, I recall Tom McAdam telling me that for the first time the Celtic players were earning more than their Rangers counterparts. Tom had been speaking with his brother, Colin, who was a Rangers player, and the pair of them had been discussing wage scales. I took that as a compliment, because I have always believed that players should be rewarded according to their achievements.

The Lisbon Lions certainly didn't reap the financial benefits our success should have brought. In today's world we would all have become millionaires. The basic problem was that Celtic played on loyalty. I remember director, Jimmy Farrell, asking during my first stint as Celtic manager why the players were not as loyal as we had been. 'Mr Farrell,' I replied, 'if freedom of movement had existed when we won the European Cup the club would not have managed to hold the team together for one year.' I sometimes wondered if these people lived in the real world. I am also convinced that Jock Stein looked around at his colleagues in the South – Don Revie, Bill Shankly and Matt Busby – and saw that they could go out and buy players at the drop of a hat, while he couldn't even hold on to the best of those he had.

That sense of frustration no doubt led to Jock very nearly becoming manager of Manchester United in the summer of 1970, in the wake of our European Cup final defeat. We were playing Bari in Toronto, as part of a month-long, close-season tour to Canada and the States, and none of us had any inkling that moves were afoot to take Jock to Old Trafford. The game, as it happened, was eventually abandoned with five minutes remaining, after the Italians had stormed off in a rage when we were awarded a penalty. Bari, who were one of the most undisciplined teams I played against, had also had a couple of players sent off, but my abiding memory of that ill-fated tour was seeing Jock walking round the perimeter track and disappearing up the tunnel. He was nowhere to be seen at the end of the game and it transpired that he had flown home without saying a word to anyone. Jock never explained his sudden disappearance. In fact, he rarely volunteered explanations. It was certainly an odd occurrence, but I don't know why Jock felt the need to behave in what was effectively a clandestine manner, although I remember thinking at the time that he had acted in a way that suggested he'd had enough of being manager of Celtic.

It was just one of several bizarre happenings on what was undoubtedly the unhappiest trip the club ever undertook. In addition to Jock's 'disappearance', Tommy Gemmell and Bertie Auld had also been ordered home for disciplinary reasons. Our nerves had also been stretched to breaking point by the events of a flight from New York to Toronto which took sixteen hours, because of various delays, and included a hairy landing in Montreal, when a tyre burst on touchdown. By coincidence, our first game in Canada was against Manchester United and we lost, 2–0, despite having more of the play. No doubt Jock was involved in talks with United officials at that point, but it was only when the team returned to Glasgow that I discovered the extent of United's bid to lure him away from Celtic.

Rumours were by this time abounding and I felt it was necessary to confront Jock on behalf of the players, so I drove to his home in an effort to have the situation clarified. Jock was up front with me. 'I've been offered the Manchester United job, Billy, and I think I'm going to take it,' he said. 'You would be daft not to,' I replied. But I hadn't anticipated his next comment. 'Will you come with me?' he asked. I didn't hesitate. 'Yes,' I said. 'That's not a problem.' Like Jock, I felt the time was right for me to change the direction of my life and the prospect of playing for Manchester United had considerable appeal. I felt that I should put myself and my family first and cash-in. But that was the last I heard about Jock going to United.

I don't know for sure what happened to change his mind, but I suspect he turned United down for family reasons. Jock's wife, Jean, was a home bird and, as later happened when he was manager of Leeds for a very brief spell, she was not keen to move away from her friends and family in Glasgow. It was a shame, because I believe that it would have done Jock the world of good at that point in his life to have accepted a fresh challenge. When he did eventually venture south, to Elland Road, it was too late. He had become thoroughly disillusioned by that stage. The loss of players like Macari, Hay and Dalglish had hit him hard. Jock should have made the move eight years earlier. The car smash in 1975 had also taken a great deal out of him and he was never the same man after that. The physical effects of the accident sapped his energy and desire to the extent that he was no longer capable of handling the demands of management at the top level.

From a personal point of view, I have always regretted that I missed out on the chance to play in England, but, given that I might have become a Manchester United player on no fewer than three occasions, fate decreed that it was not to be. However, balanced against that enduring disappointment is the fact that I achieved the proud distinction of captaining Celtic to nine successive championships. People have often said that it must have become easier as we went along, reeling off one title after another, but, if anything, it became increasingly more difficult to sustain the run.

We placed ourselves under constant pressure to succeed. No sooner had one season ended than we began focusing on the next. It was a relentless slog and it required great management to maintain the levels of desire required to keep the run going. By the final season – 1973–74 – only three of the Lions remained at Celtic Park: Jimmy Johnstone, Bobby Lennox and myself. But we were extremely fortunate throughout the run that the competitive nature of the Lisbon Lions shone through and manifested itself in the players who followed. We gave them a legacy of aggression and determination and instilled an attitude full of ambition. There was also an air of arrogance about us in as much that we believed that, at our best, we had no reason to fear any team.

Having a twelfth man in the guise of our wonderful support was another key factor. I have often wondered how many times the fans gave us the extra five or ten per cent needed to secure a victory. Nowadays I hear references to 'bonding' sessions. The expression wasn't in vogue at the time, but I reckon we 'bonded' during our close season tour of the States in the summer of 1966. Nowadays if you told players they were going to be away from their family for five and a half weeks they would probably threaten to stage a revolt, but none of us had been to America before. It was like a great adventure and living in such close proximity of one another we developed lasting friendships. We got to know each other's little quirks and likes and dislikes.

Being so close knit must have made it doubly difficult for the players who came immediately after when the Lions began breaking up bit by bit. We had worked hard, played hard and established an unshakable belief in ourselves. Entry to our exclusive little club was not easy to come by. So, I suppose it's testimony to the talents of players like Davie Hay, Jim Brogan, Harry Hood, George Connelly, Kenny Dalglish and Lou Macari, to name but a few, that they were able to prove themselves in the manner they did and to such great effect.

It also says much about the quality of the Rangers team during our run that they finished runners-up on no fewer than six occasions. Aberdeen were twice second and Hibs once. The margin of our earlier successes was not great. In the first three seasons we pipped Rangers to the post by two, three and two points respectively, and it came right down to the wire. Rangers' sense of frustration must have been all the greater when we clinched the title at Ibrox in the penultimate game of the 1966–67 season with two goals from Jimmy Johnstone earning us the single point we required. The 1972–73 championship was even closer. We outdid our arch rivals by a single point after travelling to Easter Road on the final day of the season and running in three goals in front of a packed crowd of 45,000.

One fact that I have always found fascinating is that we clinched all nine championships away from home. The sequence was Fir Park,

Ibrox, East End Park, Rugby Park, Tynecastle, Hampden, against Ayr United (Celtic Park was under reconstruction), Bayview (the former home of East Fife), Easter Road and Brockville Park, Falkirk.

But there was a grim reminder of the absurdity of Bill Shankly's claim that football is not simply a matter of life and death – it is much more important than that.

On 2 January 1971, the blackest day in Scottish football, sixty-six people died in what became known as the Ibrox Disaster. There was no hint of the tragedy that was about to unfold when 80,000 Old Firm fans anxiously began checking their watches with two minutes remaining and the scoreline blank. It had been a typical Old Firm encounter, frantic and hard fought, and the majority of the fans were presumably satisfied to settle for a share of the points. I missed the game because I was injured and I remember sitting in the stand thinking that a draw was a decent result for us. However, with just a minute or so remaining, it seemed that we were destined to snatch the victory that had appeared beyond either team when Jimmy Johnstone scored. There was barely enough time left for the referee to restart the game, but the fifteen seconds that remained turned out to be long enough for Colin Stein to equalise.

No goal in the history of football has had costlier consequences in terms of human lives. If any one of us could have turned the clock back just a couple of minutes and stopped it there, we would have happily done so. Hundreds of Rangers fans, who had been making their way down stairway 13, believing Celtic had won, made an attempt to clamber back up to celebrate Stein's goal, only to be met by a floodtide of humanity sweeping down on top of them. The consequences were disastrous. In addition to the sixty-six who died, 145 others were injured – some very seriously – and the country was left to mourn a genuine sporting tragedy.

Initially, few, other than the poor souls caught up in the collision, were aware that an incident had taken place and I recall thinking to myself at the moment when Stein equalised that he hadn't previously managed to score against me in an Old Firm game. It actually took several minutes for word to begin filtering through that police and other officials were dealing with a major incident, by which time I had joined my team-mates in the dressing room. My first awareness was seeing the club doctor, John Fitzsimmons, deep in conversation with Jock Stein, Sean Fallon and Neil Mochan, and of the four of them suddenly disappearing through the door.

Jock returned a short time later and his strained expression told us that something extremely serious had occurred, but he had no time to offer any explanations as he herded us on to the team coach. Presumably still unsure as to exactly what was unfolding, he was clearly anxious to ensure that we left the stadium as quickly as possible for fear that there might be further unforeseen ramifications. Then, as the coach headed away from Ibrox, we heard the first radio reports and quickly realised that there had been a major accident and a number of fans were feared dead.

The atmosphere hanging over the country in the days that followed was a little unreal. For probably the only time in the past hundred years, Old Firm fans were united – in grief. For once, all rivalries were put aside as the mourning began. I personally attended several of the funerals and it was a period in my life when I felt that football and the importance of winning and losing had been put into' perspective.

The players had been spared the sight of the dead and dying in the immediate aftermath of the tragedy, but others were less fortunate and for days Jock, Sean and Neilly bore the look of haunted men. Celtic were active in arranging various fund-raising activities for the dependents of those who perished and I don't recall hearing a single dissenting voice whenever anyone associated with the club was asked to play an active part.

Not surprisingly, the remainder of the season was overshadowed by the magnitude of this devastating disaster and it hardly seemed to matter that we were crowned champions for the sixth consecutive season. Rangers had beaten us, 1–0, in the League Cup final the previous October, when teenager Derek Johnstone headed a first-half winner to ensure himself of a place in the record books. Derek also struck in the Scottish Cup final in May, forcing a replay with an equaliser three minutes from the end. However, Lou Macari and Harry Hood enabled us to extract revenge in the replay, despite Jim Craig suffering the misfortune of scoring an own goal.

It was a measure of our dominance of the Scottish game that, in addition to nine championships, Celtic appeared in every League Cup final between 1964 and 1978, but, somewhat surprisingly, our success rate didn't even begin to compare with our achievements in other areas. Celtic managed to win just six of these fourteen finals. Various theories were put forward for our run of seven defeats in the eight finals between 1970 and 1978. That contrasted sharply with our previous five straight wins, but I have always held the view that it was simply down to luck and an increased desire on the part of the opposition to upstage the best team in the land.

The League Cup was certainly not Celtic's favourite competition, although I had the good fortune to miss what turned out to be the most embarrassing loss of all, to our Glasgow rivals, Partick Thistle, in season 1971–72. Thistle weren't expected to pose too many problems and I was initially disappointed to be sidelined by an injury. However, from my seat in the Hampden stand I reflected that I was never more glad to miss a game when Thistle raced into a four-goal lead. It was all over by half-time and the 4–2 result constituted one of the biggest cup upsets of all time – until another Thistle, Inverness Caley, came along in February 2000 and inflicted an even more embarrassing defeat on Celtic in the Scottish Cup.

As well as featuring in nine League Cup finals and having the good fortune to lift the trophy on six occasions, I also achieved the distinction of playing in no fewer than twelve Scottish Cup finals. That's a record, I believe, and one of which I am extremely proud, even if not all of those games were filled with happy memories. Not having been renowned as a goal-scorer, I am especially proud of the fact that I scored in three Scottish Cup finals; the winner when we beat Dunfermline, 3–2, in 1965 and in the 4–0 and 6–1 victories over Rangers and Hibs respectively in 1969 and 1972.

For the record, I also scored three Scotland goals, against Poland, Wales and Cyprus, but forty-one goals in 861 competitive games highlights that scoring was not the strongest facet of my game. Mind you, when you had strikers of the calibre of Joe McBride, Stevie Chalmers, Willie Wallace, Bobby Lennox, Harry Hood, Dixie Deans and Kenny Dalglish banging them in, that hardly mattered.

In terms of importance, the 1965 Scottish Cup final has to rank as the most significant as it kick-started the club's sustained glory run under Stein. However, beating Rangers, 4–0 in 1969 probably gave me and my team-mates most pleasure, for obvious reasons, and offered further illustration of our superiority over our great rivals at that time.

Incidentally, that was the game that effectively finished Alex Ferguson's Rangers career, when he was made the scapegoat for the defeat. I have always felt that it was unfair to blame Fergie, after he was given the task of man-marking me at set pieces. That wasn't his game. He was a striker who used his flailing elbows to great effect. Fergie freely admits that he was culpable when he lost me at a corner after only a couple of minutes and I headed the first goal, but you have to ask, where was Ronnie McKinnon, the centre-half, at that moment?

My final haul of seven winners and five runners-up medals in the Scottish Cup took my total career haul in all competitions to twenty-three winners (and nine losers) and, while I gave Celtic my best efforts for eighteen years, I must also say that I was fortunate to enjoy so much success. I was lucky, too, to avoid major injuries. Apart from the broken leg I suffered playing against Kilmarnock at Celtic Park in 1963 which sidelined me for three months and the occasional problem with my knees, I missed very few games either through being crocked – or sent off. My disciplinary record was such that I saw red only twice. The first time I was sent off was in a match at East Stirling when my 'crime' amounted to trying to protect a team-mate in my capacity as captain. I felt that Stevie Chalmers was being unjustly treated by the 'Shire full-back, Jake McQueen, and told the referee so. Clearly, I did so rather forcibly, because the referee pointed in the direction of the dressing room.

The second occasion when I failed to finish the game was during a tour match in Bermuda. Again, I fell foul of the referee for expressing the view that Jimmy Quinn – a youngster at the time – required protection from a local player who kept aiming swinging kicks at him. I shouldn't have reacted in the way I did on either occasion, but two red cards in eighteen years wasn't bad, given that I have a bit of a temper when riled.

The most serious incident I was involved in as a manager occurred in November 1982, when I was sent to the stand by referee Andrew Waddell, during a game against Aberdeen at Celtic Park. We ended up losing, 3–1, and I was convinced that their third goal – incidentally scored by Mark McGhee, who was later to join me at Celtic – was offside. I was also unhappy that Danny McGrain had been red-carded and questioned the validity of the penalty award that had enabled Aberdeen to go in front. The combination of emotions led me to challenge Waddell's competence and there is the famous photograph of the pair of us standing eyeball to eyeball at the side of the track. The scene took place in full view of the crowd and I was formally cautioned by the referee and sent packing. I was later fined £200 by the SFA and severely reprimanded. On reflection, it was a serious error of judgement on my part and I am none too proud of the way I reacted.

Clearly, nothing could surpass our achievement in winning the European Cup, but not all of my European and international experiences were happy ones. Two occasions stand out in my mind: the World Club Championship games with Racing Club of Argentina in 1967 and Celtic's European Cup semi-final against Atletico Madrid seven years later. Significantly, both Racing and, subsequently, Atletico were coached by the notorious Juan Carlos Lorenzo, who had managed Argentina in the 1966 World Cup finals, when Rattin was ordered off against England in the quarter-finals.

The die was cast in the first leg at Celtic Park, when Racing's cynicism shone through, as they clearly didn't care what methods they employed in their efforts not to concede a goal. They failed, as it happened, when I headed home a corner kick from John Hughes to give us a slender lead for the return in Buenos Aires. As we came off the pitch, one of the Racing players, Basile, gestured that they would cut our throats in the return – and he wasn't kidding.

When we arrived in the Argentine capital we were put up in a third-rate hotel and received appalling treatment, with the locals going out of their way to be awkward. The accommodation we were offered wouldn't have rated even one star and Jock immediately put his foot down, insisting on a change of hotel. He won his point, but there was nothing the manager could do about the sub-standard training facilities and it turned out that this was just a foretaste of what was to come in the match itself. We ran onto the pitch, in front of 120,000 baying fans, carrying the Argentine national flag in an effort to curry favour. But, instead of winning them over with the gesture, we were pelted with missiles. Ronnie Simpson was cut by a piece of flying metal and John Fallon had to take over from him in goal, so bad was the injury.

Once started, the game quickly degenerated into farce. They scored a goal which was blatantly offside, after Tommy Gemmell had given us the lead from the penalty spot and Jimmy Johnstone had a goal disallowed without reason. That, of course, had nothing whatsoever to do with the fact that a Uruguayan referee was in charge of the game!

The upshot was that Racing won, 2–1, necessitating a play-off in neighbouring Uruguay, where the atmosphere at Montevideo's Centenario Stadium was every bit as hostile as it had been in Buenos Aires. The pitch was ringed with barbed wire and a moat and the police were armed with guns and tear-gas. All that was missing to complete a sinister and depressing picture was a sign saying, 'Welcome to hell'. With hindsight, Celtic should have refused to agree to a third game and flown home, for what followed disgraced the game of football.

No fewer than six players were sent off by the Paraguayan referee, a buffoon by the name of Rudolfo Osorio, who on two occasions had to call on the services of the local constabulary to try to restore order on the pitch. We made the mistake of reacting to the intimidation. The Racing players wound us up by kicking everything and everyone above ground level and Bobby Lennox, Jimmy Johnstone and John Hughes saw red.

Basile, who had threatened mayhem after the first leg, also went. The final crime count should actually have reached seven, when Bertie Auld was also ordered off, but the bold Bertie simply refused to walk. The referee kept screaming, 'Off' at Bertie, but my team-mate replied,

'I've already told you, I'm not going.' Cardenas scored a second half goal to win the cup for Racing, but it was victory without honour. Our mistake had been to lose our cool.

I am convinced that the Argentinians reacted in the manner they did because of what had happened the previous year at Wembley. Interestingly, they called us 'animals', in a clear response to Sir Alf Ramsey branding them as such. However, after experiencing just how low Racing were prepared to sink, in my opinion Sir Alf was fully justified. Sure, we shouldn't have fallen into the trap, but, given the circumstances, there was no justification for Celtic's decision to fine each of us £500. Clearly this action was taken to turn the players into scapegoats for the club's failure to anticipate the potential for trouble.

The dreaded Juan Carlos Lorenzo clearly remembered Jimmy Johnstone from seven years previously when, in April 1974, he brought Atletico to Celtic Park for the European Cup semi-final first leg. How else do you explain the outrageous treatment Jinky was subjected to over 180 minutes of football? Atletico's vicious assault on Jinky, and most of the rest of us, resulted in three of their players being red-carded and another seven cautioned, yet the referee did not note a single name!

The Spaniards secured the draw they had come for when the game finished goal-less, but they paid the price of a £14,000 UEFA fine and had six players banned from the return. A more appropriate punishment, in my view, would have been to have booted Atletico out of Europe, but, having escaped expulsion, our opponents indulged in psychological warfare. We were intimidated from the moment we arrived in Madrid, to the extent that a death threat was issued against Jinky. A local newspaper carried a story claiming that Jinky would be shot by a sniper during the course of the game. There is little doubt in my mind that it was a complete fabrication, designed to put the wee man off his game. If so, it worked. Jinky didn't play well, but then who could give of their best with that sort of sinister threat hanging over us?

Atletico even protested about us warming up on the pitch immediately prior to kick-off, but, fortunately, there was little evidence of the thuggery that had characterised the first game and Atletico won with two late goals, but I felt cheated out of playing in a third European Cup final. There was a measure of quiet satisfaction, though, when, in a victory for football over malevolence, Bayern Munich hammered Atletico 4–0 in a replay, following a 1–1 draw.

# CHAPTER 11

# THE KING AND
# THE PRINCE

Kenny Dalglish was an outstanding footballer – and the world's worst babysitter! Kenny was in a league of his own as a player, but when it came to looking after my kids, he was definitely lacking commitment. Thankfully, my former team-mate left the domestic chores to others and concentrated on becoming arguably the finest player ever to wear a Celtic jersey.

Some critics have claimed that Kenny failed to replicate his outstanding club form when he swapped the hoops for the dark blue of Scotland, and there may have been a modicum of truth in that assertion, but he would not have amassed a record 102 appearances for his country if he had repeatedly fallen short of expectations.

Kenny did, however, fail spectacularly when he took over as manager of Celtic in June 1999. He preferred the title 'director of football operations', but it amounted to being manager and I find it impossible to defend his time at the club, in what I consider to be one of the most prestigious jobs in football. To be perfectly blunt, I think Kenny may have underestimated the magnitude of his task to such an extent that his downfall became inevitable.

For all his greatness on the field, even as a player Kenny wasn't a fans' favourite in the same way as, say, Jimmy Johnstone and, in more recent times, Henrik Larsson. It may have had something to do with the suspicion that he was a Rangers fan at heart and the fact that, at times, Kenny could appear off-hand probably didn't help either. Unlike Charlie Nicholas, for example, Kenny was not given to outwardly sharing his joy with the supporters when he scored.

Kenny didn't seek my advice when he was appointed successor to Jozef Venglos and, indeed, there was no call on him to do so. He has, after all, always been his own man and once his mind is made up nothing will shift him. However, I like to think that I know something about what is involved in being manager of Celtic and had Kenny sought my council I would have stressed the need for a strong bond with the fans, because if you have the people at the heart of the club on your side it's half the battle, but, as manager, I don't think Kenny really had this.

In my opinion, Kenny made some horrendous mistakes and I was dismayed by what I witnessed during his brief reign, but that didn't change how I feel about him. Through it all I could never forget the moment I first set eyes on Kenny and instinctively knew that he was a unique talent. Jock Stein often introduced young players into pre-season training, to give them a feel of what it was like to be in the first team squad, and Kenny participated with relish. The fresh-faced 16-year-old with the blond hair wasn't in the least bit fazed by the company he was mixing in. He joined in one of the many 'bounce' games Jock regularly staged to round off our training and it was like watching a thoroughbred enter the parade ring. Rangers must still be kicking themselves that they missed out on signing such a talent. Kenny was brought up in a high-rise flat overlooking Ibrox and his dad used to take him to watch Rangers play. Mercifully, Rangers failed to spot the potential living in their own back yard, as players like Kenny Dalglish are extremely thin on the ground.

It was a measure of the emerging talent Celtic had at that time that Kenny was by no means the only eye-catching youngster at Celtic Park – Lou Macari, Danny McGrain, Victor Davidson and Paul Wilson also stood out – but Kenny was the pick of the bunch. He displayed a level of confidence that belied his tender years, but no one just walked into the team at that time – no matter how talented. In an effort to speed up Kenny's development, Jock farmed him out to the junior side, Cumbernauld United, and arranged for them to play an exhibition game against the Lisbon Lions. I suspect that Jock wanted to give Kenny an early taste of football at that level, to whet his appetite, and we took it upon ourselves to ensure that he didn't run away with the idea that it was an easy game. However, there was no holding the teenage Dalglish and his progress was such that the cub was soon sharing a dressing room with the Lions.

Initially, Kenny was blooded in the first team as a midfield player, because it was still unclear at that stage what his best position was. It wouldn't have mattered where Kenny played, though. He blended in straightaway. I can't say he displayed the same flair as a babysitter, however. When we enlisted his services it turned out to be a big mistake. Kenny had started seeing Marina Harkins, who would become his wife, and Liz and I happened to be friends of her parents, Pat and Martha. One evening we had arranged to have dinner with Pat and Martha, but we were experiencing problems in finding a suitable babysitter. The difficulty was resolved when Martha volunteered Marina and Kenny for duty. When we returned home Kenny was nowhere to be seen, though. Being a conscientious, dedicated lad, who believed in always getting a good night's sleep, he had left Marina holding the fort. She, meanwhile, had dozed off and when I looked through our lounge window I was greeted by the sight of our one remaining babysitter sound asleep in an armchair. After constantly ringing the door bell we resorted to telephoning her from our next door neighbours' house, but we couldn't wake her and I eventually had to climb through the kitchen window to gain entry, skinning my knee in the process.

Kenny and Marina married and bought a home close to our own in Newton Mearns, on the outskirts of Glasgow, and we travelled together to training. I quickly learned that Kenny was every bit as superstitious as me and we drove each other mad by insisting on certain rituals being enacted. I would insist on picking up Kenny from the exact same spot every day, for example, and if he was carrying his raincoat over his left arm and we had a good result he had to continue the ritual. Invariably, I did the driving, because Kenny fancied himself as a bit of a rally driver and whenever he was behind the wheel it turned into a white-knuckle ride.

But if Kenny's driving left much to be desired, his talents as a footballer were beyond compare. He was the most complete player I played with, blessed with a God-given talent, but it would be wrong for anyone to try to suggest that he didn't have to work hard to bring it to the fore. Great players are born with a gift, but in Kenny's case it was his ability as an all-rounder which made him so exceptional. Kenny also had a potent weapon – his backside. He was well built round the rear and he used it to great effect to hold off opponents and shield the ball in a way I have seen few others manage to do.

I can't claim to have known straightaway that Kenny would become one of the truly outstanding players of his generation, but he had the look of someone very special and he often managed to make those around him appear better than they actually were. Kenny was rarely the leading scorer, but the striker playing directly alongside him usually was. That was because he was the consummate team player. He was also the obvious choice to succeed me as captain, when I hung up my boots in 1975, and for all that Kenny is a quiet and fairly private person, he was able to motivate other players, largely by example.

Kenny is also ruthlessly single-minded. Once he has made his mind up there is no going back with him. Trying to dissuade Kenny from a certain course of action is well nigh impossible. His move to Liverpool, in 1977, was a classic example of that single-mindedness. Liverpool didn't pick Kenny – Kenny chose Liverpool! He had decided that Liverpool offered him the best vehicle for his talents and ambition, that with the players they already had in place Liverpool was the club most likely to help him further his career, and that was it. I had left Celtic by then, but I did my best to try to talk him into remaining at Celtic Park. I wasted my time. By then, Kenny was 26 and had won everything with Celtic, with the exception of a European Cup medal. Liverpool were about to record the first of four European Cup triumphs.

Much as I regretted seeing Kenny leave for what was a pittance of his true worth, I couldn't blame him, and I am far from convinced that Kenny could have been dissuaded from following the path he had settled on had he been offered a significant increase in wages. He felt he had gone as far as he could with Celtic and that it was time for a fresh challenge. Liverpool got their man for a mere £440,000 and Kenny was probably the only player who could have replaced Kevin Keegan – both in terms of his value to the team and in the affections of the fans. I recall being at the 1977 European Cup final in Rome when Liverpool beat Borussia Monchengladbach, 3–1. Keegan was already earmarked for a move to Hamburg and the Liverpool fans told me that the club would be taking Dalglish from Celtic. I responded by informing them that Liverpool had no chance of doing that, but just a few months later Kenny was at Anfield and Keegan was quickly forgotten. Keegan was perhaps a more dynamic personality, but Dalglish was a more complete player, in my opinion; the type you build a team round.

Of course, it's one thing to carve out a reputation with your first club, but it takes a unique personality to move on and enhance that reputation elsewhere. Having said that, I believe Kenny would have been a success no matter where he chose to go. Kenny would have been capable of playing anywhere in the world. He could have handled the pressures of Italian or Spanish football, for instance. Once he sets his mind to something, Kenny believes that anything is possible and he seems to have been a success at almost everything he has done. He is also a very fine golfer, for example.

The one blemish on Kenny's CV was the way he handled his return to Celtic. Having achieved so much as manager at Liverpool, Blackburn and Newcastle, I thought that Kenny would prove every bit as successful at Celtic Park. But his approach to the job both surprised and disappointed me. I saw nothing wrong with him appointing John Barnes as coach. I imagined that, with the benefit of access to Kenny's vast experience, Barnes would grow into the role and there was no reason to think that, with Kenny's assistance, Barnes wouldn't have eventually developed into a fine manager in his own right. The impression given initially was that Kenny would be the dominant figure in the partnership and Barnes the willing apprentice. I did not imagine for one moment that Barnes would be thrust into such a prominent position.

Kenny's decision to appoint himself director of football operations and leave Barnes so exposed was, frankly, bewildering. Understandably, bearing in mind that he had no previous experience in a managerial role, Barnes seemed out of his depth as a front man and I remain mystified as to Kenny's reasons for seemingly wishing to take a back seat. I feel he should have been much more hands-on. I can't for the life of me understand what Kenny was thinking about, but it was a decision that impacted severely on the club and the Dalglish–Barnes partnership turned into a disaster.

Some of the other things Kenny did were equally bizarre, such as staging press conferences in pubs. By asking journalists to sit among Celtic fans at the Supporters' Club and Baird's Bar in Glasgow's Gallowgate, Kenny was subjecting them to a potentially hostile reaction and that did not endear him to the sporting press. Naturally, it would have helped him if the press had been on his side, but in doing this he alienated certain members of the media. Perhaps Kenny was trying to give the fans an insight into how press conferences are conducted and didn't care so much whether some journalists found the experience uncomfortable. Whatever the case, it was ill-advised. Celtic Park was the proper setting for any press conference.

Consequently, relations between Kenny and the press appeared to worsen and it became a no-win situation for him when the team was turfed out of the Scottish Cup by Inverness Caledonian Thistle at Celtic Park in February 2000. Given that Inverness was a first division club it was perhaps the most embarrassing result in Celtic's history. The press were in no mood to forgive and forget in the aftermath of that defeat.

The final indignity was a comment Kenny made about that humiliating game on his return from a short golfing break to Spain. He was met at the airport by a group of journalists and quizzed about his thoughts on the result. 'Why are you asking me that? I've been away working on my sun tan,' he replied. It was a tactless remark and if Kenny was making an attempt at humour, no one laughed – least of all the Celtic fans. I am sure that most regarded the comment as being downright degrading, although that period of Kenny's career shouldn't be allowed to overshadow his remarkable achievements as a player.

I bump into Kenny from time to time and our relationship remains cordial, but I don't think we will see him back in football management. He has found another niche, working as a media pundit, and he seems content. Kenny is also a wealthy man who enjoys the luxury of being able to pick and choose what he wants to do with his life. I believe that had he desired to carry on in management we would have been back in the game before now.

While Kenny was the most complete player I have seen, Charlie Nicholas was the most exciting youngster I managed. Kenny was king; Charlie was the young pretender to his throne. Charlie was blessed with outstanding talent and he possessed a quality missing from Kenny's game – that wee bit of cheek that endeared him to the fans. Kenny's ability was channelled into assisting the team. Charlie was much more of a showman. Usually, Kenny's face broke into a wide smile only when he scored a goal or did something exceptional. Charlie was rarely seen without a cheeky grin on his face.

But Charlie's flashier style couldn't disguise the fact that he was an outstanding talent. He possessed a silky touch, wonderful close control and scored outstanding goals. He was also precocious to the point of being a real Jack the Lad. Nothing and no one fazed the teenage Nicholas. It was brought to my attention that Charlie never wore socks, winter or summer, and, as feet are the principal tools of a footballer's trade, it concerned me that he might be doing himself some damage because of this unusual habit, which, I felt, was unhygienic. Presumably, it was some sort of fashion statement and Charlie was always in the height of fashion, but no matter that Charlie had quickly become a key player, I warned him that if he didn't conform I was going to fine him and leave him out of the team.

However, typical Charlie, having promised to start wearing socks, as soon as he left the ground after training he would head straight for his car and promptly remove his footwear. I got to hear of this and one day waited until Charlie was about to get behind the wheel before telling his closest buddy at Celtic, Danny Crainie, to relay the message that I wanted to see him straightaway. Having done his usual quick change by the time Danny reached the car park, Charlie had no option but to report to my office minus his socks. 'How much did your socks cost?' I asked. 'A fiver, gaffer,' replied Charlie. 'Right,' I declared, 'I'm fining you a fiver and I'll go on doing so every time I catch you disobeying my instructions.' Charlie protested that I couldn't do that, but I could, of course, and I did. Mind you, it was a bit of fun more than anything and a light-hearted way of demonstrating to Charlie exactly who was boss.

On another occasion, Charlie and Danny reported to my office one day to reveal that they had been charged by the police with breach of the peace following an incident in Kilsyth. When I pressed the pair for a fuller explanation, Charlie was happy to oblige. 'All we were doing was playing football in the street. Honest, boss,' he said. I immediately shot back, 'Charlie, you don't get hauled into court for playing football in the street these days. There must be more to it that that.' But the pair of them insisted that they were telling the truth. What they failed to add was that their impromptu kick-about had taken place in the town's main street and had involved them lobbing a tennis ball over the roof of double-decker buses and other passing traffic. That was typical of Charlie. He was full of daft fun, but there was no maliciousness in his nature.

Charlie had a tough streak as well, though, and I saw that side when he had the misfortune to break a leg playing against Morton reserves at Cappielow in early 1982. The injury was potentially serious and such a blow might have proved too much for some young players, but Charlie worked hard to regain his fitness and he returned fitter and stronger. I believe the experience also had the effect of making him realise the precarious nature of a career as a footballer and may have contributed to his desire to cash-in on his talents as quickly as possible.

I first became aware of Charlie when I was helping out at Celtic Boys' Club, immediately after I stopped playing, and it was evident that he was a cut above other kids of the same age. He was unquestionably the most naturally skilled young player I worked with, but his flair and ability perhaps partially obscured the fact that Charlie was also a hard worker. In addition to his natural predatory instincts, he led the line with real authority. So, when I became manager of Aberdeen I made an immediate move to take Charlie to Pittodrie, because I'd had my card marked that Celtic had not made an official signing offer. As soon as Celtic heard about my interest they swooped to prevent the loss of a player who should have become one of the true greats. Ironically, Charlie later found his way to Pittodrie, but by then much of the authority he had displayed previously with Celtic and, for a time, at Arsenal had disappeared from his game.

Charlie was still a teenager when he exploded on the scene in my third season as manager. He very nearly had it all – talent, the ability to excite and an air of supreme self-confidence, combined with a refusal to be intimidated by the demands placed on Old Firm players. He was seemingly nerveless. In short, Charlie was a star and the fans loved him. But, like most young players with a few bob in their pocket and the world at their feet, Charlie thought he knew best when it came to advancing his career, and there was certainly no shortage of clubs desperate to entice him away from Celtic Park. Arsenal, Liverpool and Manchester United headed the queue in the summer of 1983 and it was obvious from the start that his talents would soon be lost to Scottish football because we simply could not – or would not – compete with the big guns from the South. After several weeks of uncertainty, Charlie eventually settled for a move to Highbury, for a fee reputed to be £625,000. I personally believed him to be a £1 million player. I was also of the view that he was not ready for such a move.

It was the wrong time. Charlie was attracted by the bright lights of London and a showbiz lifestyle, but I had seen what such a move had done to the career of another extremely talented Scot, Peter Marinello, years earlier. When Marinello was transferred from Hibs to Arsenal in January 1970 for £100,000, he was talked about as the next George Best. There was a lot of truth in that statement, as Marinello's career unfortunately followed a similar downward spiral to Bestie's!

Peter was little more than a kid and I don't think he had matured sufficiently to cope with the demands of suddenly becoming a star and signing for a club of the status of Arsenal. He was a good-looking young bloke and he was a magnet for the advertising agencies. His face featured on billboards after he was encouraged to promote various products, including extolling the virtues of drinking milk. He was marketed more as a pop star than a football player and he got caught up in the showbiz lifestyle. There was no shortage of newspaper pictures of Peter surrounded by pretty young models and he probably got carried away with his sudden exposure to life in swinging London.

It was hard to be critical of Peter. What young man wouldn't have had his head turned? But his career undoubtedly suffered as a consequence of living life in the fast lane.

He joined Arsenal when the club was building towards a League and Cup Double in 1971, but his time there was short-lived and he never fulfilled his glittering potential. Eventually he ended up playing for Portsmouth and Motherwell.

Charlie was also marketed as having a playboy image, and I think his agent was largely responsible for that, but it was Charlie's choice to turn down Liverpool and Manchester United. No one had to twist his arm to persuade him to become a Gunner, but by electing to join Arsenal I believe that Charlie effectively shot himself in the foot. He put himself into a difficult situation, whereas if he had gone to Anfield or Old Trafford I am sure that he would have been given greater protection from the media and steered away from the bright lights.

Perhaps it had something to do with not wanting the responsibility of trying to fill Kenny Dalglish's boots. If so, who could blame him? But, whatever the reason, Charlie was never the same player he had been at Celtic. He should have remained at Celtic Park for a couple more seasons, to develop as a player and a man. Dalglish was twenty-six and a complete player when he joined Liverpool. He was also a married man with family and was settled. Kenny was equipped to cope with the demands placed on him, whereas Charlie was twenty-one and still a boy in many ways; a fun-loving youngster with money to burn.

I have always had a fondness for Charlie and I tried to warn him of the potential pitfalls, both as his manager and as a friend. But his mind was made up. Desmond White, too, had made the decision to cash-in on Charlie's talents. I recall the chairman coming to me and saying that a deal had been agreed and that Charlie was going to Arsenal. I responded by asking him why he had to be sold in the first place, but I might as well have talked to the wall. The answer I got – if indeed you can call it that – was a rambling reply to the effect that Celtic had concluded a sound piece of business. That really annoyed me and I retorted, 'Mr White, why has he got to leave this club?' The chairman said that was just the way it was in football and I snapped, 'No, Mr White, that's the way it is at Celtic. As soon as we unearth a good player he is sold.' I then implored Mr White that if his mind was truly made up to sell our prize asset, at least make it a Dutch auction. By placing Charlie on the open market I reckoned we would receive a small fortune, but I was wasting my time. The board, or at least the chairman, had ruled and Charlie was going to Highbury, because, Mr White explained, Denis Hill-Wood, the Arsenal chairman, was an honourable man. What that had to do with it, I wouldn't know.

To this day I can't say with absolute certainty the precise sum Celtic received for one of the finest players to wear the hoops. The chairman simply refused to tell me. When I asked him what I should tell the press with regard to the transfer fee, which I knew would be the first thing they would want to know, I was told to say that both parties were perfectly happy with the deal. I tried again. 'Fine, but what is the fee?' To no avail. 'There is no need for you to know,' Mr White declared. 'So,' I replied 'in other words, your manager is not considered trustworthy enough to be told such details.' The writing was now firmly on the wall. Just a short time later I would be following Charlie out of the door at Celtic Park. I considered that my position as manager was being undermined and that my situation was close to untenable. Charlie's final appearance for Celtic was a 4–2 win at Ibrox and he signed off with a double. It was also my last competitive game in charge.

Charlie won just twenty Scotland caps, a fifth of Dalglish's tally, but do I think Charlie could have emulated Dalglish's feats in the game had he been more patient? The answer is yes, for Charlie was the sort of charismatic individual who was capable of lifting you out of your seat with one flash of brilliance. If only Charlie had copied his predecessor's freedom of movement and expression we would have had a player to compare with Dalglish.

By the time he was finished at Arsenal, Charlie no longer appeared to possess the same desire and enthusiasm he had shown as a youngster at Celtic Park. The skills and touches were still evident, but were in somewhat shorter supply. Part of the problem may have stemmed from Arsenal's style of play at that time. They were not renowned as an attacking force and Charlie probably found it difficult to adapt to a different type of game to the one he had been used to at Celtic, but maybe his failure to excel had more to do with having to shoulder the heavy weight of expectancy. Having said that, I would not have hesitated to re-sign Charlie at the start of the 1987–88 season, following my return as manager, but he never gave me any indication that he was keen to do so and elected to join Aberdeen instead.

The pair of us would eventually return to Celtic Park, older and presumably wiser, but whereas Kenny's career was fulfilled, I believe Charlie fell someway short of reaching the heights he was capable of achieving. I know that Charlie will claim that he enjoyed considerable success and point to the fact that he made a lot of money from a career that saw him serve Celtic, twice, Arsenal, Aberdeen and, finally, Clyde, and who can argue? But whereas Kenny's haul of medals and trophies would fill a display cabinet to overflowing, Charlie requires somewhat less space to display his. Ironically, just weeks before joining Arsenal, Charlie was named Scotland's Player of the Year, an award that eluded Kenny, but, in the final analysis, football is part of the entertainment industry and Charlie Nicholas gave a great deal of enjoyment to a lot of people. Plus the question has to be asked, would Charlie have been the same exciting player had he been blessed with Kenny's dedication and adopted a much more serious approach to playing football? Probably not.

# CALLING
# TIME

I was thirty-five when I called time on my playing career. On reflection, the decision was premature. I could have carried on for another couple of seasons at least, but I was partially influenced by the fact that my right knee had begun playing up. Initially I feared that the injury – damaged cruciate ligaments – would force me to quit. For quite a while I suffered excruciating pain and was forced to lie in a hot bath when I came home from training to try to ease the discomfort and get my leg moving freely. Then, one day, without warning my knee clicked back into place and I was able to regain my fitness, but there was a price to be paid and I have certainly suffered in recent years.

If I am honest, I had also become increasingly irked by the constant references to me being a 'veteran'. Call it paranoia if you like, but it seemed that every time I picked up a newspaper and read an article pertaining to Celtic, I was referred to as some sort of old guy. I should have ignored what the hacks were saying because, even at thirty-five, I still had something to offer. I also still enjoyed playing the game. Another mistake I made was not following my own advice. I had repeatedly advanced the view that the end of the season is not the time to make a decision about retirement, because that's when, inevitably, you're tired. The best time to judge how you feel is in the early months of the season.

Almost from the moment I announced my retirement I regretted the decision, but I wanted to go out at the top and the Scottish Cup final against Airdrie seemed as good a time as any to sign off. So, on 3 May 1975, I pulled on a Celtic jersey for the last time in a competitive game and, after thirteen years as captain, led the team into action at Hampden.

By then I was Billy McNeill MBE. The previous year I had been honoured by Her Majesty in a ceremony at Buckingham Palace for my services to football. It was one of the proudest moments of my life, but I cannot, for the life of me, recall what the Queen said as I bowed before her during the investiture. I can, however, recall making my way through what seemed like miles of corridors with the weightlifter, Precious McKenzie, at my back. The wee man was in good form as he tapped me on the shoulder and pointed to a huge picture dominating almost an entire wall. 'Will you look at that,' said Precious. 'It's bigger than my f****** house!' Liz accompanied me to the Palace, although because each recipient of an award is restricted to just two guests, the girls missed out. But there wasn't any time to celebrate in London. As soon as the investiture ceremony was over we had to dash to Heathrow Airport to catch a flight to Glasgow. The reason for our haste was Kenny Dalglish's wedding. I'm not sure that Kenny would have been very understanding had we put the Queen first and missed his big day altogether!

We were naturally short-priced favourites to beat Airdrie, but I had learned to my cost that there is no such thing in sport as a 'certainty' and I approached my final ninety minutes in the hoops with the same commitment as I had the first time I pulled on a Celtic jersey all those years before. In the event, Celtic won, 3–1, with two goals from Paul Wilson and another from Pat McCluskey, and I began planning for a new life as a businessman away from the football world.

However, it could so easily have been a short-lived retirement when fate intervened that summer to leave Jock Stein seriously injured following the horrific car smash I mentioned earlier. Liz and I were in the process of disembarking from the Canberra at Southampton, following a Mediterranean cruise, when we received the news. It had been our intention to spend several days with friends, Tony and Annette Church, in Woking, but when it became clear that Jock had been badly injured we decided to head north immediately. I had expected to find Jock lying at death's door, but was taken by surprise when we arrived at Dumfries Royal Infirmary to find him looking incredibly healthy for someone who had been pulled from the wreckage of a head-on collision. Jock was connected to several tubes and was unable to speak, but he had all his wits about him and communicated by scribbling notes. I joked that I was enjoying the fact that for once I was able to out-talk him.

However, for all that Jock gave the appearance of having sustained fewer injuries than had at first been feared, it was clear that he would require a lengthy period of recuperation before returning to Celtic Park. I felt, in the circumstances, that the club might turn to me to assist them in a crisis, but the call never came. That hurt at the time and still rankles to this day. Perhaps I should have been the one to make the approach, but I didn't feel that it was my place to offer my services, even though I knew I was good for another two or three seasons at least. The Icelander Johannes Edvaldsson had been signed and Roddie MacDonald was being given his chance in the first team, so those in charge clearly felt that they had adequate cover.

Vancouver Whitecaps had wanted me and I was offered all sorts of inducements to join the NASL, but, having decided to hang up my boots, I turned them down. Ayr United were also keen to keep me in the game. I was offered the managership at Somerset Park and the job appealed. I hadn't given a great deal of thought to becoming a manager, but I felt that Ayr had potential and that it would be an ideal opportunity to cut my teeth away from the pressures associated with a top club. However, after discussing the offer with my business partners, Frank McCormack, an accountant, and Joe McBride, my former teammate, we agreed that it was more important for me to concentrate all my efforts on establishing the company.

We had set up as Milnrow Development and I sank all the proceeds from my pension fund and the bulk of the £25,000 I received from my testimonial match against Liverpool into the company. I also sold a small pub that I had in Bellshill to help finance the operation. However, the venture turned into a disaster. Initially we renovated properties and rented them out, but it was a business that had been tarnished by unscrupulous landlords and we sold off our stock of flats and moved into the licence trade instead. Soon we owned several hotels in Ayrshire and for a time business was good, but interest rates suddenly went through the roof and we began to feel the pinch. Perhaps we were the architects of our eventual downfall by being over-ambitious, but we were also unlucky.

The realisation that the company would have to find ways to reduce overheads coincided with my move into management with Clyde and, when I moved on to Aberdeen a short time later, I resigned as a director. When I tried to recoup my investment in Milnrow, though, it proved impossible to get my money back and, by the time I returned to Celtic in May 1978, the company was in a serious financial state. It eventually went bust several years later and I was very nearly ruined. I lost £85,000 and we were forced to sell our beautiful home at Pollokshields in Glasgow. After eighteen years playing at the top level I was damn near skint.

I will never forget the moment when I was given the news. Liz and I had been for dinner with friends and when we returned home one of the kids had left a note telling me to phone Joe McBride. I got an immediate sinking feeling in the pit of my stomach and I instinctively knew what I was about to be told, but the words, 'gone bust' were still a dagger to the heart. Thankfully, Liz handled the situation very much better than me. She was remarkably philosophical, in fact, and a tower of strength at the time. Had I not enjoyed the staunch support of my wife, I am not sure that I would have been able to have bounced back as quickly as I did.

My ill-fated venture into the world of big business might never have happened had my career taken a different course when, in 1972, Tommy Docherty became manager of Manchester United and offered me the chance to join him at Old Trafford. He had quit as Scotland boss to take over from Frank O'Farrell at Old Trafford and he wanted me. 'Big Man, I desperately need a centre-half and I know you can do a job for me,' said the Doc. 'I'll give you a three- or four-year contract and you'll earn more money here than you have in your entire career at Celtic.' Was I tempted? You bet. I didn't know very much about the Doc as a manager, apart from the time we had spent together at Largs with the Scotland squad, but I liked his style. The fact that the scars of the 1970 European Cup final defeat had not healed either was influencing my thoughts about the future.

Earlier that year, on the advice of Jock Stein and to my lasting regret, I had already turned down Doc's invitation to go to Brazil and play in the world famous Maracana Stadium, and, this time, again I listened to Jock. Playing for Manchester United would have been a wonderful adventure, but he told me how important my influence was on the team at Celtic Park and I allowed his pandering to my ego to override my gut feeling.

I was proud that Jock regarded me as being so important to him, but it was the old loyalty thing rearing its ugly head once again. Celtic always called for loyalty, but it was a one-way thing. I should have considered the fact that the bulk of my Lisbon Lion team-mates had already been discarded. Tommy Gemmell, John Clark, Stevie Chalmers, Willie Wallace and John Hughes had all gone. But, of course, you never think it will happen to you and I have to admit that when the end came for me it was through choice. I also enjoyed the financial rewards of a testimonial match, so I can't really complain, although after eighteen years and 832 appearances for Celtic surely I merited that much?

The truth is that the Lisbon Lions were paupers compared to our Italian, Spanish and Germany counterparts, yet the revenue poured into Celtic Park on the back of our success. Celtic generated incredible sums of money from gates that were regularly in excess of 50,000, sometimes considerably more. Where all that money disappeared to I have no idea, but it certainly didn't find its way into the players' pockets. It was a standing joke the way the attendance figures were massaged. If the attendance at an Old Firm game was 70,000, it was invariably returned at 50,000, and 50,000 crowds mysteriously became 35,000!

It wouldn't have been so bad had the surplus cash been spent on the training facilities, but, not to put too fine a point on it, they were crap. At Barrowfield, we trained on what was little better than a mud heap. When the Belgian side, Mechelen, played St Mirren in the Cup Winners' Cup in 1987, I received a telephone call from the coach, Aad de Mos, asking if we could provide training facilities. I readily agreed to the request, because I have always enjoyed watching

Continental sides train, but de Mos probably wished I hadn't agreed to accommodate him. The Mechelen players changed at Celtic Park before I accompanied them the mile or so to Barrowfield, but when de Mos saw the condition of the small training pitch and the red blaze pitch alongside, he was convinced I was winding him up. 'Billy, this is a joke. You are pulling my leg,' he said. 'Surely this is where the boys train.' Somewhat shamefaced, I replied, 'No, Aad, this is where the first team do their training.' Little had changed in thirty years!

It would have been wonderful to have enjoyed the facilities provided for the Manchester United players in those days at the Cliff, but it wasn't to be. Perhaps if I had known then what life in Manchester was like, I would have pushed harder to make the move, but it was to be another eleven years before I eventually headed down the M6.

# CHAPTER 13

# LEGENDS
# AND HEROES

If there is such a creature as a complete footballer, **George Best** is the closest I have seen to the perfect player. Best had the lot – skill, flair, pace, tenacity, bravery, timing, remarkable speed of thought and he could also score goals. What more could you ask for? But Franz Beckenbauer ran the Irishman close. The 'Kaiser' was the outstanding defender of his generation, yet he could probably have filled every position in the team and done an outstanding job.

I encountered Bestie several times at both club and international level and he was murder to play against, because he was a mix of everything. You could never be sure exactly what he planned to do next. Best's dribbling skills were such that he could take the ball up to an opponent and in one flash he was past his man and away. The fact that he was capable of running at defenders on either side of the pitch or setting off on a diagonal run across the defence, because of his electrifying burst of speed, made him almost impossible to man mark. Once he was clear, Best rarely wasted a shot. Some very skilful players lack a finish, but Best had total self-belief. He was simply sensational, without any obvious flaw that I could see.

I played against Beckenbauer only once, for Scotland against West Germany in the 3–2 defeat in Hamburg, in October 1969. Beckenbauer's reading of a game was his greatest strength. His razor-sharp brain meant that he saw a situation developing two moves ahead of most other players. That enabled him to step in and take the ball off an attacker with perfect timing. Once he had possession, Beckenbauer initiated a counter-attack out of defence. His vision, allied with his wonderful ball control and ability to hit short or long passes with great precision, meant that he was able to orchestrate so much of Bayern Munich and West Germany's play. Beckenbauer also had stature and a natural presence. In other words, he looked the part and in doing so exuded importance. That characteristic had an intimidating effect on the opposition and was almost worth the headstart of a goal to his team.

Fate decreed that Celtic were drawn against Italian opposition at a time when Serie A was generally regarded as the finest and most feared league in the world. That gave me the opportunity to test myself against some of the most talented players in world football. There were three, in particular, who left a lasting impression: the Inter pair of Giacinto Facchetti and Sandro Mazzola, and Gianni Rivera of AC Milan.

Facchetti was essentially an over-lapping full-back and a tall and imposing figure. His height also allowed him to dominate in the air at set-piece moves, but Facchetti was not a typical Italian defender of that time, in the sense that he carried himself with great dignity and was skilful and creative. The physical aspect he left to his defensive partner, Burgnich, at least when we faced Inter in the European Cup final. Burgnich was the one who clattered opposing forwards and had the toughness associated with the Italian sides of that generation.

Mazzola typified what was needed in a striker capable of unlocking a well-organised defence and that was an area where the Italians excelled. The front players had to be lightning quick to stand any chance of losing the markers, who shadowed them constantly throughout the game. The top class strikers were sharp off their mark and quick to read situations. They also had to be able to display instant control and electric-fast reflexes in the box. Mazzola possessed all of those qualities and you had to be constantly on your guard against him.

Rivera must have been a dream to play alongside. It was a measure of his talents that he was voted European Footballer of the Year in 1969, seven years after exploding on to the international scene at the age of just eighteen. He was the strategist of the Milan attack and the architect of our European Cup third round defeat at Celtic Park in 1969, after we had managed to hold them to a 0–0 draw at the San Siro. Rivera's technique was flawless and, for one with a fragile physique, he was surprisingly strong and determined and could ride tackles and ghost away from opponents. He was able to do that because he was blessed with instant control and his passing was wonderfully imaginative and accurate.

Less than a fortnight after we won the European Cup, Celtic provided the opposition in a testimonial match for Alfredo di Stefano of Real Madrid, in the magnificent Bernabeu Stadium, and this gave me the opportunity to study the great man up close. Di Stefano and Ferenc Puskas were at the end of their careers, but they remained icons. I could see why. Di Stefano made the play for others and also scored goals. He was withdrawn slightly behind the main strikers and was given the freedom to express his marvellous talents of close control and brilliant inventiveness. Puskas' portly build belied his speed of movement and remarkable stamina. He took up positions where he could dart in behind defenders and punish a moment's slackness. He fed off the likes of Di Stefano, whose linking with the strikers was a key feature of Real's many successes. Players of the genius of Di Stefano and Puskas didn't need to be told how to blend into a team. They instinctively knew what was required of them and added to their overall contribution with delightful off-the-cuff flashes of brilliance.

After what they did to Scotland in 1961 I am not absolutely sure that I should be paying tribute to the English trio of Johnny Haynes, Bobby Charlton and Jimmy Greaves, but it would be churlish not to. Haynes was perhaps the best long-passer in the game at that time. He was the master of everything he did and pulled the strings of what was a very good England team. He demanded the ball and began many of his side's most enterprising moves with a single pass. England always seemed to have quality, quick, wide players and Haynes knew which passes to play to release them.

I never had any difficulty understanding why the Italians wanted Jimmy Greaves. Greavsie was quicksilver. No matter how vigilant a defender was, he had the knack of losing his marker by suddenly bursting into life. His bursts of speed over a short distance and his mental reflexes allowed him to out-think the majority of defenders.

The first time I faced Bobby Charlton, I couldn't believe how explosive he was. Charlton posed a hellish threat, because even if you succeeded in holding him off, his ability to hit screaming shots from long range was such that he was still capable of doing real damage. I recall one game in particular, a League International at Villa Park (these games featured teams comprising players playing in the English and Scottish leagues and were often used to gauge the potential of players emerging on the full international scene), when Charlton pulled the trigger and unleashed one of his piledrivers. The ball must have been travelling at something like a hundred miles per hour. Fortunately, it flew a foot wide of the post. Otherwise it would probably have burst the net and lifted the goalposts out of the ground.

Kevin Keegan came later and he was a different type to Charlton. Keegan, whom I played against a couple of times, epitomised perpetual motion. He never seemed to need to stop to recharge his batteries. He drew his opponent in and then played his pass. He was electrifyingly sharp and his strength was the way he played the ball to a team-mate and ran into space to take the return pass.

Bobby Moore was as classy a defender as any I have ever seen. He was in the same league as Beckenbauer, the way he could read passes, and was quite brilliant at opening up the opposition. Moore never looked to be under pressure. He had a commanding air and a genuine presence on the pitch, which made other players look up to him. Bobby passed the ball with the same accuracy as Beckenbauer, but he didn't attack people. His pace was suspect, but his judgement and timing were such that he was able to compensate for what he lacked in terms of mobility by winning the ball and delivering it on a sixpence. For me, Moore was the best defender on show at the 1970 World Cup finals in Mexico. He also used to annoy the hell out of the Scotland fans, who gave the impression that they hated him, but, to be honest, I think the Scots secretly admired Moore, because he appeared dignified and was so much in control. It was also a fact that the more abuse he had hurled at him at Hampden, the better he seemed to perform.

It would be easy to overlook the stars I played with and against much nearer home, but it's a measure of how highly I rated the Celtic trio of Danny McGrain, George Connelly and Kenny Dalglish that I would have replaced three of my Lisbon Lions team-mates with them. That is no reflection whatsoever on Jim Craig, John Clark or Steve Chalmers. It is simply a recognition of just how outstandingly good McGrain, Connelly and Dalglish were. McGrain was the finest right-back I played with and Connelly could have become one of the true greats of the game had he not walked away from football at such a young age. Dalglish was simply outstanding in all departments of the game.

I may surprise a lot of people by putting forward John Greig as a player I would want alongside me. Given that Greigy is a Rangers legend that may not go down terribly well with Celtic fans, but the truth is Greigy was an outstanding player. Besides his strength and ability he was wonderfully adaptable and could play in either full-back position or midfield. He was also noted for scoring the occasional goal, none more important than the winner against Italy at Hampden in 1965.

I was always a big fan of Dave Mackay, the former Spurs and Scotland star. When it came to wholehearted commitment and steely determination, no player ever wore the jersey with more pride or captained his country with greater zeal. He was also able to stabilise a game.

The late Billy Bremner was another who typified the Scottish spirit. Bremner was a lionhearted wee man and a skipper who led by example. His flame-coloured hair embellished his fiery temperament and his sheer tenacity, but to suggest that Billy was simply a battler who snapped and snarled at the heels of opponents would be to do him a grave disservice. He was also a talented individual who thought deeply about the game and could make passes that sliced open defences.

The most skilful midfield player Scotland has ever produced was undoubtedly Jim Baxter. Jim was a contender for the status of world class and was imbued with genius. One flash of Baxter could transform any game and he was a typical showman, who performed best on the big stage. Some observers claimed that Jim was lazy and had a selfish streak. They espoused the view that Jim contributed little unless he had possession of the ball. That was nonsense. Jim also did a lot of work off the ball and, for all that he had an aversion to training, he was capable of covering a great deal of ground, at least in his earlier days, before his lifestyle caught up with him.

My former Celtic team-mate, Jimmy Johnstone, would not have been out of place in any football company. Jinky was simply sensational at times. Blessed with a God-given talent, Jinky was a throwback to the age of the 'tanner ba' winger who could beat defenders for fun, and sometimes he chose to start all over again and go past the same luckless opponent a second time, just for the sheer hell of it. It's a pity that Jinky never had the chance to headline his talents on the World Cup stage. He would have loved to have had the opportunity of taking the ball up to an Italian or Brazilian full-back and mesmerising his opponent with his trickery. The rest of the world would have enjoyed the sight, too.

Denis Law did make it to the World Cup finals, in West Germany in 1974, by which time his best days were behind him, but Denis was another truly outstanding player in his heyday.

# CHAPTER 14

# DICK

Aberdonians have a reputation for being tight-fisted. I can't say that was my experience in the eleven months I spent in the Northeast working for a club chairman who was a cut above the rest. One of the first people I met when I arrived in the Granite City was a fellow by the name of Charlie Rettie, who gave the lie to the popular myth that the inhabitants of Scotland's oil capital have zips on their pockets. More than a quarter of a century on, Charlie remains a close and valued friend, who is invariably first at the bar to buy a drink.

We met by chance after Faye MacLeod, wife of Ally, my predecessor at Pittodrie who sadly passed away in February 2004 after being struck down by Alzheimer's Disease, advised us to book into Charlie's hotel, where, she said, we would be made most welcome. The Aberdeen chairman, Dick Donald, had arranged for Liz and me to stay at the plush Caledonian Hotel in the city centre, but Faye said that she and Ally had spent some time there and, while they had found certain aspects of their stay pleasant enough, being a large hotel it had lacked the personal touch. So we opted for the much smaller Ashley House instead and Faye's advice turned out to be spot-on. Charlie and his wife, Ruth, couldn't have done more to make us feel welcome.

Unlike Charlie, Dick gave the distinct impression that he wasn't all that keen to part with his money and I quickly discovered that he would never sanction any move for a player without being utterly convinced that the signing would turn out to be a sound investment. I suspect that Dick's apparent reluctance to part with his cash was largely a misconception, but he seemed happy enough to foster the image. However, when Dick made his weekly rounds of his many leisure interests on a Friday afternoon, invariably sucking one of his favourite mints, he certainly looked the part of an old-style tycoon, thinking of ways to save a few bob here and there.

The chairman was a genuine class act. I don't recall ever seeing him dressed in anything other than a pin-stripe suit, collar and tie, topped off with his soft hat set at a jaunty angle. Dick always looked the part. He was a great believer, too, in letting his managers get on with the job of managing, without any unnecessary interference. He saw his role as that of father figure and, to this day, I have not heard a bad word said against him.

He would arrive at the ground most days after training and walk round the perimeter track surveying his kingdom. If you wanted to discuss any matters with Dick you had to join him on his daily stroll. Once a week, he would have a member of the ground staff accompany him. The object of the exercise was to spot any flaws, such as tiles missing from the roof of the stand or other repairs that required attention. Dick took great pride in seeing Pittodrie looking clean and tidy. He cared deeply about the appearance of the place and it's a testament to his thorough ways that, to this day, the stadium always looks immaculate.

Another of Dick's legacies is the warm welcome that awaits you when you arrive at the ground. In many ways, Dick was ahead of his time. When the idea of all-seater stadia arose, Aberdeen Football Club was ahead of the rest. Dick decided to install seating round the ground and when I pointed out to him that it might prove rather cold for fans sitting out in the open just a few hundred yards from the North Sea, his reply was typical. 'Aye,' he said, 'but at least we'll bring them in. We'll not be able to do that if we put up a roof first, before we install the seats.'

Dick also formed a strong bond with my eventual successor, Sir Alex Ferguson. Fergie and he were a team, just as Dick and I had been, and Dick deserves great credit for the part he played in the remarkable success Aberdeen went on to achieve under Fergie.

I had known Dick when I was a player at Celtic, but when I was offered the Aberdeen managerial post, following Ally MacLeod's appointment as Scotland manager, I was taken completely by surprise. My managerial experience amounted to just three months as boss of Second Division Clyde when the call came and the person on the other end of the telephone was none other than Jock Stein. 'How do you fancy the Aberdeen job?' enquired Jock. It didn't take me long to say yes. Aberdeen are, after all, one of the biggest clubs in the country, outside the Old Firm, and such a move represented rapid promotion for someone whose experience of management was so limited.

I hadn't even given a move into management much consideration after I decided to hang up my boots, but when Clyde approached me in April 1977, nearly two years after I had stopped playing, it seemed natural to accept the offer without further thought. I had been helping out with Celtic Boys' Club Under-16s and enjoyed having the opportunity to coach youngsters, who always seem keener to listen and learn than their senior counterparts, but this represented a wonderful opportunity to test the water at a higher level.

Initially, after I quit playing I rather enjoyed the freedom of concentrating on my various business interests and I also aspired to become a TV and radio pundit as spectating at matches struck me as being somewhat less stressful than calling the shots from the touchline. But my time with the Boys' Club had whetted my appetite for a more direct involvement in the game, so, when Willie Dunn, the Clyde chairman, asked if I would be interested in managing his club, it seemed like a good idea.

Frankly, some of my friends thought I was mad to take on such a challenge, because Clyde didn't have a penny to their name, but I knew the Dunn family well and I also realised that I would gain valuable experience of how the other side of football operated from a board of directors who were both knowledgeable and fair-minded. I also came into contact with Steve Archibald for the first time. I could see straightaway that Steve had the potential to make it big, and his subsequent success with Aberdeen, Tottenham and Barcelona proved me right, but Steve was very nearly anonymous when Clyde were drawn against Celtic in the Glasgow Cup. Because of a colour clash I was forced to ask Umbro to rush through a fresh set of strips, but when they arrived one jersey was minus its number, so I had to dash to a local sports shop to buy the figure eight. My wife was kind enough to get out her needle and thread and Archibald was none the wiser, but, knowing Steve, he would not have been best pleased had he taken the field as the only player without a number on his back.

The cup-tie against Celtic, which we lost, 4–2, turned out to be the highlight of my brief reign at Shawfield. I felt bad about leaving the directors in the lurch so soon after agreeing to become manager, but, thankfully, they understood and there was no bad feeling. A move from Newton Mearns, on the outskirts of Glasgow, to Aberdeen, with five kids to contend with, obviously represented a considerable upheaval in all our lives but, typically, Liz gave me every encouragement and took it all in her stride.

My initial meeting with Dick Donald took place at the Wheel Inn at Scone in Perthshire. It turned out to be a relatively short one, because, as I was soon to discover, Dick preferred to come straight to the point. It was only when I returned home that it dawned on me that I hadn't even asked what sort of salary I would be on or the duration of my contract. Later, when I broached the subject, there was no need to haggle. The chairman told me that the salary was £10,000 a year and added, 'As far as the contract is concerned, you can have what you want, Billy. Three or five years – the choice is yours.' Not surprisingly, we struck up an instant rapport and our relationship remained warm until the day Dick died in 1993. I never did sign a contract, largely because I had complete trust in the man who had considered me a worthy successor to Ally MacLeod.

When you have spent all your life in the West of Scotland, a move east calls for certain adjustments. Glasgow and Aberdeen are only 150 miles apart but the cultural differences are considerable. Glaswegians are noted for their sharp, often cutting, sense of humour, which tends not to spare the feelings of outsiders. They are also warm and generally helpful to strangers. Aberdonians tend to be a little more reserved and perhaps a touch suspicious of newcomers, but I quickly warmed to my new surroundings and we were made welcome wherever we went.

I suppose in some senses it was an adventure for all of us. Liz and the kids loved life in the Northeast from the moment we arrived, even if it did take all of us a little while to get used to the local dialect, which must sound like a foreign language to the uninitiated from south of the border. The Aberdeen supporters differ from their Glasgow counterparts in terms of their noise levels. It's often been said that, when there's a lull in the play, you can hear the rustle of the sweetie papers at Pittodrie, and there is perhaps some truth in that claim, but they are a passionate and knowledgeable bunch for all that and their team is very important to them.

Aberdeen had enjoyed success under Ally, winning the League Cup the previous year when they beat Rangers, 2–1 in extra-time, with Davie Robb assuring himself of a permanent place in the hearts of the Dons fans when he headed the winner. I was naturally expected to pick up from where Ally had left off, but I had my own ideas on how the team should try to play and these differed in some ways from Ally's approach. I was young and inexperienced, but I was determined to be my own man.

Unfortunately, one of my first tasks was to oversee the transfer of winger Arthur Graham to Leeds. I didn't want to lose a player of Graham's undoubted ability, but I was powerless to prevent him going. The chairman had given Graham his word that he would be allowed to leave if the right offer was made and Dick was an honourable man, but there was no shortage of talent at the club. We had players of the quality of Willie Miller, who became an outstanding captain and who was, for me, the lynch pin on the field for so much of the success that followed under Fergie. Little Joe Harper was also an important cog in the wheel. His goal-scoring abilities belied his size and shape, even though he could be a rascal at times and I always had to keep a close eye on him, but he was also a likeable character who was popular with the fans and could always be relied on to make life difficult for the opposition centre-half.

John McMaster was another I rated highly. John, a highly creative left-sided midfield player, had the misfortune to suffer a serious knee injury in a challenge with Ray Kennedy of Liverpool, in the 1980 European Cup second-round first-leg match, and was never quite the same after that. Complicated surgery to repair the damaged ligaments in his knee reduced John's effectiveness and he eventually left the club to join Morton, where he became a member of Allan McGraw's backroom team, doing a fine job as coach.

But it was Miller who stood out. Willie, who comes from Glasgow, was a born competitor and a tenacious tackler. He was a genuine hard man who was rarely injured and who had even fewer poor games. Proud, positive, uncompromising and determined, Willie was the ideal captain. He had complete confidence in his ability and set a remarkably high standard of consistency. Willie wasn't the nosiest player in the dressing room, but he was blessed with a dominant personality and he was capable of moaning his head off, for the right reasons. Perhaps the word that summed Willie up best was 'winner'. He read the game brilliantly and timed his tackles to perfection. His lifestyle reflected his dedication. Whenever the players were given a day off, Willie would spend most of it resting in bed to ensure that his energy levels were topped up. It didn't surprise me in the least that Willie went on to enjoy such an outstanding career, winning sixty-five caps for his country in the process.

The Aberdeen team that won the European Cup Winners' Cup in 1983 owed a great deal of its success to the defensive partnership of Miller and Alex McLeish, who, I am pleased to say, I introduced into the first team when he was still only eighteen.

McLeish, known as 'Big Eck', has gone on to become one of the country's finest managers, following a highly distinguished playing career which included seventy-seven Scotland appearances. A commanding centre-half who, like Miller, achieved an astonishing level of consistency, he cut his managerial teeth with Motherwell and did an outstanding job at Fir Park. Motherwell, hardly the most fashionable club in Scotland, finished second and third in the championship and qualified to play in Europe during McLeish's time in charge, so it was hardly surprising that he became a target for other, bigger clubs. Hibs eventually persuaded him to advance his managerial career at Easter Road and, as he had done previously at Fir Park, Alex made a big impression – big enough to be appointed a worthy successor to Dick Advocaat as manager of Rangers in December 2001.

Alex has never been the sort to court controversy or mouth off in public, but he isn't a soft touch and operates a strict code of discipline, although it was as a consequence of two players misbehaving that I gave Alex his debut against Dundee United in January 1978. We had played Clydebank away on Hogmanay and managed to maintain a good run of form by winning 1–0. By the time we arrived back in Aberdeen it was mid-evening and as Garner and Glennie were both single blokes I arranged for them to stay at Ashley House, the hotel owned by my good friend Charlie Rettie.

I didn't want the pair of them going out on the town to join in the celebrations so I asked Charlie to keep an eye on them. But I also told Garner and Glennie that I didn't mind them having a couple of drinks provided they made sure that they got to bed at a reasonable hour. Unfortunately, they abused my trust. They had more than a couple and I felt that I had no option but to take a firm stand to demonstrate to other young players that I would not tolerate indiscipline.

When I broke the news to Alex that he would be playing, I swear he grew another six inches. He was still on a high when we beat United, 1–0. I recalled Garner for our next match and Alex winds me up to this day by reminding me that no sooner had I introduced him into the first team than I left him out, but it was clear even then that Alex was a special talent and his development was rapid, largely, I believe, because of Miller's influence. Miller was the perfect partner for a young player seeking to feed off the experience of those around him, but McLeish soon became an accomplished performer in his own right. Eventually, it was difficult to say which of them was the more dominant force. What was never in doubt was that McLeish and Miller were the perfect combination and the backbone of the team. They could read each other's minds. Like Miller, McLeish read the game superbly. He was strong in the air, tackled powerfully and positively and had confidence in his ability.

Jim Leighton was at the apex of the triangle. But during my spell as manager I didn't have room for him, because we already had sufficient cover for our first choice goalkeeper, Bobby Clark, so I sent Jim on loan to Deveronvale to gain experience. They are a Highland League club who had achieved little – until Jim arrived on the scene. That season Deveronvale won a trophy with Leighton in the team. Soon it would be Aberdeen and Scotland who would benefit from having such an outstanding goalkeeper.

The board at Pittodrie at that time consisted of only three directors: Dick, Chris Anderson, who acted as vice-chairman, and Charlie Forbes. They made for a tight-knit group and there was rarely any dispute among them. Dick and Chris were the movers and shakers, while Charlie saw his role more as that of social convenor. All three were very different types, but, collectively, they made an ideal team. Board meetings tended to be short-lived affairs, lasting between thirty and forty-five minutes at the outside and were not occasions for in-depth discussion. We had a meal first, before gathering in Dick's office directly across from His Majesty's Theatre in the city centre, but they were social occasions rather than detailed business meetings and there was no requirement for me to give a long-winded report on the team's current progress.

That period was a wonderful learning curve for me. I was taught the financial structure of the club. I had never been made aware of the business side of a football club as a player, but, by the time I left to become manager of Celtic, I'd had a detailed grounding. I imagined all clubs operated the same way as Aberdeen, but, as I soon discovered on my return to Celtic Park, that was most certainly not the case. Desmond White was a very different character to Dick. When it came to persuading Dick to part with money, Chris Anderson was a useful ally. He was the architect with the ability to construct a powerful case for bringing certain players to the club, and Dick always listened to what he had to say.

Dick, who was very much a family man, also felt it important to concern himself with the welfare of others and would regularly phone Liz at home to ask how she and the kids were settling in. That meant a lot. After looking at various houses in the area, we had elected to live fifteen miles south of Aberdeen on the coast at Stonehaven. We had a lovely home overlooking the North Sea and it was an ideal setting in which to raise children. Stonehaven has a village feel to it and the bracing sea air and almost rural lifestyle added to the feeling that we were on a permanent holiday. Liz felt much the same way and it's an indication of just how much we enjoyed our time in the Northeast that I faced a family revolt when I announced that we would be returning to Glasgow.

My time at Aberdeen coincided with the start of the oil boom and there was a real vibrancy about the city and its surrounds. The people were wonderful to us and we have retained several friendships to this day. Stewart Spence, Dick's son-in-law, epitomised that friendly air. Stewart looked after Liz when she came to Pittodrie for games and the pair of them regularly travelled together to away fixtures. Stewart would phone on a Friday to tell Liz what train he and the directors would be on the next day if the team was playing in Dundee, Edinburgh or Glasgow. The sight of Dick leaning out a window of the first-class carriage when the train pulled into Stonehaven station, gesturing to Liz, still brings a smile to my face.

However, there was a serious side to life as well and that involved trying to achieve success on the pitch. From the point of view of results, I couldn't have wished for a better start. Aberdeen were unbeaten in the first eleven games of the season, starting with a 3–1 home win over Rangers, and that run continued until the Belgian side, RWD Molenbeek won, 2–1, at Pittodrie to end our UEFA Cup aspirations at the first hurdle. We also beat Rangers, 3–0, at Ibrox later in the season, but they extracted a sizeable measure of revenge in the League Cup, when they thrashed us, 6–1, in the away leg. A 3–1 victory in the return helped restore some of our battered pride, but Rangers had the last laugh that season. Aberdeen, in fact, finished runners-up to the Ibrox side in both the championship and the Scottish Cup, and the latter competition taught me several lessons in the art of football management.

I had genuinely felt we were more than capable of beating Rangers at Hampden, despite their remarkable record in Cup finals, but I had not foreseen that our players might freeze on the big occasion. My mistake was that I didn't apply any verbal de-icer! Our first-half performance was, frankly, awful and we were perhaps fortunate to go in at the interval only one goal down. However, instead of aiming a blast at the players I elected to adopt a softly-softly approach in order to try to talk them out of producing another lack lustre forty-five minutes. I endeavoured to offer words of comfort and encouragement, when I should really have let rip and reminded the players that thousands of our fans had made the journey to Glasgow expecting to see a performance they could be proud of, not one that lacked passion.

What made our Cup final flop all the more exasperating was the fact that there was no shortage of players with battling qualities in that

Dons team – individuals such as Stuart Kennedy, Willie Miller, John McMaster, Drew Jarvie and Ian Fleming – but fate had clearly chosen to conspire against us. Alex MacDonald, a lion-hearted little midfielder who went on to enjoy a successful managerial career with Hearts and Airdrie, headed Rangers into the lead and when Derek Johnstone, with whom I'd had several tussles as a player, scored a second early in the second half it was more or less all over. Steve Ritchie got a consolation goal five minutes from the end, when he mishit a spinning shot over Peter McCloy's head and found the net via the crossbar, but, to all intents and purposes, it was not an occasion that lives fondly in the memory.

I also have to hold my hands up and admit to having made a catastrophic mistake in not signing Steve Archibald straightaway when I became manager of Aberdeen. Had I done so, I believe that we would have won the cup and maybe also the championship. Steve was this very interesting character who could play centre-half, left-midfield, outside-right or centre-forward. I was so impressed, in fact, that when Jock Stein asked if we had any players at Clyde who I considered capable of doing a decent job for Celtic, I urged him to sign Archibald. I knew Clyde were in desperate need of funds and had no hesitation in recommending Archibald. I admitted that I wasn't sure what Archibald's best position was, but Jock had already seen him play and wasn't entirely convinced. I also got it wrong. I was embarrassed at having left Clyde after just three months and, as a consequence of my discomfort, I delayed making a move for Archibald. By the time I did pluck up courage to approach Clyde about signing him, he was already cup-tied. If only I had made my move for Archibald the moment I took over at Pittodrie, I'm convinced he would have made the difference between us finishing second to Rangers and achieving the double.

Inexperience also led me to make another costly mistake in my team selection – I left Gordon Strachan out of the Cup final squad. Strachan, whom I had signed from Dundee the previous November in a cash-plus-player exchange deal involving Jim Shirra moving to Dens Park, was young and relatively inexperienced. Consequently, he initially found it difficult to settle and he lacked consistency. However, on reflection, I should have included the wee man. Who is to say whether a player of Strachan's undoubted ability would have made an appreciable difference in the final, but subsequent events were to prove that he was a player capable of creating something out of nothing and producing the spark necessary to transform a game.

Still, considering that I was still wearing L-plates, I don't suppose the new boy had done all that badly in his first full season as a gaffer. There were no complaints from the chairman and the fans seemed happy enough that we had at least upstaged one half of the Old Firm! However, the Cup final was my last game in charge of the Dons. When the call came to return to Celtic Park, I simply couldn't say no. Jock Stein again acted as the middle man and when Dick Donald was made aware of Celtic's approach, he realised that the pull of a return to Celtic Park would be too much for me to resist and didn't even try to persuade me to stay at Pittodrie.

At the time, though, I thought the chairman wasn't all that bothered one way or another and I was frankly disappointed that he didn't at least try to talk me out of the move. It was only some time later that I was made aware of the reason for what I had seen as his apparent indifference. On a later visit to Aberdeen, Liz happened to mention to Stewart Spence how upset I had been at not hearing from the chairman. Stewart was glad to have the chance to set the record straight. He told Liz: 'I went to my father-in-law's house and said that I was going to drive him to Stonehaven to speak with Billy in the hope that he could be talked out of going to Celtic, but Dick would have none of it. He looked at me and said, "Stewart, Billy has been a Celtic man all his life and he might never get another chance to manage the club. He is entitled to go back to Celtic and I am not going to try to stop him." ' That reaction was typical of Dick Donald. He could have made things difficult for me, but instead chose to smooth my path back to the one club that has meant more than any other to me, and I will always be grateful to him for that.

Would I have changed my mind had Dick tried to talk me out of the move to Celtic? Probably not. But I was about to learn that not every football chairman is blessed with the same sense of decency as Dick Donald. I also remember the chairman's words when I broke the news to him that I had decided to become manager of Celtic. 'You'll nae enjoy working for that board as much as you've enjoyed working with the one here,' he had declared in his broad Aberdeen accent. How prophetic those words turned out to be.

# DESMOND

I should not have agreed to succeed Jock Stein as manager of Celtic. With the benefit of hindsight, I realise now that I was not equipped to assume such an awesome responsibility. I didn't lack drive and ambition – I was full of both – but I didn't have the necessary experience to make the step up at that stage in my managerial career. I had not long since turned thirty-eight and had little more than a year as a manager under my belt. Great strides had been taken at Aberdeen and I had laid the basis of a very good team, but there was a great deal of learning still to be done. Looking back, though, compared to the squad I inherited at Celtic, the one I had in place at Pittodrie was much better equipped at that stage to achieve success.

On reflection, it was probably wrong of Jock to approach me at that particular time. I had hoped that Celtic would ask me to come back at the time of his horrific car crash, but neither he nor the club had responded positively. This time, though, the goal posts had moved. The Celtic directors were apparently keen for change and both they and Jock felt that it was time for a younger man to take charge, so how could I resist the lure of a return to the club where I had enjoyed so much success as a player? I should have said no, but the pull was simply too great, so Alex Ferguson inherited the fruits of my labours at Pittodrie and, to his great credit, became by far and away the most successful manager in Aberdeen's history.

Naturally, I have often wondered what direction my life would have taken had I not allowed my heart to rule my head, but it would have been too great a gamble to have rejected Celtic's approach. There might never have been a second chance. For me, managing Celtic was a vocation, not just a job. Maybe sometimes it is wise to stand back and take an objective look at a situation before jumping in with both feet, but I was never able to do that when it came to the club I love – and you know what they say about love often being blind!

Over the years I have read suggestions and heard whispers that I engineered my return to Celtic Park and that I was responsible for the club getting rid of Jock Stein. Not only do I find such comments offensive, they are also without foundation. The offer to become manager came from big Jock himself. Jock never did anything without a reason and I think he had already made up his mind to go to Leeds. Jock approached me at an awards lunch in Glasgow, where I was being honoured with the accolade of manager of the year. I must confess that I have never understood why I was chosen ahead of Jock Wallace, considering that Rangers had won the treble, but the fact that Jock Stein espoused the same view ruined the occasion for me. He might at least have kept his opinion to himself and just let me enjoy the moment. That wasn't Jock's style, though. He had a tendency to be blunt. He also told me that he was keen to speak to me on another matter and asked me to drive to a spot near to the hotel where the lunch was being held, so we could discuss what was on his mind.

I certainly didn't anticipate that our clandestine meeting would change my life and I had hardly parked my backside on the front seat of his car when Jock asked, 'How do you fancy coming back to Celtic?'

After a moment I asked, 'What do you mean?' I had always secretly harboured the hope that Jock would ask me to work with him at Celtic Park and it had annoyed me that the invite had not been forthcoming. Was this it? 'I mean as manager,' said Jock. 'I've had enough and now I want to merge into the background. You won't have a problem with the board.'

I was stunned, but mobile phones didn't exist in those days, so I waited until I had driven back to Stonehaven to break the news to Liz. Her response was as I had feared. Liz and the kids loved life in the Northeast and she wasn't at all keen on returning to Glasgow, but I appealed to my wife's compassionate nature. 'Liz,' I implored, 'I can't say no. You know what Celtic means to me and this may be the only chance I get to manage the club.' I could fully understand Liz's reluctance. We were happy with our lot and we were far removed from Old Firm aggro. The religious divide that blights life in the West of Scotland and is a cancer in society does not exist in Aberdeen, at least not in the nightmarish way it overshadows the Old Firm.

However, Liz eventually gave me her blessing and I immediately contacted Jock with the news. I also pleaded with him not to whisper a word of what was happening to the press. Some hope. The news that I was to succeed Jock as manager broke in the *Evening Times* newspaper. I was attending a local Junior Cup final when I was made aware that the story was out. I was annoyed, because I had wanted to inform Dick Donald and the Aberdeen board of my decision in person. I hadn't signed a contract so I knew the club couldn't prevent me from leaving, but I considered it a matter of courtesy to make Dick aware before he heard from elsewhere. Perhaps I should have known better than to expect Jock to keep it under his hat until the moment was right. He had many contacts among the football press and one in particular at the *Evening Times*.

As far as I am aware, Dick never held it against me, but it was embarrassing nonetheless, as not even my assistant, John Clark, was aware of what was happening. However, as soon as I asked John if he would be my number two at Celtic his reaction was exactly what I had expected. Like me, he found the lure of a return to Celtic Park simply too great to resist.

I'd had my eyes opened at Pittodrie by the way Dick Donald did things. Aberdeen was a club striding boldly into the future and, indeed, one marching ahead of Celtic. I left board meetings at Aberdeen full of excitement. On my return to Celtic I was soon to discover that Desmond White was caught in a time warp. The chairman seemed content to maintain the status quo, no matter the long-term implications of such negative thinking, and I knew very little of what was happening behind the scenes. I had known Desmond White during my time at Celtic as a player, but I had never really had any direct dealings with him. That all changed on 28 May 1978.

Of course, I had seen him about the place from time to time and I recalled how he would travel with the team on foreign trips, depending on our destination. If we were headed for an especially exotic spot, such as the Caribbean, Desmond would be there. Snorkelling in the clear blue waters of Barbados, for example, had great appeal. Resplendent in his flippers and goggles, I think Mr White imagined himself as James Bond in search of Ursula Andress. In reality, he was a distant figure who had little in common with the players.

Mr White had been a goalkeeper with Queen's Park, but I can't imagine that he was ever one of the boys. He certainly never made any effort to establish a close relationship with his manager during the five years I worked for him. I remember as a player asking him for one of the fancy Cuban cigars he smoked as we celebrated winning the league title at Easter Road. It would never have crossed his mind to dish them out and I took a perverse pleasure in chucking ten quid's worth out the coach window after taking just a few puffs and immediately feeling as if I was about to throw up.

Unlike Dick Donald, who was warm-hearted and witty, Mr White was aloof and distant and I found him well nigh impossible to get on with. Within days of taking over at Celtic I realised that our relationship would always be that purely of chairman and manager. Mr White found it impossible to dismantle the barriers. Whenever he telephoned my home and Liz answered, he would find it impossible to use her name and would ask curtly: 'Is Billy there?'

While we enjoyed plenty of success on the park, off it all was far from sweetness and light. Most of the time, when it came to the chairman and the board, it was as if I had to place myself on a war footing. One day, during a board meeting, irritation got the better of me and I said to him: 'Mr White, you are the chairman and I am the manager. Are we not supposed to steer in the same direction? All we ever seem to do is argue.' It also irked me that I was rarely offered any positive suggestions by the board. At Aberdeen I had been able to seek guidance and advice from Dick Donald. At Celtic Park I always felt as if I was the lone driver. Managing Celtic seemed to be a constant struggle.

But for all that my relationship with Mr White and his fellow directors was far from cordial, that didn't prevent me from guiding the team to the championship in my first season back. It came down to what was effectively a dramatic title-decider against Rangers at Celtic Park in our final fixture and we triumphed, 4–2, despite being reduced to ten men for much of the second half. The late Johnny Doyle, who tragically died when he was electrocuted while carrying out repairs at his home, saw red ten minutes after the restart, when he became involved in a flair up with Alex MacDonald. We were trailing, 1–0, at the time and I was furious with Doyle, warning him that if we lost he would be in even bigger bother with me. At that point you wouldn't have given a five pence piece for our chances, but the players displayed astonishing character to transform our situation and achieve a quite remarkable victory.

Roy Aitken took the lead role and scored an equaliser midway through the second half, but we needed much more because Rangers required just a single point to be crowned champions. In an effort to introduce fresh legs to our attack, I decided to substitute Mike Conroy with my Lisbon Lions team-mate, Bobby Lennox. It had nothing to do with sentiment. Bobby had made a sizeable contribution to our season, in spite of his advancing years, and I knew he still possessed the necessary stamina and drive to run at Rangers. The odds were still stacked against us, though, so when George McCluskey scored to make it 2–1 for Celtic, I can't claim to have been anticipating a goal in our favour. But no sooner had we taken the lead than Rangers regained the initiative through MacDonald and the title looked to be once again heading for Ibrox.

However, the Celtic supporters have often acted as a twelfth man and that May evening was no exception. They succeeded in almost drowning out the roars of the Rangers fans in the 52,000 crowd, to the extent that our players became inspired. With just five minutes remaining, had there been a roof over Celtic Park it would surely have been lifted off by the roar that greeted the sight of the unfortunate Colin Jackson heading into his own net after Peter McCloy had pushed out an effort from McCluskey. Then, with barely one minute left, Murdo MacLeod gathered the ball and it was all over. Murdo couldn't hear my screams from the bench to boot the ball for safety, because of the unbelievable noise, and he elected to shoot for goal. Happily, he found his target to devastating effect! Afterwards, I was amazed at the sight of so many of my former team-mates dancing a victory jig around the Celtic Park foyer. Their reaction characterised what Celtic means to so many people.

One of the defining moments of that season was our away fixture against Rangers. The game was scheduled to take place on 24 March, three days after Rangers had faced Cologne in a European Cup tie. Ibrox was being renovated at the time and the Old Firm game was set to take place at Hampden, but the weather had been particularly severe for the time of year and heavy snow had put the fixture in doubt. A pitch inspection was arranged for the Friday afternoon. Our opponents had had a tough midweek fixture and I was concerned that the referee, Brain McGinlay, might be pressurised by Rangers officials into calling the match off, so I made a point of being present to ensure fair play. We had enjoyed a free midweek and, not unnaturally, I was especially keen that the game go ahead in the hope that we would be able to take advantage of Rangers' European exertions.

When I arrived at Hampden, along with John Clark, the first thing I did was speak to the groundsman, John Docherty, who assured me that the pitch was fine. He did, however, express some concern over the state of the terracing. As a thaw was forecast, John saw no reason for a postponement, provided he could acquire sufficient quantities of salt to spread on the terracing to ensure the fans' safety, so I immediately arranged for extra supplies to be delivered from Celtic Park. I was further heartened when Brian McGinlay told me that, in his opinion, the pitch was playable. He added that he wanted to check the weather forecast first though, but I knew from my own enquiries that the local met office was sounding upbeat.

By then, John Greig, the Rangers manager, whom I knew well from our many tussles and times together with the Scotland team, had arrived along with another Ibrox legend, Willie Waddell, who had been both player and manager before his appointment as a director. But I wasn't prepared for what happened next. Greigy approached me and announced: 'The game's off.' I reacted furiously and asked Greigy what he was playing at. 'Are you telling me that you are afraid to play us?' I taunted. At that point, Waddell jumped into the discussion and began spluttering about taking exception to my suggestion that Rangers were scared to play us. Now, I happened to have a reasonable relationship with Waddell, but I didn't hold back on that occasion. 'Mr Waddell,' I intoned, 'this is manager to manager. I don't think a director should be interfering.' Greigy was clearly embarrassed by the altercation and quickly added that the game was being called off because the authorities could not guarantee the safety of the fans. I was very annoyed, especially later when a photograph in the *Evening Times* the following day showed there wasn't a snowflake to be seen!

As it turned out, the postponement until 5 May worked against Rangers. Although we lost, 1–0, to an Alex MacDonald goal, we had by then hit a decent run of form and were competing strongly for the championship, while the postponement added to their backlog. Perhaps if the teams had met two months earlier and the result had favoured Rangers, that would have weakened our resolve. As it was, Rangers' victory gave them only a single point advantage over us, with the final Old Firm game of the season still to come.

In that first season I made two highly significant signings: Davie Provan from Kilmarnock and Murdo MacLeod from Dumbarton. Provan, whose fee was a then record between two Scottish clubs, cost £120,000, while MacLeod was bought for £100,000. The pair of them repaid these fees several times over. Unfortunately, Davie, who has since gone on to become a highly successful newspaper columnist and Sky TV broadcaster, was forced to cut short his career after falling victim to ME, but he was a pivotal figure in the Celtic team for several seasons and his talents as a winger were recognised by Scotland on ten occasions. Provan is also fondly remembered by Celtic fans for scoring the equalising goal against Dundee United in the 1985 Scottish Cup final.

Both Murdo and Davie would very probably have ended up at Pittodrie had I remained manager of Aberdeen. I had been tipped off by the club's veteran scout, Bobby Calder, that Dumbarton had one or two players worth looking at and I followed his advice. Murdo stood out, but I was also taken by Dumbarton's centre-forward, a fellow by the name of Graeme Sharp. However, I reckoned that it just wasn't possible for Dumbarton to have two players who were capable of making the grade at the highest level and made the mistake of deciding that Sharp had just had one of those days. I didn't feel I could gamble on signing two players at the same time from a lower league club, but, considering that Sharp went on to become a key player at Everton and for Scotland, I hold my hands up to having made a monumental misjudgement.

Circumstances dictated that I never did get round to making a bid for Murdo while I was still at Pittodrie, but I didn't waste any time in tabling an offer once I had moved to Celtic. Murdo was just the sort of player we needed. He was powerful and aggressive and I sensed that he would be a huge asset. The first time I watched Murdo I was convinced that he was naturally left-footed. It was only when he arrived at Celtic Park that I realised that he was, in actual fact, right-footed, but that gives you some idea of just how talented he was. Murdo was always striving to improve himself and he had the confidence to try things. His best assets were his quickness of thought and movement, and the fact that he could hit the ball powerfully with either foot. Murdo specialised in scoring spectacular goals and he was almost guaranteed to notch fourteen or fifteen a season – an impressive return from a midfielder.

Davie made his debut against Partick Thistle at Firhill and within a couple of minutes I instinctively knew I had signed a player who would become a big favourite with our fans. He cut inside and whipped over a great cross that created immediate panic in the Thistle defence. The ball fell perfectly between the defenders and the goalkeeper. In that situation the defender is reluctant to go for the ball in case he knocks it into his own net, and the keeper is scared to come for it for fear of missing the ball and being made to look stupid. Neil Mochan, our coach, leapt off the bench, shouting about it being the best cross he had seen in years, and Neilly wasn't a bad player himself. Davie played with his feet on the touchline and his level of fitness was so great that he was able to work up and down the park all day long. His value to the team was demonstrated to great effect on the evening of our championship triumph over Rangers. His remarkable stamina meant he was able to make intelligent runs or back-track as the circumstances demanded. If Davie had a weakness it was – and he would probably be the first to admit this – that he wasn't the greatest finisher in the world, but he was more than capable of setting up chances for others.

I wonder where all the wide players have gone? Scottish football seemed to produce that type in abundance not so terribly long ago. It also used to be the case that the Old Firm could sign quality players from other Scottish clubs, but not any more, and that concerns me greatly.

Considering the poor state of the first team squad when I returned from Aberdeen, our achievement in winning the championship surpassed all expectations. But, if the truth be told, we were not entitled to win the league and in an effort to further strengthen the squad I signed Dom Sullivan, for £80,000, from Aberdeen, to supplement our determination and aggression with a bit more class. I also acquired the services of Frank McGarvey from Liverpool, for a record £250,000 fee, but the season was drawing to a close by the time McGarvey arrived and we eventually had to settle for the league runners-up spot in my second season, behind Aberdeen, who won by a single point. So much for my judgement in quitting Pittodrie for Celtic Park, but at least we managed to win one trophy when we beat Rangers in the Scottish Cup final, thanks to a George McCluskey goal in extra-time.

Real Madrid had put paid to our European aspirations two months earlier, though. Having beaten them, 2–0, at Celtic Park, we had fancied our chances in the return in the Bernabeu, but we were denied a stonewall penalty, when Benito clearly handled in the box, and then conceded a goal almost on the stroke of half-time. The timing of Santillana's strike shattered the players' confidence and we conceded two more goals in the second half to Steilike and Juanito.

I cannot overemphasise the part played by Danny McGrain during my first spell as manager and his influence on the team that won back-to-back championships in 1981 and 1982. Danny had everything you could want in a competitive full-back. He was very strong and fit and had the ability to push forward and give the team added width. He isn't the biggest guy in the world, but when Danny put in a tackle his opponent knew all about it. There was never anything half-hearted in his challenges. If Danny had a weakness in his game it was his final ball. Having got himself into a great position, Danny often didn't finish off the move as he would have wanted, and he didn't score many goals either, but he had a wonderful appetite for the game and was one of the many great Scottish players who had he chosen, could have achieved success in English football over the years. I have always held the view that the principal reason for English clubs being so keen to have one or two Scots in their teams was because of the competitive spirit Danny epitomised.

Danny had the misfortune to develop diabetes and, for all that he dealt with his illness in a way few others could have done, it undoubtedly had a fairly dramatic effect on his career. It caused him to miss the 1978 World Cup finals in Argentina and the ankle injury which blighted his career at that time took very much longer to heal as a consequence of the diabetes. The condition didn't prevent him from winning sixty-two caps, but one wonders how much more Danny would have achieved had his health not been affected. Danny was such an outstanding player that it was not difficult to understand why so many people described him as the most accomplished full-back of his generation and others went as far as to label him world class.

Frank McGarvey was another vital cog in the wheel and when he arrived from Liverpool in March 1980, he had an immediate impact, both on the field and in the dressing room. In Glasgow parlance, Frank can best be described as a gallus individual, an infectious character with a droll sense of humour and a lively personality. I was never quite sure what Frank was going to do in a game and, I suspect, most of the time neither did he. His football was played off-the-cuff and he scored goals for fun. Football was a game to be enjoyed as far as he was concerned and his enthusiasm shone through. No cause was ever lost as far as Frank was concerned. He was prepared to run and chase all day long and he was also quick and sharp, with complete faith in his ability. He was also always on the go off the park as well, winding up the others and indulging in all sorts of harmless japes. In short, Frank was a breath of fresh air to all of us, because he was great for morale.

Roy Aitken, who was later to become my captain, was a comparative youngster at that time, but he was already setting an example to his team-mates in terms of his enthusiasm and wholehearted approach. I remember the first time I saw Roy in action was when Celtic sent a team to play Bellshill Athletic in what, I think, was a charity match. He was just sixteen, but I was immediately impressed by his solid stature and determination to be involved in the game. Roy invariably led from the front and, for a big man, he possessed decent ball control and had two good feet, but his biggest strengths were his fitness and athleticism. Even at training, Roy did everything at maximum pace. You could always rely on him to dig you out of a hole, because he had a pride in the job.

Unfortunately, despite the influence of players such as McGrain, McGarvey and Aitken, our progress in both the 1981–82 and 1982–83 European Cup campaigns was extremely limited. We had the misfortune to be drawn against teams of the calibre of Juventus, Ajax and Real Sociedad. There was a degree of compensation in eliminating our Dutch rivals, who included Johan Cruyff in their line-up, but we were fated to lose by the odd goal to the other two. At least I managed to maintain my record of winning at least one trophy a season, though, when in December 1982 we defeated Rangers, 2–1, to land the League Cup.

However, we lost out in the championship race by a single point, when Dundee United took the title for the first, and so far only, time in the club's history. Our fate was sealed when we lost to both United and Aberdeen in the space of four days in the run-in, but it would be churlish of me to attempt to detract from the magnificent job done by Jim McLean. Wee Jim was perceived as taciturn and dour. It was suggested that whenever United flew off to play in Europe, as the plane taxied on to the runway a sign flashed up ordering that all smiles be extinguished! There was perhaps some truth in the claim that Jim rarely smiled or formed close relationships with his players and staff, but his achievements bordered on the remarkable, given United's limited resources and geographical location. With two teams in the city drawing their fan base from a population of around 185,000, Dundee United commanded a fraction of the support enjoyed by the Old Firm, even during the club's most successful period, but few provincial teams have even come close to matching United's achievements under Jim McLean.

He transformed the face of Scottish football almost single-handedly, by upstaging the Old Firm for a time, and he did so by casting his net across the length and breadth of the country to land talented youngsters from all areas. Traditionally, Celtic and Rangers had effectively had the market place to themselves. Bobby Calder, Aberdeen's legendary talent scout, had bucked the trend to an extent previously, but it was Jim who set in motion a youth system that became the envy of the majority of the other clubs. Paul Sturrock, who has gone on to emulate at least part of his mentor's success at Plymouth and Southampton, after a spell as manager at Tannadice, and David Narey, whose memorable goal against Brazil in the 1982 World Cup finals was famously described as a 'toe poke' by Jimmy Hill, were two of the most notable. Jim blended his mix of youngsters and shrewd buys into a potent force and one powerful enough to upstage the Old Firm.

In addition to Sturrock and Narey, United fashioned a team packed with international players: Richard Gough, who went on to captain Rangers to a host of honours, Paul Hegarty, Eamonn Bannon, Raymond Stewart, who was sold to West Ham, Ralph Milne, a player considered good enough to wear the colours of Manchester United, and, prior to their emergence, Andy Gray. They were outstanding individuals who gelled into an exceptional team, but the catalyst was Jim McLean.

Jim wasn't everyone's cup of tea, but the fact remains that he made Dundee United. Football was his life and it remains so to this day. An illustration of how deeply Jim thought about the game was to be found one day when they were playing us at Celtic Park. When I was handed a copy of the United team lines I discovered that he had changed his line-up at least four times. The sheet of paper was full of scribbles. I could only assume that Jim had sat on the team coach on the journey from Dundee, constantly going over in his mind the different permutations we might adopt and how best he could combat the various threats we might pose. Yes, Jim, who had been a skilful and thoughtful midfield player with Clyde, Hamilton and Dundee, was probably excessive at times in the way he disciplined his players and demanded the same level of professionalism from them that he himself strived to achieve, but I personally found him a decent enough individual. We never became close, but I have always admired Jim's achievements.

Jim deserved his success and I remember feeling deeply for him when United reached the last four of the European Cup in 1984, only to be cheated out of their place in the final by Roma. Having secured a two-goal lead from the first leg at Tannadice, United were subjected to appalling intimidation in the return and were eventually beaten, 3–2 on aggregate. The events of the UEFA Cup final three years later were even more heartbreaking. IFK Gothenburg was, I suspect, a team too far after United had lost to St Mirren in the Scottish Cup final just five days earlier.

The other half of the so-called New Firm, Aberdeen, had forced us to accept second spot in season 1979–80 and it was no coincidence that Jim and Fergie were close. I also enjoyed a reasonable relationship with Fergie, who had started out in management ahead of me. We had been rivals as players and enjoyed several interesting tussles. Fergie had served his apprenticeship with lowly East Stirling, before moving on to take charge of St Mirren, and I recall him telling me that it was best to get out of the bottom end of the market as quickly as possible. 'Starting out in the lower leagues is fine for gaining experience,' said Fergie, 'but it's soul-destroying and when the chance to better yourself presents itself jump at it.'

Jump Fergie did, when he was offered the chance to become my successor at Aberdeen, but no one could have imagined then that he would go on to become the one man whose achievements rival those of Jock Stein. Yet, initially, Fergie experienced certain difficulties at Pittodrie. I think he underestimated the depth of talent he had at his disposal and continued to adopt the same principles and tactics he had employed at Love Street, but he gradually realised that he had a squad capable of achieving a lot more than St Mirren.

We had differences of opinion at times and that led to arguments, but managers disagreeing in the immediate aftermath of games is part and parcel of football. There was no lasting animosity. Fergie is a highly volatile and argumentative bugger, but we always managed to patch up our differences and move on. It's that volatility and aggressive streak which makes Fergie the driving force he is, in my opinion. His ruthless ambition borders on the ridiculous at times. Fergie's own personality is reflected in his players. He encourages his team to be aggressive and to argue the toss in an effort to put referees and opponents under pressure. But it's also an aspect I like to see in managers. It's a strength, rather than a weakness, and illustrates Fergie's enthusiasm and sheer will to win all the time.

Looking back on that period of my life I wish I could say that all was rosy. Much of the success I and the team enjoyed was soured by ongoing tensions behind the scenes. My relationship with the chairman was certainly not helped by an incident that occurred in September 1980, en route to a European Cup Winners' Cup tie in Hungary. Leading 6–0 from the first leg at Celtic Park, the return was no more than a formality, so there was a reasonably relaxed air about the squad when we checked into the Excelsior Hotel, near Heathrow, for an overnight stay.

My relationship with the media was such that it was quite normal for me to socialise with the travelling press party when circumstances allowed. We had our disagreements from time to time, of course, and there was the occasional heated exchange, but most fall-outs lasted no more than a day or two. Having ensured that the players were bedded down for the night, I joined half a dozen reporters at the bar. The directors were seated at a nearby table. To start with, the mood was cordial, but, suddenly, one of the press corps, Gerry McNee, launched into a criticism of the players and alleged that they had displayed an unacceptable level of indiscipline in the recent Old Firm match, which we had lost, 2–1. I did not share that view and was surprised at his comments. I had been disappointed to lose the game, of course, but I could not understand where McNee was coming from. The game had been keenly contested but it had not been overly physical by Old Firm standards in my view. Frankly, I felt that Rangers had been fortunate to survive sustained Celtic pressure and Alex Miller's match-winner thirty seconds from the end was more than the opposition deserved. McNee's attack became increasingly more vitriolic and I made it clear that I was not prepared to tolerate his verbal onslaught at what I had perceived as a friendly late-night gathering. I should stress that none of the assembled company was worse for wear from the effects of alcohol, but passions were by now running high and McNee shocked me by suggesting that the pair of us go outside to settle our differences.

McNee may have meant to continue the discussion in private, but the suggestion meant only one thing to me. I took this to mean that we should settle the matter in the time-honoured fashion, with our fists. I should never have agreed, of course, but my temper was up and any semblance of common sense went out of the window. It was a monumental error of judgement on my part. McNee was walking in front and was already outside when he turned towards me I assumed he was about to throw a punch and instantly retaliated first! My blow hit him on the cheekbone and what was really only a minor injury was made to look worse because my ring aggravated the damage. Down went McNee on all fours and covered his head to protect himself from any further blows. He need not have bothered. I realised the moment I threw the punch that I had reacted to McNee's goading like an idiot. Several of his colleagues came running towards us and I immediately knew that there would be potentially serious ramifications.

In an effort to defuse the situation, I called the press party together at the airport the following morning and confessed that I had been wrong. I also apologised to all of them, including McNee, for my unacceptable behaviour. When McNee responded by offering to shake hands I imagined – somewhat naively, as it turned out – that the incident might soon be forgotten. I also spoke with the chairman and he advised that we should wait to see what happened before reacting further. A month later, I was confident that I had weathered the storm. There had been no witnesses and McNee was denying anything had happened, but the balloon went up with a vengeance on the first Sunday of October. The story had hit the front pages and my home was under siege from a posse of press photographers. Someone had blabbed. The effect on my family was devastating. To this day, I cannot say with any certainty where the hacks got their information from, but suffice to say that I did not tip them off!

My father, Jimmy, always a calming influence, offered the view that the unwelcome publicity would soon blow over, but, with complete justification, he also upbraided me for having reacted the way I did. 'Billy, you were severely provoked,' he agreed, 'but no matter the level of provocation, it is wrong to lift your hands.' As usual, Dad was correct. I had allowed my occasional explosive temperament to get the better of me and we were all paying a high price for my indiscretion. I felt that I had no choice but to offer my resignation, but the chairman rejected it. Instead, I was reprimanded by the board and fined £500. In spite of assurances that the board's action would be kept private, within a very short time it was public knowledge on the streets of Glasgow. I was not amused.

It was clear that McNee did not approve of many of my managerial decisions. He is a fan of Celtic and was certainly closer to the club than the majority of his colleagues. McNee also appeared to have contacts among the players and was highly critical of my decision to allow Johannes Edvaldsson to leave the club. Fate decreed that he was given further ammunition when Roddie MacDonald and Tom McAdam were suspended for the 1980 Scottish Cup final against Rangers. The situation was made worse when Jim Casey, whom I had intended to play at centre-half in the final, went over on his ankle in training, forcing me to field Mike Conroy in an emergency, but someone up there took pity on me and Conroy was outstanding in a 1–0 victory.

I was, frankly, thoroughly fed-up with McNee's constant sniping and matters came to a head following a match against St Mirren at Love Street. I noted that McNee was among a group of reporters gathered outside the away dressing room, seeking my views, and I indicated that I was not willing to discuss the game as long as he remained. As I had not called a press conference, I took the view that it was up to me which journalists I chose to speak with. My employers did not agree, however, and I received a letter from the board advising me to that effect.

My action in refusing to speak to McNee at Paisley had been prompted by an incident that arose following our European Cup

Winners' Cup tie with the Romanian side, Politehnica Timisoara. We led, 2–1, from the home leg, but fell victim to arguably the worst referee I have ever seen, who red-carded Roddie MacDonald and Frank McGarvey and also allowed the Timisoara match-winner to stand, despite our keeper, Peter Latchford, having been blatantly fouled. Following the match, which resulted in the Romanians going through by virtue of the fact that they had scored an away goal, Timisoara held a reception at the hotel where we were staying. The referee and linesmen were invited, along with the media, and I was stunned to see McNee approach the match official and remonstrate with him about his handling of the game. A short time later, the referee eye-balled McGarvey in a very aggressive manner and accused him of inciting trouble. I immediately intervened and ordered the players to their rooms in an effort to avoid any further unpleasantries. I then took the precaution of going to see the chairman to appraise him of what had taken place. Imagine my surprise when I was confronted by the sight of McNee giving his version of events.

I'd had a bellyful of McNee and his meddling, and I made my feelings plain to him and the chairman, adding that because of McNee's continued criticisims of me I had no wish to have any dealings with him in future. My assistant, John Clark, ended up being banned from attending UEFA functions for two years, apparently for insulting the referee, and both MacDonald and McGarvey received three-month bans.

McNee, meanwhile, has continued on occasion to have a go at me in his newspaper column and I thank him most sincerely for his continuing interest in my life. In fact, he has done more than most to ensure that my name remains prominent. Thankfully, my relationship with most members of the media has always been very good and I have developed several lasting friendships with journalists.

# THE ROAD
# SOUTH

I think most people would agree that three league titles and two cup triumphs in the space of five years would satisfy the demands of the majority of football directors and supporters. Indeed, I will go as far as to suggest that the majority of club chairmen would consider that the manager is doing a decent job if he averages one trophy a season. Desmond White clearly did not fall into that category. By the time Charlie Nicholas was sold to Arsenal in June 1983, the cracks in our relationship had grown to the extent that they could no longer be papered over. The chairman and I were constantly at loggerheads and I was, frankly, sick of the bickering.

It had reached the nit-picking stage. Every niggle had become a major point of dispute and I could no longer contain my frustration. If I said black, the chairman said white – and White ruled! The situation came to a head at the same time as Charlie was pondering his future. Mr White informed me that the board was keen to see several changes and one of them involved me getting rid of my assistant, John Clark. He added that he wanted me to appoint Frank Connor as my new number two. Besides having been a team-mate, John had also been my assistant at Aberdeen and I rated him highly. I also valued him as a coach and for his extensive knowledge of the game. So, hardly surprisingly, I told Mr White in as blunt a manner as possible, 'I am not sacking John Clark. If you want him out, you sack him.'

I had nothing against Frank Connor. Indeed, he is a thoroughly decent fellow and was a hard-working and enthusiastic coach, but I had every reason to remain loyal to John and there were no grounds whatsoever for me to replace him. I was also concerned that my authority as manager was once again being undermined and that this was yet another blatant attempt by the chairman to throw his weight about, irrespective of the consequences of his action. Having won that particular argument, I sensed that it would not be long before I found myself once again at odds with my employers. I wasn't wrong.

A story appeared in *The People* newspaper, linking me with the Manchester City job. Mr White jumped at the chance to accuse me of going behind his back in a deliberate attempt to manoeuvre my way out of Celtic Park. That was absolutely nonsense. I hadn't spoken to a soul at City or let it be known that I was considering my future as Celtic manager. It was true that I had been sounded out about whether I would be interested in becoming Manchester City manager by someone claiming to be acting on behalf of the club, but I had brushed the enquiry aside. So, I was somewhat taken by surprise when the question was put to me by several journalists. Clearly, City had leaked their interest in the knowledge that further newspaper coverage might help their cause.

Had I actively encouraged the publicity, no one could have blamed me, because I had been informed during a conversation with Ricky McFarlane, who was manager of St Mirren, that I was the sixth highest paid boss in the Premier League. Now, with all due respect to men like Sir Alex Ferguson and Jim McLean, who had transformed the fortunes of Aberdeen and Dundee United respectively, I don't think it's unreasonable to suggest that the managers of Celtic and Rangers are entitled to expect at least parity with their colleagues elsewhere. My salary was in the region of £15,000 a year. Others were apparently earning a great deal more, so was it any wonder that money had become an issue?

However, Mr White jumped on the speculation – with glee. When I turned up at his city centre office the day after the story had appeared in the papers, his desk was littered with copies of the various publications. Brandishing one of the many newspapers, in the manner of a headmaster who has caught one of his pupils smoking behind the bike shed, Mr White went on the offensive. 'Mr McNeill, we see that you have been busy speaking to other clubs,' he said. I had nothing whatsoever to hide and replied: 'Mr White, I spoke with a reporter who telephoned me regarding the story that has appeared, but if you read the articles carefully you will see that at no point have I declared an interest in becoming manager of Manchester City.' Mr White had the bit between his teeth, though, and he wasn't about to let go, choosing to ignore what I had just told him. 'Well, as far as I am concerned, if you wish to continue your negotiations you are free to do so,' he added. The steam was coming out of my ears at that stage. The other board members – Jimmy Farrell, Kevin Kelly, Chris White and Tom Devlin – heard me tell the chairman, 'I don't know what your game is, but if you want to get rid of me, do so.'

Just the week before I had played in the Glasgow Classic golf tournament at Haggs Castle in the company of Howard Clark, the former Ryder Cup player, and I remember thinking to myself that it wasn't such a bad old life. Now my world was about to crash. By the time I reached home I was at boiling point and I discussed my situation with Liz. I also spoke to my dad, whose advice I always valued, but I knew in my heart of hearts that the writing was now firmly on the wall.

In the space of just a few days, the sunshine of Haggs Castle had been replaced by storm clouds gathering over Celtic Park.

I suppose in many ways it was the straw that broke the camel's back, for I had also recently seen my business interests go bust, forcing us to sell our home in Pollokshields to balance the books. We had bought the property, on the south side of the city, on my return from Aberdeen and we had spent a lot of money and effort turning the house into a home we could be proud of. Now the house, and what was effectively my pension fund, had gone and we had moved into a much smaller property. The timing of my latest run-in with the chairman couldn't have been worse. What made his accusation, that I was deliberately manipulating a move to Manchester, all the more absurd was the fact that we had been in the new house barely one month. If I had been planning my escape, it would hardly have made sense to put my wife and family through the trauma of moving home for the sake of just a few weeks.

My dad's advice, as usual, was offered after careful consideration of the facts. 'Anyone who treats you in that way isn't worth bothering about,' he said. 'I certainly won't be back at Celtic Park and, if you have any pride, you will walk away from them.' Walk I did, to Maine Road, metaphorically at least. *The People* story had been spot-on. City did want me as their manager. The club made an official approach and soon afterwards I met Peter Swales for the first time. The meeting took place in Carlisle and, from the first moments, I was impressed by the chairman's forthright manner. However, I didn't accept his offer straightaway. In truth, I was in a state of shock. I loved being manager of Celtic. I derived great pleasure from working with the players and the many other aspects of the job. It was the chairman and most of the directors I couldn't stomach. To be honest, my head and my emotions were in turmoil and I asked for twenty-four hours to make up my mind. Maybe I hoped I would wake up to discover that it had all been a bad dream – but it wasn't.

On returning to Glasgow, I contacted Mr White to inform him of my situation. He responded by offering to increase my salary to £25,000, but there was a catch. Mr White reiterated his demand that I sack John Clark and appoint Frank Connor as my number two. Not satisfied with that, the chairman sought a few extra drops of blood in the form of a newspaper retraction to the effect that I had wronged the club through certain statements attributed to me. There was nothing more to be said! My days as Celtic manager were at an end – for the time being at least.

I told Liz and then Peter Swales that I was taking the job, but I headed down the M74 in July 1983 with very mixed emotions. On one hand there was the excitement of a new challenge, on the other the heartache of having broken up with my first love. I lived in a hotel initially and it was a lonely existence at times, away from my wife and family. The feeling of isolation was offset to some extent by the friendliness of the locals and, in particular, my new chairman. At Celtic Park I had never called the chairman anything other than, 'Mr White' or 'Mr Chairman'. It was the same with the other directors. Indeed, I was never invited to address them by their Christian names. My new boss was somewhat different. When I called him 'gaffer', the chairman quickly set the record straight. 'My name is Peter,' he corrected. 'I am not comfortable being addressed in any other way.'

It would be wrong of me to try to claim that all my troubles at Celtic were the fault of Desmond White. I do have an explosive temperament at times and there were occasions when I might have been better advised to have held my tongue. My only excuse for a lack of diplomacy and tact is that I was a young manager, still feeling my way. I wasn't yet fully schooled in the politics of the boardroom, but

Mr White never appeared to make allowances. Instead of putting a fatherly arm round my shoulder, as Dick Donald had done on more than one occasion, he seemed to thrive on confrontation, in the belief that he was always right and I was invariably wrong. Things would be very different at Maine Road, but I very nearly didn't stay long enough to find out.

I realise now that I was suffering from a severe bout of homesickness. So severe, in fact, that one evening I packed my bags and headed north, vowing never to return to Manchester City. It was hardly what could be described as the responsible actions of a 43-year-old man, but, fortunately, Liz quickly made me see sense. My wife pointed out that I wasn't in a position to quit my new job. With the business having gone bust there was no other source of revenue. So back I went. It was far from easy, though. I missed my kids like hell and I found the solitude of a hotel room hard to handle. When my family was finally able to join me we all had many adjustments to make, but the move affected our youngest girl, Paula, more than the rest of us. Paula was just about to begin secondary school and she was upset at being parted from her friends at what is a difficult age. It was much easier for Martyn to make the adjustment. He was still attending primary school and he handled the transition smoothly. He was also fortunate that his new school was next door to our home at Hale Barns. Our other three girls had begun work in Glasgow so they stayed behind and we purchased an apartment for them in the Kings Park district of the city. But Liz and I missed not having them around and they eventually joined us in Manchester the following year.

We lived in rented accommodation to start with but soon moved into a home of our own and we were fortunate to have good neighbours who made the settling in process easier.

As it happened most of our friends were United fans because of my relationship with Paddy Crerand. But we were fortunate to enjoy a nice lifestyle in a lovely area of the country.

My predecessors at City, Malcolm Allison and John Bond, had operated a spend-spend-spend policy. Now the club was well and truly skint. The situation was so bad that we actually had to release certain players to reduce the overall wage bill. I appointed a fellow Scot, Jimmy Frizzell, as my assistant. John Clark had left Celtic at the same time as I did and went on to become manager of Clyde. He later returned to the club and is now the kit-man and a highly respected figure at Celtic Park. My decision not to appoint John as my assistant at City was taken on the basis that I felt I needed to have someone on hand with an extensive knowledge of English football to advise me. Jimmy had been manager of Oldham and knew the local scene, which helped.

I didn't need Jimmy to tell me about Derek Parlane, though. I was aware of what the former Rangers striker was capable of from his time at Ibrox, so, when he became available, on a free transfer from Leeds, I was first in. Jim Tolmie, a midfielder who was playing for the Belgian side, Lokeren, at the time, was another whose credentials were known to me from his days with Morton. Another two Scots were purchased from Brighton, Neil McNab and Gordon Smith.

Is it any wonder that the City fans feared that we were in grave danger of turning the place into a rest home for ageing Scottish footballers? But my faith in the trio was repaid through their performances, particularly during the early part of the season. We were also boosted by the arrival of Mick McCarthy from Barnsley. I was able to sign Mick with part of the proceeds from Tommy Caton's transfer to Arsenal for £450,000, and it was one of the best pieces of business I ever did, because he became the heart of the team.

Tough as teak and an inspirational force, Mick was perhaps not the most naturally gifted player in the world, but he was nonetheless a tower of strength at centre-half. It hasn't surprised me that he has gone on to carve out a successful career in management. His blunt, no-nonsense approach is not to everyone's liking, but he's a typical Yorkshireman without any airs or graces. No matter what people thought of his handling of the Roy Keane situation during the 2002 World Cup finals, Mick's refusal to allow his authority to be undermined said much about his strength of character. It was unfortunate that his time as the Republic of Ireland's manager ended in acrimony, but he has picked up the reigns again with Sunderland and, after a difficult start, has begun turning the team around.

Peter Swales wasn't everyone's cup of tea either. Some thought him brash, because of the loud suits he wore, but underneath the flash exterior, Peter was a down-to-earth bloke and a joy to work for. Invariably attired in a powder blue suit and Cuban-heeled shoes in an effort to appear a few inches taller than he actually was, as a member of the FA he also sported the three lions badge in his lapel with pride.

When it came to discussing the club's financial state, Peter always played it straight with me. He took me into his confidence and never tried to hoodwink me over money. In fact, when we met to discuss my becoming manager, he painted such a bleak picture of the club's financial plight that at first I thought he was kidding. However, Allison and Bond had done such a thorough job of emptying the coffers on a series of transfer deals that Manchester City was in a truly parlous state. The situation was graphically illustrated when the youth team travelled to the Northeast for an FA Cup tie.

I had decided that, as a reward for the team having done so well in the competition, I would invite the players' parents to accompany us, in the hope that they would be impressed by the way City did things and encourage their youngsters to commit to the club long term. So we organised a second coach for the mums and dads and made a reservation for lunch at a hotel where the first team had dined prior to a match at Middlesbrough. However, when we arrived, coach Tony Book suffered the acute embarrassment of being told by the hotel manager that he was unable to provide a meal unless he received cash up front. Tony explained the situation to me and I decided to try to talk the manager into a rethink, but it soon became evident that I was wasting my time. 'It's more than my job's worth,' he explained. 'Payment for the previous bill is outstanding and I have been instructed to withdraw all credit facilities.'

I could see the manager's point, but I had a coach-load of parents to consider and I didn't think it would do Manchester City's reputation much good for them to discover that their sons were playing for a club who couldn't even afford the price of a meal. So, I asked the manager if he would accept payment on a credit card to which he replied, 'Only if it's a personal card and not a business card.' In the event, it took me quite some time to get the expense of that lunch reimbursed by the secretary, Bernard Halford. Not that I held that against Bernard. He's a lovely fellow and he did a first-rate job in almost impossible circumstances.

As it happened, the youth team lost to Newcastle in the semi-finals, but the following season they won the FA Youth Cup, beating Manchester United in the final, so these kids were very important to the future wellbeing of Manchester City and several of them went on to achieve considerable success at a higher level. David White and Earl Barrett represented England and several others made it into the first team.

Peter had heart problems and his health must have been affected by the intense pressure he was under, constantly trying to balance the books, so it was perhaps not surprising that he died at a comparatively young age, but he never tried to duck his responsibilities. He faced his critics and took the blows. I remember on one occasion he asked me to accompany him to a meeting with the fans, held for them to air their grievances. Peter listened patiently to all they had to say and held his hands up to the mistakes he had made in allowing Allison and Bond to almost bankrupt the club. Eventually, though, Peter stood up and had his say. 'Normally, the chairman takes stick for not providing money for players,' he said. 'I did the exact opposite and now there is nothing left. You will have to be sensible. I wish I could tell this man sitting beside me that there is money to spend on players, but I can't and I am sorry.' In my book, it took courage for Peter Swales to stand up and tell the blunt truth.

Peter was a smashing guy – and a very generous one. When we won promotion to the First Division at the end of my second season, Peter put his hand in his pocket and splashed out a small fortune on booze. Paul Power, our captain, told me that the players had arranged a celebration party at a popular country club and asked if there was any chance that the club might chip in for the drinks. I approached the chairman and he agreed to personally foot the drinks bill, provided the players didn't order champagne. When he also learned that I was hosting a private function at Geoff Baker's, a well-known Altrincham establishment, for thirty or so friends and family, he informed me that he would pick up the tab.

My bash turned into a memorable evening and the drink flowed long into the night. At one stage the red half of Manchester was represented by several United players in the shape of Bryan Robson, Gordon McQueen, Paul McGrath, Mark Hughes and Arthur Albiston, who turned up to offer their congratulations. I appreciated the gesture and the fact that they arrived armed with bottles of champagne, but we still managed to run up a bill for £900 and I felt awkward about presenting the chairman with a tab for that amount, so I offered to halve the cost with him. But Peter wouldn't hear of it. 'You certainly know how to enjoy yourself,' he quipped with a smile, 'but, so what, we're going to take £1 million in season ticket sales.'

Contrast that attitude with Desmond White's reluctance to splash out just a few hundred pounds when Celtic beat Rangers, 2–1, in the 1982 League Cup final. The competition was sponsored and I think Celtic received in the region of £100,000. It was a big result for us and everyone was in the mood to party after goals from Charlie Nicholas and Murdo MacLeod had sent the Celtic fans home happy. I hastily arranged a celebration meal for the players and officials at Glasgow's Grosvenor Hotel and, at the end of the evening, I asked the manager, Tim Kelly – himself a Celtic fan – if there was any chance that he might see his way to sending a couple of cases of champagne to my home in Pollokshields, where we planned to carry on the celebrations. Tim readily agreed to my request and added that he would 'disguise' the cost of the additional champagne in the bill, which was to be sent to Celtic Park for payment.

However, I thought I had been rumbled when I turned up for the next board meeting to be told by the chairman, 'Billy, that meal the other night was very expensive. Have you any idea how much was spent on champagne?' I tried my best to keep a straight face as I speculated that it must have run to several hundred pounds and, in the hope of avoiding detection, added, 'You and I alone must have drunk £100 worth, Mr White.' I don't know if he was taken in by my outrageous claim, but it transpired that the bill for champagne came to £300! You couldn't have made it up.

No more was said, but I wonder what White's reaction would have been had he found out I also took the League Cup on a tour of one of Britain's toughest districts in the early hours of the Sunday morning following our Hampden victory. The Gorbals, home of the infamous

Glasgow razor gangs, who were immortalised in the novel, *No Mean City*, published in the 1930s, once boasted some of the most appalling housing conditions in Europe. These slums were, thankfully, demolished and replaced by sky-rise blocks of flats in the 1960s and 1970s, but the Gorbals remains a tough place. It is also a hotbed of Celtic supporters.

In 1982, Paddy Crerand's mother still lived there. Paddy and I have been friends since we signed for Celtic on the same day in 1957 and he had travelled from his home in Manchester to be at the final and spend the weekend with Liz and me. The party was in full flow when Paddy happened to mention that his mum, Sarah, hadn't been keeping too well and I suggested that we pay her an impromptu visit. Being a Celtic fan herself, I thought Sarah might appreciate the opportunity to hold the League Cup, which I had spirited away from the Grosvenor for safekeeping. I can still see in my mind's eye the look of sheer disbelief on her face when she opened her front door to be greeted by the sight of her son, the Celtic manager and his wife, along with one of football's most famous trophies. Paddy and I had been in no fit state to get behind the wheel of a car and Liz had kindly agreed to drive us. The next thing we knew we were standing in the courtyard of Sarah's maisonette, surrounded by dozens of excited neighbours having their photographs taken with the League Cup. It must have been the only time in her life that Paddy's mum entertained in her dressing gown and curlers!

Unfortunately, there were no trophies to show off during my three and a bit seasons with City, but I have many happy memories. As had been the case at Aberdeen, I was encouraged to become involved in all aspects of the running of the club. Looking back, we lived a hand-to-mouth existence at times, often buying players on the never-never. I also signed several players knowing that they wouldn't be there for the duration. I was forced by circumstances to look for quick fix solutions, but if the team lacked star quality, there was no shortage of battlers and we missed out on promotion in my first season after finishing fourth. Newcastle were in third place behind Chelsea and Sheffield Wednesday, thanks largely to the influence of Kevin Keegan, a player for whom I had the highest regard and the sort of inspirational individual who can transform a team almost single-handed.

By the following March we had moved into poll position in the promotion race, when we beat Blackburn Rovers at Ewood Park, where they had not lost for a couple of seasons. Unfortunately, there was a heavy price to be paid for our success when Graham Baker, who had been so influential in midfield, fell awkwardly and dislocated his shoulder. The game was played on 2 March, my forty-fifth birthday, and Liz had arranged a surprise party for me at our home in Hale Barns. That turned into quite an occasion. My old mates, Benny Rooney and Mike Jackson, who were guiding Morton's fortunes at the time, travelled down from Glasgow, along with another long-time friend, Gordon Whitelaw.

Sir Matt Busby, like me, a Bellshill man, was also invited. Liz was clearly making up for the fact that I had missed out on any celebrations when I had hit the big 4–0!

But the champagne threatened to go flat. We badly missed Baker and a defeat by Notts County in our penultimate fixture meant that we had to beat Charlton at home to go up in third place. With Mick McCarthy and Nicky Reid also injured, we were missing several key players for one of the biggest games City had faced in years. I did my best to give the impression that I was super-confident that we would achieve our target and I arrived at the ground much earlier than usual, resplendent in my best suit. I spent the next five hours telling everyone I saw that we would definitely be playing in the top flight the following season, but looks can be deceptive. Inside, my stomach was churning.

I was as much a bag of nerves as the next person, but I couldn't afford to give of any negative vibes to my players. However, when I caught sight of the Charlton players my heart sank. They all looked to be about six feet four inches tall and we had five feet eight inch Andy May filling in as an emergency central defender.

I need not have worried. May out-jumped the lot of them to head us into an early lead and we were on our way to the First Division. There was an incredible atmosphere, with 47,000 packed into Maine Road and, roared on by our wonderful fans, we proceeded to dismantle the opposition, eventually winning, 5–1. Jim Melrose, Dave Phillips, who got two, and Paul Simpson were our other goal-scorers, but it was an all-round team performance that won the day in such spectacular style. My office, which doubled as a hospitality room on match days, was overflowing. It was as if half of Glasgow had turned up to join in the celebrations.

Much of the credit for our success was due to my backroom team. I was fortunate to have the support of people whose views I valued. My assistant, Jimmy Frizzell, is a fellow Scot and he was very passionate about his birthright. He always drank whisky and water and I remember on one occasion, when we were playing Cardiff away, that he reacted with indignation when the locals began chanting, 'English bastard'. Frizz was furious – not at being called a bastard, but at being labelled English!

Tony Book was another real character. Tony had captained City during the club's glory years in the late 1960s and early 1970s, after being introduced to league football at the age of thirty-one. He also had a spell as manager and was fiftysomething by the time our paths crossed, but he had lost none of his enthusiasm and was still very fit. He loved taking part in bounce games and could mix it with the youngsters. On one such occasion, he was sent crashing to the ground following a particularly heavy challenge and we feared at first that he had suffered a broken leg. However, after receiving treatment from the physio, Roy Bailey, Tony jumped to his feet and asked me: 'Is it okay if I kick that bastard?' 'Feel free,' I said, 'if you can catch him.' Our chief scout, Ken Barnes, was another who did a remarkable job, in spite of the fierce competition we faced from United as we tried to snap up local talent.

Privately, I knew that the really hard part lay ahead. Surviving in the First Division would require a miracle, given that we had so little money and lacked the strength in depth of the majority of our rivals. But survive we did – by the skin of our teeth, eventually finishing a highly creditable fifteenth, four points above Ipswich Town, who were relegated.

The financial constraints placed on me meant that I had to wheel and deal on a very tight budget. Our local rivals, United, could afford to go out and buy the best. I had to settle for signing Mark Lillas from Huddersfield and Sammy McIlroy on a free transfer from Stoke. Both players did a fine job for us, though. Mark was a hardworking, committed centre-forward and Sammy's experience proved crucial in the big games. We hit a purple patch at New Year and went on a five-game winning run, beating Aston Villa, Southampton, Tottenham, West Bromwich and QPR, but we didn't win a single game from the middle of February onwards and lost nine out of thirteen. Nevertheless I was pleased, all things considered, but the reality was that unless we tightened up at the back the odds were stacked against us beating the drop next time round.

The previous close season I had been approached by the Spanish club, Real Sociedad, to become their manager and I was both flattered and intrigued. Apparently, I had come to Sociedad's attention when Celtic played them in the European Cup in season 1982–83. We were beaten, 3–2 on aggregate, but the club's directors must have liked the cut of my jib and the fact that I was able to converse with them in Spanish. San Sebastian is a beautiful city and I was tempted, but I was also keen to make my mark in English football and declined the offer. In the event, John Toshack was appointed manager and did a first-class job. Liz was aware of the offer, of course, but it was some years later before I informed my children of the approach and they were none too pleased at having missed out on the chance to sample life in Spain.

The family would soon be on the move again, though, albeit only as far as Birmingham. My relationship with Peter Swales hadn't changed. We still got on well and met regularly to discuss in what direction the club was headed. I also found most of the other directors easy enough to get along with. Some had invested six-figure sums in the club, and I saw that as an act of faith in my ability to take Manchester City forward, but I was not so keen on Freddie Pye. Freddie had a habit of expressing his opinions rather too loudly and succeeded in upsetting a number of players, in particular Mick McCarthy, who, I felt, had done an outstanding job for the team.

So, when the news broke that Freddie had been appointed vice-chairman and given the additional title of director in charge of team affairs, I was far from pleased. I phoned Peter Swales straightaway and expressed my concern that Pye would endeavour to interfere in team matters. Peter attempted to reassure me that would not happen. 'Freddie has made additional funds available and I felt he should be given a title, but he won't cause you a problem, Billy,' Peter said. I responded by declaring that if he came anywhere near the team I would be off. Peter tried to offer further reassurance, but I was already upset and unsettled by the news and I didn't feel I would be able to handle the situation. I suppose, too, I was impatient for success. I was prepared to remain as manager of City, but I was also ambitious to better myself.

I had found the transition from chasing trophies with Celtic and competing in Europe to managing an English Second Division club difficult. Then, having won promotion, the constant struggle against relegation was unquestionably stressful. Not having the resources to buy the players I knew we needed to maintain our First Division status was also frustrating. So, when Doug Ellis, the Aston Villa chairman, began making encouraging noises about me being the ideal man to succeed Graham Turner as the Villa manager, I was very interested in listening to what he had to say. We were just a few weeks into the season and Peter said he felt I would be making a terrible mistake if I chose to go to Villa Park. He insisted that Villa's position was no stronger than City's and stressed that he would assist me in every way possible if the right job for me came along, but I already believed that I would be improving my lot if I went to Villa and his pleas fell on deaf ears. Others also warned me that I could be making a big mistake. Sir Matt Busby said I should be very wary and Tommy Docherty, who had first-hand experience of Ellis from his time as manager at Villa Park, was even blunter. 'You would need to be aff yer heid,' declared the Doc. On reflection, maybe I was.

# CHAPTER 17

# DEADLY

The alarm bells rang louder than a klaxon when Doug Ellis offered me the job as manager of Aston Villa in September 1986, but don't ask me why I ignored the warnings. My inner senses told me to give Ellis a wide berth and there were plenty of others saying the same thing. Whoever landed Ellis with the nickname of 'Deadly' was spot-on. From my perspective, Ellis is a plausible dictator with a heart of stone and if you think that's just sour grapes on my part consider for a moment the number of managers Villa have had since Tommy Docherty famously told the chairman and chief executive where to go in 1970. The average life expectancy of the Villa manager is two and half years and they can't all have been hopeless at doing the job.

Ellis's initial approach was made through the proper channels. He contacted Peter Swales for permission to speak to me and was granted clearance by the City chairman. Soon after, Liz and I travelled to the Midlands to open discussions. We couldn't help but be impressed by the opulence and grandeur of the mansion Ellis calls home. It bore all the trappings of a highly successful businessman. Ellis himself was charm personified, but almost from the first moment my suspicions were aroused. Ellis told me that he had held a party for the players that afternoon and I was instantly on my guard. It was most unusual for a chairman to be so close to the players, so did that mean Ellis had friends among the players who were prepared to go behind the manager's back and carry dressing room tittle-tattle back to the chairman, thus undermining the manager's position? Stupidly, I dismissed the thought for the time being and listened as Ellis told me he had parted company with Graham Turner and considered that I would make an ideal replacement. Apparently, Graham Turner had actually recommended me as his successor.

'I've been impressed by the job you've done for Manchester City,' said Ellis. 'I realise that it can't have been easy for you working under such financial constraints, but you won't have the same problems at Villa. Ours is an excellent and well-run club and the team is far more secure. I would never have allowed things to slip as far as City have done.' Ellis also informed me that he was prepared to pay me £35,000 a year, an increase of almost £10,000 on what I was earning at City. To be honest, money has never been a motivating force for me. The opportunity to achieve success was always a greater incentive, so, when Ellis added that he was keen for me to take a look at the player pool and assess the strengths and weaknesses of the squad with a view to making any changes I felt necessary, I was encouraged.

However, I asked for time to consider my position and he agreed. When I returned to Manchester, Peter Swales hadn't altered his stance. Once again he warned, 'This is not the right move for you, Billy, but if you feel that Villa can provide you with a greater opportunity, you have to make up your own mind.' By now the press were aware that Villa were pursuing me and I wasn't short of advice. Looking back, I can't recall a single positive voice among the many expressing a view, but when I sat down and reflected on the three full seasons I had spent as manager of City, although Peter Swales had done everything in his power to generate funds, the fact remained that City simply didn't have the resources to enable me to rebuild the squad. Now, here was a club with a superb stadium and a terrific fan base offering me a seemingly easier ride. Initially, I decided to stay where I was, only to suddenly change my mind at the last minute, for reasons I have never been entirely sure of. The Freddie Pye situation had put me on a bit of a downer and my thought processes possibly became a little confused. Doug Ellis also talked a good game and I was probably taken in to an extent by his big ideas and his ambitious plans for the club. On reflection, if Pye had not been given the role of Director of Team Affairs, I would very likely have stayed where I was. But it is easy to be wise after the event.

My decision was certainly not driven by the prospect of earning more money. As a family we were also happy living in the Northwest, where we had made new friends and enjoyed a pleasant lifestyle. I also had an excellent relationship with my chairman. Villa, meanwhile, were propping up the First Division, having won just one and lost six of the first seven games. The club was in a sorry state, but still seemed to offer considerably more in the longer term.

Perhaps the fact that I had considered myself a prime contender for the Scotland managership, only to be left disappointed and frustrated, also contributed to my decision. Alex Ferguson had taken over the reins of the international team on a part-time basis following Jock Stein's sudden death on 10 September 1985, but Fergie had decided to move aside following the 1986 World Cup finals in Mexico. In the event, the SFA appointed Andy Roxburgh as his successor, so I was feeling pretty low when Ellis came on the scene.

In the end I fell for his sweet talk and swapped Maine Road for Villa Park. It turned out to be the worst eight months of my managerial career. I was barely five minutes in the job when I received the first of many memos from the chairman, informing me that the club had no option but to accept an offer of £650,000 from Spurs for Steve Hodge. So much for strengthening the squad! A combination of Ellis's refusal to supplement the existing squad, coupled with us not having a proven goal-scorer, as well as a succession of injuries, eventually led to the inevitable.

Did I make mistakes? You bet. I should never have gone to work for Ellis at Villa. At the time I also felt I had made a mistake in not moving my family to the Midlands. Instead, I commuted from our home in Hale Barnes and spent a couple of nights a week living in hotels. Consequently, I was always on the move and never really got to know the area or the people, but, with hindsight, it turned out to be a wise decision. Within a fortnight of becoming Aston Villa manager I realised that I had made a huge mistake. Can you imagine how much worse I would have felt had I uprooted my family for what turned out to be a short stay in the Midlands?

Ellis had said initially that he didn't have a problem with me commuting, but the whispers soon began that I wasn't committed to the club and I was told by a friend of Ron Atkinson that he was being lined up to take over from me. When I confronted Ellis he denied any knowledge of the rumours that were circulating and then asked if I was calling him a liar. Unfortunately, I wasn't in any position to be truthful! On several other occasions I approached him and alleged that he was talking behind my back.

Everything went through the chairman, who had an office at the stadium. Villa's training ground at Wishaw, near the Belfry, is some distance from the stadium, but Ellis was made aware of every single incident – large or small – within hours of it happening. Certain players were only too happy to report back to him and Ellis ensured that his door was always open to accommodate the disaffected. The chairman effectively had spies in the camp. I never did find out for sure who they were, but I knew for a fact that I had enemies in the dressing room. All of this added to Ellis's power and control and ensured he stayed in the spotlight.

Ellis loved being the centre of attraction and I felt in the early days as if I was being paraded around as his prize exhibit. Ellis took me to the motor show and had me speak at one of his social gatherings, for example. I think it made him feel even more important, but at no time did we form a close relationship.

Having realised what a mistake I had made, it murdered me to admit it to myself. It didn't help my mood, either, when I was offered an escape route and didn't take it. I received a phone call from a sports journalist, Ian Broadley, who is based in Aberdeen, informing me that, with Fergie having gone to Manchester United, the job was mine if I wanted it. But I was trying to build a reputation in England and I felt I had gone some way to doing that, so I hesitated and asked for time to consider my situation. I had been at Villa for only a couple of months and my mind was in turmoil. In the end I delayed too long and when I got back to Ian to confirm my interest in returning to Pittodrie as manager, it was too late. Ian Porterfield had been lined up to succeed Fergie. That was yet another bad call on my part.

I already had the distinct impression that it was going to prove impossible to arrest Villa's slide into the Second Division and that the chairman had accepted our fate. I had got off to an encouraging start when we travelled to Anfield for my first game in charge and drew, 3–3, with Liverpool, but it turned out to be one of the few high points during what was the only period of my life when I have not enjoyed my involvement in the game.

The squad was a mix of youth and experience. We had some exciting young players, such as Martin Keown, Mark Walters and Paul Elliott, whom I later signed for Celtic, but they couldn't be expected to shoulder the burden of keeping the club in the top flight. That was the responsibility of the senior professionals, guys like Andy Gray, Simon Stainrod and Allan Evans, but, significantly, Evans, a defender, shared the distinction of being our joint highest league scorer with Stainrod and Garry Thompson, on six apiece. Frankly, the place was crying out for a major clear-out and I told Ellis and the board as much, but I never had the full backing of the chairman and our relationship became increasingly strained.

Eventually I hated going to work. I might have survived longer had I been prepared to spend twenty-four hours a day at the club, with one eye on the players and the other on the chairman, but I never felt comfortable and I was operating below optimum performance. I didn't feel I was working with the chairman – I was working under him all the time.

When the end came I was not in the least surprised. I had been expecting the sack. Ellis had been alleging that I didn't spend enough time at the club, which I refuted. I will admit, however, that my heart was no longer in it. We had won only two games since the turn of the year and relegation had become an inescapable fact. I wanted out as soon as possible, but the manner of my removal as manager did annoy the hell out of me, as my sacking was forecast in one of the tabloids. I felt Ellis also took great pleasure telling me that I was sacked. He called me into his office and delivered the unsurprising news as coldly and clinically as he possible could, but he did do me one favour. We had only one match left and that was against Manchester United at Old Trafford. Losing 3–1 there with Fergie in charge of the opposition would not have been a pleasant experience.

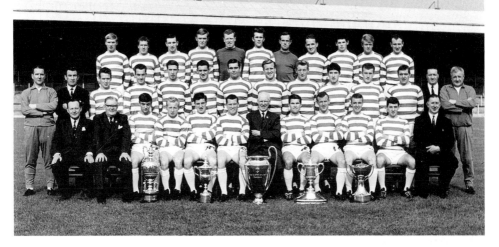

ABOVE *A pride of lions and the most successful squad in Celtic's history. The 1967 grand slam winners proudly show off an impressive collection of trophies –* the Glasgow, League, European and Scottish Cups and the League Championship Trophy. I doubt that our achievement will ever be matched by another Scottish club.

BELOW *The 1969 Scottish Cup final was a great moment for us all as we beat Rangers 4-0. Here I am heading the opening goal. (Empics)*

ABOVE *Overseeing a conversation between two football greats, Jock Stein and Bill Shankly, in 1975. Note Shanks's cropped hairstyle while I preferred a more trendy look in keeping with the times. But what about that shirt!*

LEFT *Me and Danny McGrain with the Scottish Cup in 1975. Danny was still a huge influence on the team when we won the championship in '81 and '82.*

TOP RIGHT *Out on a high. Jock Stein and I at a reception following my last game for Celtic – the Scottish Cup final win over Airdrie in May 1975.*

BOTTOM RIGHT *Billy McNeill MBE. The family share one of the proudest moments of my life. Paula points to the award I received in 1976 surrounded by her sisters (from left to right) Libby, Carol and Susan.*

LEFT *Me in a Rangers jersey! As Rod might say, 'You wear it well', but it was definitely a one-off, for charity. Bobby Shearer, the Rangers full-back, promised to kit us out in Scotland strips but turned up with a set of light blue jerseys instead.*

ABOVE *An unforgettable moment. Celtic have just beaten Rangers 4-2 at Celtic Park to be crowned Premier League champions in May 1979. This smiling trio is me, full-back Andy Lynch and my assistant John Clark.*

BELOW *Maine Road erupts. Manchester City have just beaten Charlton 5-1 to clinch promotion to the First Division in May 1985 and the joy and relief is evident on the faces of yours truly and Norman Luft, the club doctor.*

ABOVE *The lion and the mongoose. My former Scotland team-mate Denis Law, who starred for both Manchester City and United, again crosses the divide to offer his congratulations on City's promotion.*

LEFT *The double in our centenary year! Cup final celebrations after beating Dundee United. Tommy Craig is in the background. (Empics)*

TOP RIGHT *The boys of 1967 reunite for the opening of the Lisbon Lions stand at Celtic Park on 1 February 2000. Bobby Murdoch and Ronnie Simpson are sadly no longer with us.(Line up see p. 301)*

BELOW RIGHT *My dream team. Celebrating my 60th birthday in March 2000. From left to right: Libby, Susan, me, Paula, Martyn, Carol and Liz.*

*The lion king and his cubs. Liz and I surrounded by our grandchildren in 2004. From bottom left: Gerrard, Abby, James, me, Liz, baby Sean, Alexandra and Matthew.*

Under the terms of my contract, I was entitled to a payment of £25,000 as part of a get-out clause. In the end, I had to settle for £15,000. For all that I found Doug Ellis a despicable character, I can't help but admire the way he has managed to survive in the face of so much opposition from a cross-section of the Villa fans. He is clearly a shrewd and clever man. A string of managers have come and gone, but Deadly remains at the head of affairs into his eighties.

# CHAPTER 18

# RETURN TO PARADISE

Queuing up with my fellow unemployed at the local labour exchange in Altrincham was a shock to the system. It was also a completely new experience for me and one I never wish to repeat. For the first time since leaving school in 1957, I was having to collect unemployment benefit, but I did allow myself a wry smile as I took my place in the queue that morning in May 1987. What would the others have said if they realised the identity of their fellow claimant? The captain of the Lisbon Lions wasn't supposed to be doing this sort of thing, was he? The answer I am afraid was yes. I am no different from the next person. I had a wife and family to support and a living to earn.

Thankfully, having to sign on was a short-lived experience. I have no wish to sound disrespectful to those unfortunate enough to have to go through the same routine week after week, simply because they are out of work, often for reasons beyond their control, but I found the whole business utterly demoralising. However, even though I had reached a low point in my life, I couldn't afford to start feeling sorry for myself. I had already given some thought to returning to the licensed trade, following my very public dismissal by Doug Ellis as manager of

Aston Villa, but, privately, I prayed that another door would open to allow me to continue in the game that had been my life.

When that door swung open, the person behind it was Jack McGinn, now chairman of Celtic. Frankly, he was the last person I expected to be standing there offering me a way back. Others had suggested that I would eventually return to Celtic as manager. I did not share their optimism. Having left the club in the manner I did, I feared that my days are Celtic Park were over, but that was seemingly not the case when I took a telephone call from Jack requesting a meeting. He didn't go into detail and I resisted the temptation to ask what was on his mind. I had returned to Scotland for a Celtic supporters' club function at a Renfrew hotel to mark the twentieth anniversary of the European Cup win and the following day – a Monday – I attended the annual manager of the year lunch in Glasgow.

It had been my intention to return to Manchester the next day, but I was persuaded by my friends, Mike and Pat Jackson, with whom I was staying, to prolong the trip. As it happened, I was also due to take part in a radio recording about the Lisbon Lions and when I received the call from Jack I suggested that we meet in a car park near to Radio Clyde's studios at Clydebank. The meeting was viewed as having been clandestine, because of the choice of venue, but my reason for suggesting the meeting place was based on the fact that few people would take much notice of two men sitting talking in a car. The last thing I wanted to happen at that juncture was for the news to leak out that Billy McNeill was on his way back to Celtic when my predecessor, Davie Hay, had not even been told that he was being replaced as manager. So I made it clear that Davie had to be told before I met the board.

Jack didn't beat about the bush. 'We would like you to return as manager,' he said. 'This is what we can offer you.' The details were immaterial. In response to his offer my answer was an instantaneous yes. To say I was happy would be an understatement. I was, in fact, every bit as excited as I had been the first day I walked into Celtic Park thirty years earlier. I had always felt that Celtic was my club and regarded the job of manager as mine. I had managed two major English clubs, but neither compared with Celtic in status or appeal. None of the magic of Celtic had worn off for me and I experienced a real sense of excitement that I was coming home. I met with the remainder of the board four days later at the Jacksons' home in the Queen's Park district of Glasgow and the deal was formalised. However, there was one piece of outstanding business the board had to conclude before my appointment could be made public – and it was one that clearly filled the directors with dread.

The man who replaced me, when I left to go to Manchester City, had to be removed as manager. Given what had just happened to me, I could fully understand how bad the board felt about having to take the step of sacking their manager. It was a task made even more difficult by the fact that Davie Hay is a genuinely decent bloke. Naturally, I sympathised with Davie. Being given the sack is a stressful and unpleasant experience. Having called Davie to wish him good fortune at the time of his appointment as manager, I now found myself telephoning to offer my sympathies.

I want to make it crystal clear that I had nothing whatsoever to do with Davie's departure. There have been suggestions over the years that I was part of a plot orchestrated by the board. That is simply not true. The Celtic directors chose to replace the manager without any encouragement or prompting from me, but I would be lying to say that I was anything other than delighted to be given the opportunity to return to my first love. I might have done so two-and-a-half years earlier in December 1984, when I was approached by director Tom

Devlin and asked if I would be interested in returning to Celtic Park. The question was posed when Celtic played Rapid Vienna at Old Trafford in the Cup Winners' Cup second round second leg replay and I answered by informing Mr Devlin that I would be interested whenever the job of manager became available.

One valuable legacy of Davie's reign was the signing of Mick McCarthy. The deal, valued at £500,000, had been concluded shortly before Davie's departure and I was grateful that my predecessor had moved for a player I rated highly. Mick had been an inspired signing while I was at Maine Road and, as things turned out, he was a great asset for Celtic, too. But for all that I was incredibly pleased to be back, I sensed that there was much work to be done. The atmosphere at Celtic Park didn't feel right and there appeared to be a degree of unrest among certain players over their contracts. Changes would have to be made – quickly.

I wasted no time in confirming Tommy Craig as my assistant, a role he had assumed during my predecessor's time in charge. I had known Tommy for several years and had been impressed with his knowledge of the game, and it was also clear that he had a genuine feeling for the club. Graeme Souness had been appointed the previous year as player-manager of Rangers and his so-called Ibrox revolution was well under way. Rangers had been crowned league champions and had also won the League Cup. The fact that I had received a positive response from the majority of the fans was extremely heartening, but I cautioned against expectations outweighing the potential of the squad to win back the championship from our great rivals. Patience would also be required, I felt.

To be honest, I had already resigned myself to spending my first season rebuilding the squad and I was prepared to settle for a UEFA Cup place. I was not hopeful that there would be any silverware to show for our efforts. My priority was to establish a solid base and improve discipline and understanding. To that end, I arranged a pre-season tour to Sweden where we worked hard on developing into a unit. It doesn't take a genius to know that the defence, midfield and attack must gel to have any hope of achieving success. But while I was in a much happier frame of mind on our return from Sweden, where we had played a series of trial matches, I considered that the reality of our situation was that we were short of the necessary quality to mount a sustained challenge to Rangers.

I needed to bring in fresh faces to enhance the squad and I identified my targets to the board. Faced with the loss of Davie Provan, whose career was ended by his viral illness, Murdo MacLeod, Mo Johnston and Brian McClair, there was no time to waste. The club was particularly upset that a tribunal had ruled that Manchester United should pay only £850,000 for McClair. He was worth considerably more, in my opinion, but at least the directors showed willing in re-investing the money. I was able to busy myself in the transfer market and bought striker Andy Walker from Motherwell for £350,000, full-back Chris Morris from Sheffield Wednesday for £125,000 and Billy Stark, the Aberdeen midfield player with a flair for scoring, for a bargain fee of £75,000.

However, the squad required further strengthening and I persuaded the directors to release the necessary funds to purchase Frank McAvennie from West Ham. I had always been an admirer of Frank from his earliest days at St Mirren and I was convinced that he would form a potent strike force with Walker. I was not wrong. My initial approach to West Ham had been rejected out of sight by John Lyall, my counterpart at Upton Park, but I persisted and by October I had worn Lyall down sufficiently for the Hammers to accept a fee of £750,000. Frank had enjoyed an outstanding first season in London, but his form had dipped and West Ham perhaps felt that they had seen the best of him. Frank was also a loveable rascal and loved living life in the fast lane, which clearly did not endear him to his employers.

I was also keen to land Joe Miller, the Aberdeen winger, whom I felt could give us greater width and pace, but I faced competition from Liverpool and Manchester United. Fortunately, Aberdeen preferred the thought of hard cash rather than taking their chances with a tribunal and we reached agreement on a £650,000 fee. Piece by piece the jigsaw was falling into place and, happily, all the new signings fitted in pretty much straightaway. When you pay big money for a player it is always a gamble, but I enjoyed a winning run at the tables!

In addition to recognising the need to carry out a major overhaul of the squad, I was also keen to impose a standard of discipline. Without wishing to distance myself from the players, I felt this was necessary to make the point that there was only one person running the show. The buck stops with the manager and I have always believed in setting standards for dress code and behaviour, which is something I learnt from Jock Stein. I laid down certain rules that I felt were both adult and acceptable. I have never believed in imposing my will on others simply for the sake of showing who is boss, but there can only be one individual at a football club calling the shots in team matters and that is the manager. Otherwise, if they spot weaknesses, players tend to take liberties.

To that end, I decreed that jeans were an unacceptable mode of dress around the club. As a father of five I would never have been silly enough to imagine that young people will accept a ruling banning casual wear at all times, but I have always believed that football players should look the part when they are at work. My father's army training has always made me a bit of a stickler when it comes to timekeeping, so I also stressed the need for punctuality when it came to the players reporting for training. As far as I know there were no dissenting voices, but I was well aware that I would not be judged on how the players were turned out. The only thing that mattered to the fans was results.

When Arsenal stuck five past us in a pre-season friendly, I didn't exactly feel any great optimism going into the club's centenary season, but I couldn't afford to let the players see anxiety on my face. I sensed that there was a lack of self-belief and it was up to me to boost morale by giving out positive vibes. So I hid my concerns and extolled the players' virtues rather than criticise their shortcomings, but when we lost to Aberdeen in the Skol Cup quarter-finals and tumbled out of Europe at the first hurdle, I was twitching a little myself.

The irony of our UEFA Cup first round exit against Borussia Dortmund was the part played in our downfall by Murdo MacLeod, a player who had been so influential in Celtic's successes during my first spell as manager. As it happened, the first leg at Celtic Park was Murdo's competitive debut for Borussia, following his move to Germany during the close season. Andy Walker and Derek Whyte scored to give us a slender 2–1 lead, but Borussia struck twice in the return and we were free, albeit most reluctantly, to concentrate on domestic matters. However, I would not have dared to imagine that there would be such a remarkable climax to a season that had begun shakily. A league and cup double in the club's hundredth year seemed too much to hope for, but someone up there obviously liked us.

# CHAPTER 19

# DOUBLE
# TOP

I like to think I know a little bit about captaincy and what makes an ideal leader on the pitch. To my mind, there have been fewer better at the job than Roy Aitken, who was such an inspirational force during his time as captain of Celtic. A good captain does more than just lead the team out. He must set an example and Roy portrayed an attitude that rubbed off on his team-mates. I have already discussed Roy's qualities as a player, but I cannot overemphasise the important role he assumed in the dressing room.

I knew I could rely on him to rally the troops and encourage the others to adopt a positive attitude at all times. Roy worked hard behind the scenes as well, to instil a never-say-die attitude, and the team's refusal to accept defeat or simply settle for a share of the spoils was ably demonstrated during the 1987–88 season, when we won so many games almost with the final kick. The sight of Roy with his first raised in an almost threatening gesture, demanding one final push became commonplace. Roy was also invariably the first player to arrive for training and the last to leave. Scotland also benefited from having Roy as captain and he always gave the same level of commitment when playing for his country.

So, when Roy came to me in December 1989 and intimated that he wished to move, I was disappointed, but I had already seen the signs. Roy had begun to change dramatically. Suddenly, instead of being first in, he was turning up just before training and was off as soon as he had showered and changed. Roy made it clear to me that he was being motivated by financial considerations and when he told me that he had heard Newcastle were interested, I knew there was no point in trying to persuade him to have a re-think. The fact that Roy said he wanted to sign for Newcastle told me that I would be wasting my time. Roy was under contract to Celtic, and other clubs are not supposed to approach any player directly in those circumstances, but I'm not daft. Roy became a Newcastle player in January 1990 and Celtic received £500,000 for his services, but the money did not come close to compensating the club for the loss of such a key player.

My disappointment was compounded by the fact that it had been my intention to eventually appoint Roy and Tommy Burns as my lieutenants. Initially, it had been my hope that I would be able to move them on elsewhere, so that they could gain valuable experience of management at a lower level. Once they had done that, I envisaged bringing them back to Celtic Park in a different capacity and, as I became older, Celtic would have readymade replacements. But in Roy's case, at least, circumstances prevented that from happening.

Tommy was different. He was allowed to go to Kilmarnock as player-manager and, after serving his apprenticeship at Rugby Park, returned to Celtic as manager in succession to Lou Macari. I was delighted when that happened, because my belief in Tommy's ability to become a successful manager had been proved correct, although, as things turned out, his reign was much shorter than I had anticipated. Tommy did, however, win the Scottish Cup in 1995. The previous November he had suffered the grave misfortune of presiding over one of the biggest cup final upsets of all time, when Raith Rovers defeated Celtic, 6–5, in a penalty shoot-out to win the Coca-Cola Cup. Tommy's credibility never full recovered from that result. Defeat in a cup final is never easy for the fans to accept, but, when it is inflicted by a team from a lower league, the ramifications are inevitably far greater.

Roy's departure necessitated the appointment of a new captain and I elected to give the job to Paul McStay, who was already an established star with both club and country. My hope was that the added responsibility and status would help him develop a more outgoing personality. Paul is a really nice fellow, but I felt he needed to become more of an extrovert. I realised that Paul was never going to be another Roy Aitken-type, who would shout at his team-mates and cajole them to greater effort, but there was no requirement for him to behave in a similar manner to his predecessor. Paul was an outstanding football player and he led by example. It always amazed me when I heard criticisms of him, because he was a truly great player and one of the finest ever to wear a Celtic jersey.

I have heard it said that Paul couldn't tackle and that he was a 'nearly man'. Don't you believe it. Paul was as powerful as hell and was able to command a game in a manner few others could match. His attributes were that he was a good all-round player, who could tackle and fight to win the ball and make telling passes to begin moves. The only criticism I would make of him was that he did not have much of a record as a goal-scorer.

I remember that when I became manager the first time round, I discovered that Paul had not actually been signed by Celtic, so I immediately went to his home to rectify what was a glaring oversight. Paul's dad, John, left the decision entirely up to him, in the knowledge that there was no shortage of clubs keen to secure his services and, thankfully, he was persuaded to become a Celtic player. From the outset

I realised that Paul was special and I remember wrestling with my thoughts before handing him his league debut against Aberdeen in January 1982. Paul was only seventeen and I wondered at first if I was doing the right thing. He had been substitute a couple of times and eventually I said to myself, 'To hell with it, this boy needs to play.' My faith in Paul was immediately repaid when he scored our third goal in a 3–1 win. Paul also instantly looked an even better player in the first team than he had done playing for the reserves. The reason for that was his ability to identify with good players and adapt to their way of thinking. Paul was soon helping the senior guys.

I had gone as manager when there was all the talk of Paul moving to Italy. I have no idea whether that was a distinct possibility or if it was simply his agent trying to twist Celtic's arm and secure a better deal for his client. No matter, Paul could have acquitted himself with distinction in any company in any era. It was sad when Paul's career was ended prematurely by injury. His was a massive loss to Celtic and football in general.

However, in season 1987–88 Roy Aitken and Paul McStay were two of the top stars and their contribution in helping Celtic achieve a momentous league and cup double was as significant as any. As I have already stated, I did not dare even imagine that we might scale such dizzy heights, given the number of personnel changes that were necessary, but the manner of our league win at Cappielow on the opening day of the season made me stop and consider that we were perhaps in better shape than I had imagined. Morton were newly promoted to the Premier League and were, therefore, fired up to give us a tough ninety minutes, but we scored four goals without reply, with the added bonus of Andy Walker, who was a new signing, claiming two of them.

Our early season successes against Hearts, Motherwell and Rangers were only briefly overshadowed by an away defeat at Dunfermline.

That loss was, in fact, one of only three we suffered in the league all season. Consequently, by the end of the first quarter we had racked up six wins and four draws. Our passing was good and the hard work that had been done on the training pitch, learning to close opponents down, also paid off. I was also impressed with the players' work ethic and determination to persevere until the final whistle. Perhaps it was that latter quality that proved most decisive in the final analysis and enabled us to become champions.

The first Old Firm win was especially satisfying and by early October we were sitting third in the table, behind Aberdeen and Hearts. We kicked-off the second quarter of the campaign with a second win over Morton. Frank McAvennie, who had been signed from West Ham, made his debut and scored. However, one week later all hell broke loose at Ibrox. Once the dust had settled on a quite extraordinary game, even by Old Firm standards, four players faced court proceedings. The game exploded when Rangers goalkeeper Chris Woods and McAvennie clashed inside the penalty box. Frankly, I didn't feel that there was a great deal in the incident, but the involvement of Terry Butcher, the Rangers captain, and Graham Roberts, who had a bit of a hard man image from his days at Spurs, appeared to influence referee Jim Duncan. Once Duncan had restored some semblance of order following the fray, McAvennie, Butcher and Woods were sent off, while Roberts – whom I felt was extremely fortunate to escape similar punishment – took over in goal. The tension was palpable and the remainder of the game was played out in a highly volatile atmosphere. Peter Grant and Walker gave us a two-goal lead, but Rangers fought back to make it 2–2, scoring the equaliser in the final minute.

Much more significant than the result, in my opinion, was the fact that the police had become involved. The procurator fiscal's office initiated breach of the peace charges against the three players who had been red-carded, and included Roberts in the charge. In the resulting court proceedings, McAvennie was found not guilty, while the charge against Roberts was not proven. Woods and Butcher, meanwhile, were fined £500 and £250 respectively. My greatest concern was that the law had made an unwelcome incursion into football. I felt that the direct involvement of the police in a matter where the referee should have been the sole arbiter did not auger well for sport in general.

Football is a physical contact sport, after all, and confrontations inevitably take place. If you follow the argument to a logical conclusion, the question has to be asked: will boxers be charged with serious assault when they strike an opponent and jockeys summonsed to appear in court on a count of cruelty to an animal if they use the whip to encourage their horse? I would not for a single moment try to suggest that football should be above the law, but once you have outside influences meddling directly in the affairs of the referee and his assistants, it opens up all sorts of unwelcome possibilities.

As it happened, I fined McAvennie for his part in the fracas, although I never found disciplining players a pleasant duty and I don't think I could ever have been accused of punishing any individual without very good reason. However, the ramifications of the Ibrox flare-up were far-reaching and heightened Old Firm tensions among the fans. By allowing the situation to drag on for some time, all the authorities succeeded in doing was creating further unnecessary resentment. Had football been left to deal directly with the events of 17 October 1987, I feel sure that the matter would have been concluded in a much less high profile way. But it was a timely lesson for all of us that unless the game – in particular the SFA – put its house in order, there were others willing to act.

The Old Firm bust-up coincided with our shakiest spell of the season. The following week we lost, at home, to Dundee United and in our next game, also at Celtic Park, we tossed away two late goals to be forced to hang on for a 3–2 win. But the turning point came at Pittodrie on the last day of October, when Frank McAvennie scored to earn us a narrow win. Mick McCarthy, who had been troubled by injury, was also outstanding. I immediately enjoyed another victory over my former club when Aberdeen agreed to sell little Joe Miller to us. Joe's debut against Dundee in mid-November confirmed that he would give us added panache and extra width to exploit defences. By the end of November, when we beat Hibs at Easter Road, we were top of the league and we stayed there.

I think the reason for our consistency was a combination of the influence of Aitken and McStay and the fact that the new players had gelled quickly. Confidence grew steadily on the back of good results and we approached the third Old Firm game of the season, at Celtic Park on 2 January, in a mood of quiet confidence. With an adversary like Graeme Souness in the opposite corner, I realised that it would be unwise to dismiss the threat still being posed by Rangers, but I sensed from the look on the faces of my players that we were going to win. And win we did, 2–0, with McAvennie scoring both goals in a performance that was full of conviction. From that moment onwards I sensed that, barring an unforeseen collapse, the title was ours.

Rangers had attempted to give their fans a lift by signing Mark Walters from Aston Villa, but it didn't come as any surprise to me. Indeed, I had sensed, by pure chance, that moves were afoot. In view of the events surrounding the previous Old Firm game, I had gone with the chairman, Jack McGinn, to meet Souness and the Rangers chairman, David Holmes, for lunch at the Excelsior Hotel at Glasgow Airport, to discuss pre-match arrangements. It was an effort to try to defuse the tension and ensure that the fans were not more fired up than usual. The idea was for both sets of players to walk out together and mingle on the pitch, in a show of unity, to demonstrate that there was no animosity between the protagonists. After a pleasant lunch, I turned to my chairman and said, 'I have a feeling that Rangers are going to make a signing. Don't ask me why I think that. There's just something about Souness' body language that tells me he's up to something.' My hunch was spot-on. Later I discovered that Souness had stayed on after lunch to meet Walters off the Birmingham flight and whisked him to Ibrox where the deal was formalised.

Not that Walters, whom I knew from my time as Aston Villa manager, was able to influence the outcome of the game. By the time the fourth and final Old Firm fixture of the season came round on 20 March, we were four points clear of our rivals, with eight games remaining. Live TV coverage dictated that the game was played on a Sunday afternoon. I knew that a draw would suffice in the circumstances, but I told the players to forget all about playing for a point. I knew that if we could win and go six points clear, it would have a dramatic psychological effect on our rivals. Consequently, I urged a positive approach.

The atmosphere was electric when McStay put us in front with a memorable goal. Jan Bartram, Rangers' Danish defender, equalised and, if the score had remained at 1–1, honour would have been satisfied, but I encouraged our players to keep pushing forward in search of a winner. It came eleven minutes from time, when Tommy Burns's corner was headed on by Anton Rogan and chested home by Andy Walker. At that point I felt that we were virtually beyond reach in the title race. I was also proud of the character the players had shown to bounce back in the wake of Bartram's equaliser.

What was a remarkable unbeaten run, stretching over thirty-one games, ended at Tynecastle on 16 April, when Hearts beat us, 2–1, but that defeat hardly mattered, for we clinched the championship with seventy-two points, ten ahead of Hearts, in second place, and twelve more than Rangers. It was also a new Premier League record. In addition, Celtic achieved the distinction of having lost only three times in the league, which was another milestone. That defeat had the effect of delaying the title party by seven days, although in a sense it was almost beneficial, for it meant that we were able to stage a memorable shindig at our own place the following weekend.

With Hearts drawing at Aberdeen that same afternoon, we were champions anyway, but it was important to hallmark our achievement in a manner befitting champions and we did, by beating Dundee, 3–0. The record books claim that the attendance was 60,800. I suspect that the true figure was nearer 80,000, given that the crowd spilled on to the perimeter track to avoid the crush. The fans sang 'Happy Birthday' to Celtic and the ground was a sea of green and white. What had seemed extremely unlikely nine months earlier had been achieved in a way that spoke volumes for the players' appetite and refusal to give up on games that had, on several occasions, appeared to be a lost cause. Fully fifteen minutes after the final whistle, hardly a single fan had left the ground. They demanded an encore and we gave them one. It was one of the proudest and most emotional moments of my life. It was the thirteenth title I had been involved in and the most significant, given that it was achieved in the club's hundredth year.

However, we still had the Scottish Cup final to come and there could be no let up in terms of our preparations if we were to complete a centenary year double. I need not have worried. To underline that the players remained entirely focused, we beat Motherwell and Dunfermline in our remaining league games.

On reflection, winning the Scottish Cup proved somewhat more difficult. With the exception of our fifth round tie against Partick Thistle, which we won, 3–0, it was a bumpy ride to Hampden for the semi-final with Hearts. Our run began with a home tie. Stranraer, of the Second Division, were not expected to pose too many problems, especially as they had not won for some time, but I was never happy in these situations, playing against a team with absolutely nothing to lose and everything to gain. My concern was justified. The Stranraer players fought like demons and, if I am perfectly honest, we were fortunate to scrape through by dint of a Frank McAvennie goal. Otherwise, we would have been forced to travel to Stair Park for an unwelcome replay. Significantly, Stranraer also missed a penalty, with the score standing at 1–0. Hibs came next and, despite home advantage, we were held, 0–0, but Billy Stark scored the only goal in the replay at Easter Road to set up a meeting with Thistle at Firhill, where a capacity crowd watched us score three.

Hearts, who had made significant strides under the co-managership of Alex MacDonald and Sandy Jardine, would, I realised, offer a stern test of our resolve in the semi-final on 9 April, but I didn't imagine that they would take the tie right to the wire. Celtic's dream of the double appeared to be over when Hearts led with just three minutes remaining, but our players had already shown on several occasions that they didn't know the meaning of the word defeat. Pride was a motivating force. After Hearts scored with a goal from Brian Whittaker, the former Celtic player who was tragically killed in a car crash in 1997, we began to take control and, in an effort to apply further pressure, I sent on Mark McGhee in place of Joe Miller. The substitution – inspired or otherwise – had the desired effect. McGhee equalised and the sensible approach would probably have been to settle for a replay, in the knowledge that there was scope for improvement in our performance, but the players had other ideas. An epic comeback was completed by Andy Walker, after McGhee had set up the chance. There was clearly an element of luck about our last gasp victory – of course there was – but every team needs a rub of the green at some stage in any cup run and I prefer to believe that we made our own luck, because of the players' extremely determined attitude.

Having beaten Aberdeen in the other semi-final, Dundee United were our opponents at Hampden on Saturday 14 May. United were contesting their fifth final and had never won the trophy, but I didn't read too much into that statistic. After all, Jim McLean had performed minor miracles in transforming the club and his achievement in guiding United to the title in 1983 had spoken volumes for his abilities as a manager. Our preparations had also been overshadowed by injuries to two key players. Peter Grant, whose wholehearted attitude and dedication to Celtic had been an important ingredient in our season, and goalkeeper, Pat Bonner, were forced to miss out. I felt especially sorry for Granty. No player epitomised the spirit in the club better. Granty was a Celt through and through and having to tell him that he would not play in the final was one of the hardest things I ever had to do. The tears welled up in his eyes, but I had no choice. He had broken a bone in his foot playing against St Mirren the previous month and the injury had not responded sufficiently to treatment for me to take a gamble on his fitness. Packy Bonner's problem was a calf muscle injury and, although I gave him until the Saturday morning of the final, he, too, could not be risked in such an important game. So, Allen McKnight played instead.

It was a glorious day weather-wise and Celtic walked out into the Hampden sunshine bidding to win an eleventh League and Cup double, but United were not overawed by the occasion and Kevin Gallacher's strike three minutes into the second half dented our hopes of a fitting climax to a remarkable season. In fairness, it was a goal of genuine quality. Roy Aitken tried to force Gallacher off the ball, but had to be careful not to commit a foul, because he had been cautioned earlier. Gallacher managed to retain possession and then produced a superb shot to put United in the driving seat. I felt that we had been a little more inventive than our opponents in the first half, but, in truth, the tension of the occasion had created a nervousness about our game. However, I knew that with United in front I had to do something to introduce more flair.

'We've lost the cup, so now we have to go and win it back, I told my assistant, Tommy Craig, so I gambled by sending on Billy Stark and Mark McGhee for Derek Whyte and Andy Walker. That effectively meant I was leaving the team slightly exposed at the back, but managers are paid to make decisions and that one paid off. My intention in introducing Stark was to allow Joe Miller greater freedom to express himself, while McGhee constituted a fresh pair of legs in attack. We were able to stretch United's back four, but it was Frank McAvennie who emerged as the hero of the hour. Macca scored with a header in the seventy-fifth minute, after Anton Rogan had supplied the cross, and I felt at that point that we could look forward to extra-time at worst.

There was almost a feeling of inevitability about the final outcome. It was as if the result had been pre-ordained in favour of Celtic. With almost the very last attack of the game, McAvennie spotted an opening in the defence and went for it, shooting through a forest of bodies. The scenes that followed will live in my memory forever. The players reacted with a mixture of relief and sheer joy and the fans gave vent to their emotions in a manner that highlighted what Celtic means to them. Yet, I wanted to be alone with my thoughts and sought the sanctuary of the dressing room. I also felt that the moment belonged more to the players than me. It was only when the chairman approached me and said that I should join the players on the pitch that I relented. A total of twenty-one players contributed to our success in one way or another that season, underlining that it was very much a collective team effort. All of them are entitled to look back with pride.

Did I feel sorry for United and, in particular, Jim McLean? Naturally. Five finals and five defeats was more than any one person should have to endure, but, happily, United eventually went on to win the Scottish Cup in 1994, beating Rangers in the final – at the seventh attempt!

# CHAPTER 20

# THE GREAT DIVIDE

I take the view that religious intolerance is a blight on our society and serves no purpose other than to create unnecessary divisions and stir up bitter hatreds. In the West of Scotland expressions such as 'Billy' and 'Tim' are in every day use to describe Protestants and Catholics. Neither word is especially offensive and most Old Firm followers attach these titles to those of a different faith. Too many, however, view the Old Firm divide as one that must never be crossed. The venom that spews out of the mouths of a section of both supporters transcends rivalry and does nothing to benefit football or society in general.

However, it would be naive to expect a dramatic shift in attitudes in the short term, for such misguided beliefs are inbred in many cases. The absurdity of that deep-rooted intolerance is that it has its origins in events that occurred a long time ago. Frankly, I doubt the problem will ever be completely eradicated. I have even heard it said that such intense hatred suits Celtic and Rangers, because it ensures that supporters will remain passionately committed. This is not a view I have ever subscribed to. Indeed, I suspect that most sane-minded people would share my abhorrence at the sight of Celtic and Rangers fans hurling abuse at each other.

I had the good fortune to be brought up in a household free of any religious barriers. Ours was a home where everyone was treated as equal, irrespective of colour or creed. Bigotry was an alien word to my father, Jimmy. He was a man of very strong principles and never allowed himself to become involved in the religious divide. He was of the opinion that the beliefs of others should never be abused. Dad listened to, and respected, the other person's point of view. Even if he did not necessarily agree with what was being said, he believed that each of us is entitled to choose our own path. My father took people at face value. He was never influenced by what others had to say about any individual. His formed his own opinion, based on how a person reacted to him. Possibly the fact that he was a regular in the army influenced his philosophy of life. Whatever the reason, I am grateful that the bitterness that pervades so many homes in the West of Scotland never found its way into ours.

My parents were both Roman Catholic and I was brought up in that faith, but if I had ever dared express any sort of sectarian viewpoint I would have received a belt across the ear, for my dad was strict and set down certain rules which had to be observed. Dad was from Dundee and my mum, Ellen, although of Lithuanian descent, was born at Viewpark, before moving to Bellshill as a youngster. My parents encouraged me to attend chapel and when I was a kid the Catholic regime was a very strict one. The church has changed a great deal over the years, but back then in the 1940s, there was very little leeway. Looking back I don't believe it did me any harm. In fact, the strict controls practised by the church helped keep me on the straight and narrow.

I attended the Holy Family Primary School at Mossend. The chapel adjoined the school and alongside both stood the Parochial Hall, which provided a meeting place for the parishioners. There were facilities for badminton, snooker and billiards and it was, in effect, a club that fostered a strong community spirit. There were few vehicles on the roads of Bellshill in the immediate post-war years, so we were also able to play football in the streets for hours on end in comparative safety. I will no doubt be accused of living in the past, but life really did appear much simpler and less threatening when I was a kid growing up in Lanarkshire, although I am pleased that youngsters today have a good quality of life and enjoy the benefits of the National Health Service.

While I share my father's conviction that each of us should be free to choose our own path in life, Liz and I encouraged our children to embrace the Catholic faith, as we are both believers ourselves, but we have never forced religion down their throats or imposed our views on our children. Once they were of an age where we felt they were equipped to make their own judgements, they were free to do so.

Over the years, especially in an Old Firm sense, I have seen many things which I have found extremely distasteful and I will never begin to understand fully why so much bitterness exists between two faiths who worship the same God. It's an aspect of life in the West of Scotland, in particular, which I would dearly love to see disappear and I think there have been signs in recent years that the situation is steadily improving. However, while things are much better than they once were, sadly, I don't envisage religious harmony between Catholics and Protestants in my lifetime, because to many people, a Catholic is still a Fenian b****** and a Protestant is still an Orange b******.

I was delighted to discover, though, that while the origins of Celtic are closely related to an Irish identity and Catholicism, the founding principles were not based on a sectarian divide. Brother Walfrid, the Marist Brother credited with founding Celtic, did so in a determined effort to raise funds to help alleviate the appalling poverty that existed in the East End of Glasgow at that time. I did wonder if there had been a sectarian aspect when the club was founded in 1888, but Brian Wilson, the MP and noted Celtic fan, assured me when he wrote the official history of the club, *A Century With Honour*, that that wasn't the case. I talked to Brian several times during the course of his research for this first-rate publication and he explained how the club's founders had been very conscious from the outset of the need to avoid any sectarian criticisms. It was mooted by one individual that the club should be all-Catholic, but this suggestion was dismissed out of hand. So, too, was the idea that Celtic should have only a certain percentage of Protestants in the team. Of course, with its strong Irish roots, Celtic's following has always been basically Catholic, but it nevertheless pleased me there had been no deliberate attempt to create religious divisions.

I don't feel that I am in a position to comment on Rangers, because I am not versed in the club's founding principles, but it is generally held that those who are of the Protestant faith are more likely to be Rangers supporters, while Catholics automatically become fans of Celtic. While it may be difficult to dispute that widely held view I would, however, like to think that one day the rivalry will be just as intense in a sporting sense, but without the deep animosity that currently surrounds the Old Firm. Of course, not all Old Firm fans hate one another. Many have friends and colleagues of the opposite persuasion and are happy to live in peace, but, regrettably, far too many still persist in pursuing an aggressive stance.

There was a period in January 1971 when both sets of supporters felt able to put aside their differences and unite in grief for the sixty-six who died in the tragedy at Ibrox. The disaster shocked the nation to the extent that Catholics and Protestants pulled together in a manner rarely seen, to offer moral and financial support to the bereaved.

It proved to be an all-too-short unification, but at least it confirmed that it's not impossible for rival Old Firm fans to live in partial harmony. Mind you, there was absolutely no chance of that happening in the summer of 1989, when the game was rocked by the astonishing circumstances surrounding Maurice Johnston signing for Rangers.

Johnston was a former Celtic player who had moved to Nantes in pursuit of greater riches, around the time of my return as manager in May 1987. Much was made of Rangers making a conscientious effort to sign a Catholic and I don't dismiss that completely, but I have never believed that the move was motivated by religious considerations. I have always been of the opinion that it was more a case of Graeme Souness and his chairman, David Murray, sending out a message that anything Celtic could do they could do better. In other words, it was a massive show of one-upmanship. The reality of the situation was that Rangers signed Maurice Johnston on the grounds that he was a player of genuine quality, rather than a Catholic.

I was first alerted to the fact that Johnston was available by my captain, Roy Aitken. Roy was friendly with Johnston and he came to me following a Scotland training session at Gleneagles, insisting that Mo had expressed a desire to return to Celtic. My initial reaction was one of disbelief. 'Away and give me peace,' I said to Roy, but Roy was adamant. 'Honest, boss, Mo has told me that he's desperate to come back.' I replied that if that was the case, Mo should telephone me, and he did. During the course of our conversation, I warned him that I was not in the mood to be messed about, but he insisted that his intentions were honourable. I then asked Mo if his agent, Bill McMurdo, would be involved in any negotiations, but again he assured me that he would be handling that side of things himself.

My next step was to approach the Celtic board and we discussed the matter in great detail. Eventually, it was decided that an official approach should be made to Nantes and when this was done the clubs agreed a fee of £1.2 million, the bulk of the cash coming from Frank McAvennie's transfer to West Ham. The club had made a tidy profit on that deal. Having paid West Ham £850,000 for McAvennie in October 1987, the striker was then sold back to the Hammers for an estimated £1.25 million. I hadn't wanted to lose Frank, but he made several transfer requests, claiming that he could no longer stand the strains of his goldfish-bowl life in the West of Scotland. He insisted that he was regularly abused by guys coming up to him and shouting obscenities, even when he was in the company of his mother, so I finally conceded defeat in my efforts to hold on to Frank. The truth of the matter, though, was that Frank was keen to return to the bright lights of the capital because he had a Page Three model girlfriend and was fed-up dashing back and forth between Glasgow and London. It must have cost him a fortune in air fares! I have always found Frank to be a happy-go-lucky character, who invariably wears a cheeky grin and is full of mischief, but, of course, it sounded better to say that he was a victim of the sectarian divide, rather than tell the absolute truth.

So, arrangements were made for Mo to travel to Celtic Park to begin talking about his personal terms and we organised a hire car for his use. I was pleasantly surprised, because discussions went without a hitch and a deal was quickly agreed. In actual fact, we offered Mo a bit more than the minimum he had been prepared to accept. The chairman, Jack McGinn, and director, Chris White, travelled to Nantes to finalise the transfer fee and lodge a deposit of £400,000. Mo, meanwhile, signed a letter of agreement, outlining his personal terms, which he appeared delighted with. However, when he returned the rental car, he left his copy of the agreement lying on the front seat. Later, it was returned to the club, so Celtic not only had their own copy, they were also in possession of the player's documentation.

The FIFA Youth World Cup finals were being held in Scotland at the time and Celtic approached officials from the world body, seeking clarification that the document Maurice had signed complied with their regulations. FIFA responded by assuring us that the agreement was both legally watertight and binding and, eight days before the Scottish Cup final, in which we were due to face Rangers, Mo pulled on a Celtic jersey for the benefit of the media and declared, 'I don't want to play anywhere else.' The next day, he travelled on the team coach to Paisley to watch our final league game of the season against St Mirren and, when he took his seat in the Love Street stand, was given a rapturous welcome by the Celtic fans.

I was pleased. Mo was younger than McAvennie and he was at the top of his form, having scored six goals in Scotland's successful World Cup qualifying campaign. He was also a more complete player than when he had left two seasons earlier. But, suddenly, the rumours started flying. Apparently they began at the Scottish Professional Footballers' Association dinner in Glasgow, just a fortnight after we had done the deal with Nantes. Glasgow may be a large city, but it is a village when it comes to keeping secrets. It's often been said that if you want to float a story, whisper to someone in Glasgow that you're going to tell them a secret and the whole world will know the next day. The word on the streets was that Rangers had stepped in to try to sign Johnston.

It was at this point that Bill McMurdo came on the scene. He had clearly approached Rangers and alerted them to the fact that Johnston had signed an agreement with us. The confirmation that what I was hearing was true was Johnston's refusal to contact us, but he couldn't hide forever. Johnston was with the Scotland squad at Troon and I telephoned the national team manager, Andy Roxburgh, requesting a meeting with the player at the Marine Hotel, where they squad was based. Initially, Andy turned me down, explaining that he wanted his players to remain free of all distractions, but I shook Andy with my reply. 'If you don't allow me to speak face to face with Johnston you may find that you have to do without him for next year's World Cup finals,' I declared. I added that if my suspicions concerning Johnston were verified, I would make sure that he was sitting in the stand when Scotland kicked off in Italy. Not surprisingly, Andy relented.

As soon as I met Johnston, my suspicions were confirmed. He was both evasive and, I think, a little embarrassed. In my previous dealings with him, when I had returned to Celtic as manager in 1987, I had found him perfectly amiable. I hadn't managed to persuade him to stay, but he had impressed me. I knew when I left Troon that Celtic had a fight on their hands, but I was also encouraged by the fact that FIFA had assured the club that the letter of agreement was binding. It was not a contract as such, but it was a letter of intent, not dissimilar to the pre-contract agreement players sign nowadays, pledging there services to a club. I was due to go on a family holiday to the States and I flew out convinced that the board would be able to put a stop to Johnston and McMurdo's plan to conclude a deal with our arch rivals.

It was my avowed intent to prevent any further monkey business. I was given to understand that all Celtic had to do to put the kibosh on Johnston was pay Nantes the balance of the fee. Once they received the £800,000, which was still outstanding, Johnston would officially become a Celtic player. Whether we could have succeeded in getting Johnston to play for us was, of course, a different matter, but had Celtic followed the course I implored the board to take, Johnston could not have signed for another club without our blessing and, as far as I was concerned, he would never have been allowed to become a Rangers player.

However, while I was still on holiday, I received a call, out of the blue, from a very dear friend and journalist called Alex Cameron, informing me that Celtic had issued a statement to the effect the club had decided, on a matter of principle, not to proceed with the transfer and were withdrawing their bid for Johnston. That left the door wide open for Rangers to step in and take Johnston from under our nose. I was furious, but there was no more I could do. The *Scottish Sun* broke the exclusive story that Johnston was poised to sign for Rangers and on 10 July the paper had its confirmation. So much for McMurdo's earlier claim that the suggestion that Johnston was about to become a Rangers player was compete fabrication. He even had the cheek to add that the story could run for ten years and it still wouldn't be true.

Celtic were ridiculed in some quarters and accused of incompetence. Johnston, meanwhile, maintained that he had not signed a contract with Celtic, but I could not for the life of me understand why the club did not produce the evidence of the two agreements they held. It should also be remembered that Johnston approached me. He was the one who did all the running in the initial stages, but I don't believe he acted in the way he did through malice. I genuinely believe that he wanted to return to Celtic. I cannot say with any certainty what level of influence McMurdo and Souness had on Johnston, but I couldn't complain. It was a massive step by Rangers and the club had to withstand widespread criticism from their supporters.

As I have said, I have never believed that Rangers moved for Johnston simply because the club was determined to break its tradition of not signing Catholics. Rather, it was an opportunity to acquire the services of an exceptional player and, in doing so, rub their biggest rivals' noses in the dirt. Johnston turned out to be a marvellous signing, because they bought a player who was at his peak and one who had returned from France stronger, sleeker and sharper than the one who had left Celtic two years earlier. It was also a courageous decision by Souness to sign Johnston and he and David Murray were to be admired. The pair of them had to weather a storm of criticism and they must have known in advance what the reaction of many Rangers fans would be.

Since that momentous day in July 1989, Rangers have signed an increasing number of Catholic players and, if Johnston influenced the dramatic switch in policy, the move has to be welcomed with regard to improving relations between the rival factions. If it didn't completely dismantle the barriers that exist, at least it had the effect of dislodging a few bricks, but it sounded the death knell for Celtic at that time and it should never have been allowed to happen, in my view. I have never understood why the Celtic directors chose not to make the evidence they held public. The club was deeply embarrassed, so why didn't the directors stand up and tell the world the truth? The signing of Maurice Johnston would have been wonderful for Celtic. Instead, his defection to Rangers had horrific consequences for us and the club didn't recover for a very long time.

I, personally, don't bear any grudges. If Bill McMurdo was the one who instigated the moves to steer Johnston in the direction of Ibrox, he was only doing his job and looking after his client's best interests as he saw them. I'm forced to say that it was a brilliant idea – a public relations coup that had Rangers' principal rivals squirming. In May we were parading Johnston in front of the TV cameras and telling the world that he was a Celtic player. Two months later he was being paraded in the colours of our rivals. You really couldn't have made it up.

# CHAPTER 21

# TEARS FOR SOUVENIRS

I asked the Celtic board for £5 million to combat Rangers' huge investment in players – they offered me £1 million. Neil Mochan had said to me, immediately after our Scottish Cup win over Dundee United in May 1988, that I would need to reinvest at least £5 million to stay ahead of Rangers. I wanted three players: a defender, a midfielder and another striker. Stuart Pearce was available – at a price – and I was a huge admirer of the Nottingham Forest left-back, but 'Psycho' was way out of our league. Left-back is perhaps the most difficult position to fill adequately, because there are so few naturally left-footed defenders of quality in the game. Pearce fitted the criteria. Winning the double in the club's Centenary Year should have been the springboard to even greater achievements, but not everyone at Celtic Park appreciated the need for us to consolidate our position from a base of strength. I was aware that Rangers would not simply sit back and accept the situation. It was evident that they were prepared to spend big in a determined effort to regain the upper hand.

We had won the double with a mix of experience and enthusiasm, but at the end of the 1987–88 season, Pat Bonner was suffering from a troublesome back injury and Allen McKnight, who had replaced

Packy in the Cup final, decided to pursue his career elsewhere. Billy Stark had made a significant contribution in midfield. The strikers, Frank McAvennie, Andy Walker and Mark McGhee had been outstanding, but I sensed that the players we had would not do for another season. When I returned to Celtic, I had already had to mix and match to some extent. Danny McGrain had retired and the quartet of Murdo MacLeod, Brian McClair, Alan McInally and Mo Johnston has sought pastures new. Funds were limited, but I managed to bring in three new players for a combined total of £565,000: Chris Morris, an overlapping right-back, cost us £115,000 from Sheffield Wednesday, Walker arrived from Motherwell for £375,000, and Aberdeen sold us Stark for what turned out to be a bargain £75,000. Billy was a veteran by that stage, but he added a new dimension to our play in the way he was able to slip almost unnoticed into the opposition's penalty area from midfield and score goals. He was the consummate professional.

Later on in the season, I splashed out a further £1.5 million to bring McAvennie and Joe Miller to Celtic Park. Both proved to be excellent signings, but while the fans revelled in the team's success, I wasn't fooled into believing that we were likely to retain the championship without some serious money being invested in strengthening the squad. The board, however, appeared almost complacent. They were happy to bask in the glory of the double, but were blind to the reality of our situation. As usual, I found myself fighting against the directors instead of working with them.

It was as clear as the nose on the end of your face that Rangers would streak ahead of us with the quality of player Graeme Souness was bringing in. Souness, with the backing of his chairman, David Murray, flooded Ibrox with big-name players. Eventually Rangers had the England goalkeeper, the England captain and a whole host of top internationals. In addition to Chris Woods and Terry Butcher,

Souness introduced Ray Wilkins, Graham Roberts, Gary Stevens, Trevor Steven, Richard Gough, Mark Walters, Ian Ferguson and Mo Johnston at various stages, but while Rangers dominated Scottish football during the Souness era, they never quite made it to the very top in Europe, which was their ultimate aim.

Rangers' spending policy also had an adverse effect on the club in the longer term and the impact has been felt in recent seasons, with spiralling debts curtailing the current management team's ability to compete on equal terms with the top European sides. However, David Murray is to be congratulated for making such a huge commitment to the club, while the Celtic directors appeared content to sit back and marvel at events unfolding across the city.

In addition to watching my principal rival strengthening his squad, I was also wrestling with the problem of McAvennie's repeated transfer requests. I hugely admired Frank as a player and considered him to be one of the most accomplished centre-forwards I had ever seen, but he was always a restless soul and was keen to return to the bright lights of London. Eventually, in March 1989, he was sold back to West Ham for £1.25 million, but, in truth, Frank caused massive disruption before he was transferred.

By then the championship was gone. Rangers had built an impressive points lead and we were toiling in third spot. Worse still was the fact that we had suffered two humiliating defeats, 5–1 and 4–1, at the hands of our Ibrox rivals. A 3–1 victory at Celtic Park in November had eased the pain to an extent, but another Old Firm defeat – this time by two goals to one – at the beginning of April heaped on the misery. The Skol Cup was no more rewarding, when Dundee United dumped us out in the quarter-finals. Europe, too, was a graveyard for our aspirations. Having beaten Honved in the first round of the European Cup, we exited at the next stage, beaten by Werder Bremen.

So, is it any surprise that I wasn't filled with great optimism when we made it to the Scottish Cup final, where we were presented with the prospect of a fifth Old Firm game.

Rangers were going for the treble. We were simply trying to save face. For once, Rangers were hot favourites and I must confess that I feared the worst, but fate was kind to us that May day. Our man-marking was superb. We also fought for every ball and Rangers were eventually reduced to punting long balls down the middle, which was meat and drink for Mick McCarthy and Derek Whyte. Shortly before half-time we made the breakthrough we were looking for, when Rangers perpetrated a series of mistakes at the back. Roy Aitken caught them on the hop with a quick throw-in and Peter Grant sent a long ball into the penalty area. It was eventually cleared as far as Gary Stevens, who mishit an attempted pass back. Little Joe Miller was alert to the surprise opening and darted forward, before hitting a low shot past Chris Woods. I had given Joe the chance to play as the main striker, which was his favoured role, because McAvennie had been transferred and Tommy Coyne, whom I had recently signed from Dundee, was cup-tied.

So, we won the Cup, but it had been an extremely hard slog and, in the event, our joy was short-lived, when Mo Johnston signed for Rangers instead of Celtic. Still, there was nothing I could do about that, so I turned my attention to signing Mike Galloway from Hearts, for a fee of £500,000, and Paul Elliott, who cost £600,000 from Pisa, to replace Mick McCarthy, who had quit at the end of his contract to join Olympique Lyon. Mick was a big loss. Like Peter Grant, who was troubled by injuries, Mick was a solid, dependable citizen and a player I could trust, and we also lost Mark McGhee to Newcastle that summer. I couldn't guarantee Mark a regular starting place, so I could understand his desire to move on, but I was reluctant to see him go, because he was a first-rate professional and inspirational in the dressing room.

However, I felt Galloway would give us greater versatility, because of his ability to play in defence or midfield, while Elliott was a tall and dominant centre-half, but I also knew that Paul would be a short-term acquisition and that he had agreed to join us at least partly to prove to English clubs that he was over his injury problems. I knew Paul would head south at the first opportunity and I couldn't criticise him for that. Paul struggled to establish himself, but after a slow start he developed into a super player for us, before eventually signing for Chelsea for £1.4 million – a tidy profit, I think you'll agree.

But finance – or rather the lack of it – was still a major headache. If Celtic wanted to be a big club, they had to behave and react like one and accept that players' wages had suddenly spiralled beyond anything that had been imagined just a few years previously. The club across the city embraced the reality of the situation, but the Celtic directors saw things differently. Consequently, I had to lower my sights. Having cast my net wide, I was tipped off that there were a couple of Polish international players who were available and keen to move abroad. Dariusz Dziekanowski had established himself as a proven goal-scorer with Legia Warsaw and, after watching him in action, I was satisfied that he had the credentials to do a reasonable job for Celtic and got my man for £500,000. Dziekanowski's team-mate, Dariusz Wdowczyk, a highly competent full-back, came slightly cheaper at £400,000. Rangers, meanwhile, were dealing in millions.

Dziekanowski was an immediate hit with the fans. His performance in the European Cup Winners' Cup tie against Partizan Belgrade, within a couple of months of his arrival, cemented the relationship. Jackie, as he became known, scored four goals and made another for Andy Walker, but we still went crashing out. It was inconceivable that we could score five goals at home after losing the first leg, 2–1, and not qualify for the second round, but a series of defensive mistakes enabled Partizan to score four and go through on the away goals rule. I still recall jumping up and down with sheer frustration when they scored after a breakaway in the eighty-ninth minute to seal our fate.

For all that he was an excellent player, Dziekanowski was also a thorn in my side. His undisciplined lifestyle involved him in several scrapes, but it was never Dziekanowski's fault, according to him. I never felt I could trust him and eventually I did not believe a single word he said.

His fellow countryman was an entirely different character. The other Dariusz was quiet and unassuming and never gave me a moment's bother. Wdowczyk's trouble was that he was an underachiever. He was with the club for five years and gave good service, but I always felt that he could have offered much more with the skill and ball control he possessed. However, for reasons I never fully understood, Wdowczyk was content to play within himself.

Having lost to Aberdeen in the semi-final of the Skol Cup and fallen behind our great rivals in the championship race, we were hit by two further set-backs during the winter of season 1989–90. The first, in December, involved Tommy Burns's departure to become a player with Kilmarnock. The second was the transfer request I received from my captain, Roy Aitken, almost at the same time as Burns was on his way to Rugby Park. Aitken's loss was an especially damaging blow. I am convinced that outside influences were responsible for Aitken seeking a move, but, whatever the reason, Aitken manipulated his transfer to Newcastle and we lost a highly influential leader on the pitch.

I chose to replace Roy as captain with Paul McStay, and perhaps that was unfair of me, because Paul was not a natural dressing room leader. On reflection, he was thrust into a situation that he was not equipped to handle at that stage in his career. It was suggested at the time that I should have given the job to Paul Elliott and I am sure that he would have been a first-rate captain, but, as I have already stated, I felt that for Paul Celtic was, to some extent, simply a stepping stone.

Once again, for all that our league campaign had turned into a bit of a nightmare, we battled our way to the Scottish Cup final. That presented us with a second possible route into Europe the following season. A fifth place finish in the championship highlighted the shortcomings of the squad and emphasised just how short-sighted the board's policy of not freeing up funds had been. Rangers won the title by a seven-point margin over Aberdeen and we were also trailing in the wake of Hearts and Dundee United, having managed only thirty-four points from thirty-six games. The statistic that we had actually lost more games than we had won – twelve defeats compared to ten victories – just about said it all.

Aberdeen, who had already beaten Rangers in the Skol Cup final, were our opponents at Hampden on 12 May. The fact that we had accounted for Rangers the previous February, thanks to a Tommy Coyne goal, underlined that we were still capable of raising our game when required, but, on reflection, it was a poor final. We lacked self-belief and the ability to be creative, and the ninety minutes finished goal-less. So, too, did extra-time, so it came down to a sudden-death penalty shoot-out. After 120 minutes of football without a goal, the floodgates opened with a vengeance, but with Aberdeen holding a 9–8 advantage, Theo Snelders, the Dons' Dutch goalkeeper, guessed correctly and dived to his left to push Anton Rogan's shot round the post.

The dream of a third successive Scottish Cup triumph died at that moment. I felt sorry for Rogan, a thoroughly decent lad and a dedicated professional. He hit his shot well enough, but the keeper got lucky. I accept that there is no perfect solution to decide the outcome of a game, but in a match as important as a cup final, I question the fairness of asking any player to take a penalty kick under such intense pressure, knowing that if he fails to score the memory will stay with him the rest of his life. The golden goal is a more satisfactory method of settling it. At least that way no individual is forced to endure any finger-pointing.

Defeat by Aberdeen also had the effect of denying the club a place on the European stage for the first time in twelve years. Given the importance of European competition to the supporters, that was a particularly savage blow.

Following the disappointment of the Cup final, I returned to the transfer market that summer and brought back an old Celtic favourite, Charlie Nicholas, from Aberdeen, in the belief that he would provide the team with a bit of extra spark. Unfortunately, neither Charlie, who cost £450,000, nor Martin Hayes, the midfielder I purchased from Arsenal for £650,000, justified their fees in the longer term. Injury contributed to Hayes's ineffectiveness and he was eventually handed a free transfer, after I had left the club. The problem is, when you are forced to take chances with players in the transfer market, the gamble doesn't always pay-off. John Collins became Celtic's first million-pound signing when I persuaded Hibs to part with his services. Collins took a little time to settle, but he went on to become a key player for Celtic and Scotland.

Around the same time that Nicholas, Hayes and Collins were entering the fray, major changes were taking place in the boardroom. Brian Dempsey, a successful Glasgow property developer, and Michael Kelly, nephew of the former chairman, Sir Robert Kelly, and himself an ex-Lord Provost of the city, were co-opted onto the board. However, relations between the pair quickly cooled and within months they were at each other's throats over Dempsey's desire to see a new stadium built at Robroyston. The board, too, was split. Eventually, matters came to a head at the club's AGM in October 1990, when Dempsey was informed that Kelly and another director, Chris White, were opposing his ratification as a director and the former was duly removed.

The fact that we had a Skol Cup final to play against Rangers two days later, on 28 October, seemed to be of little importance compared to the turmoil taking place behind the scenes. Celtic was a club in disarray and the in-fighting was to continue for four more years, until Fergus McCann arrived on the scene to give the club some much needed stability. Looking back to that period, the atmosphere at Celtic Park was the worst I had ever experienced. The boardroom was riven with divisions and the backroom manoeuvring and jockeying for position was appalling. Kelly had a massive influence on events and the board seemed incapable of pulling together and forming some semblance of a united front.

On the park, our situation didn't improve at Hampden. We had won only three of our first nine league games and defeat by Rangers intensified the mounting pressure on me and the players. We were the better side in the first half and Paul Elliott emphasised our superiority when he scored with a header seven minutes after the restart. I opted for a more defensive strategy after we had taken the lead – perhaps wrongly – and replaced Joe Miller with Chris Morris. Rangers appeared to take heart from our change of tactics and, after enjoying a period of fairly sustained pressure, equalised through Mark Walters to force the game into extra-time. Dziekanowski had a chance to put us back in front in the early stages, but wasted a glorious opening when he shot straight at Woods after being sent clear. That miss proved even more costly, when the defence hesitated and Richard Gough got in behind our back four to seal their victory.

Defeat, especially by our oldest rivals, was hard to take and when Rangers then moved six points clear of us in the league, following a 2–1 win at Celtic Park one month later, I could sense that the conspiratorial mood behind the scenes was growing. The run of poor form in the league continued and, when Rangers increased their lead in the title race to fifteen points, it was obvious that certain elements in the boardroom wanted me out. People have said that my days were numbered after 2 January 1991, when Rangers inflicted a third successive defeat on us in the space of ten weeks. I don't agree. I believe that my fate was sealed the previous month with the appointment of the board's hatchet man, Terry Cassidy.

Cassidy was given the title of chief executive. Chief executioner would have suited him better. I have never been absolutely sure who was behind the move to appoint Cassidy. The board had become so secretive in their dealings that I was usually one of the last to know what was happening. Cassidy had previously been a professional footballer, night club entrepreneur and had, most recently, acted as managing director of a newspaper group. I am neither interested nor do I care what roles he had filled in his previous working life. In my dealings with Cassidy I found him to be a thoroughly unpleasant, untrustworthy, overbearing, offensive individual.

Cassidy seemed to have a staggering ability for upsetting just about everyone he came in contact with. His abrasive, arrogant manner did not go down well with the press, either. He quickly antagonised several members of the sports writing fraternity, to the extent that the knives were out within weeks of his arrival, but he had the knack of ruffling feathers wherever he went. Supporters' groups, sponsors, players, the manager and, eventually, the board ran out of patience. In the twenty-two months Cassidy was at the club in my view he succeeded in doing untold damage.

I have since read that the Celtic directors held a clandestine meeting at the SFA offices in the wake of the Rangers defeat, where a decision was taken in principle to sack me. I cannot say with certainty if that is in fact true, but, if so, I scuppered their plans. Celtic went on an eleven-game unbeaten run, including successive victories over Rangers at Celtic Park in the space of eight days in March.

On 17 March we staged our very own St Patrick's Day celebrations by beating Rangers, 2–0, in the Scottish Cup. Unfortunately, the occasion was marred by events on the field during the second half. Peter Grant was red-carded when he was cautioned twice in quick succession for dissent. Worse was to follow, when the Rangers trio of Terry Hurlock, Mark Walters and Mark Hateley joined Grant. A week after ten-man Celtic had beaten eight-man Rangers, we inflicted a second defeat on the champions-elect and this time Scott Nisbet of Rangers saw red. These results, it would seem, earned me a temporary stay of execution, but I was back in the condemned cell when Motherwell beat us, 4–2, in the Scottish Cup semi-final. I knew deep down that winning our last four league games to clinch a UEFA Cup spot would not be enough to save me.

It would be absurd to try to suggest that what happened was all the fault of the players and the board. I also made my share of mistakes, but there were occasions when I felt that the players could have given more in certain games. The board, meanwhile, spent more time squabbling than trying to assist the manager. They also lacked the courage to act independently and brought Cassidy in to do their dirty work for them.

Cassidy's ideas on how a football club should be run differed from mine, at least on the playing side. I deeply resented his attempted interference and marvelled at his obsession with memos. Indeed, there were so many flying about the place that he must have threatened the existence of a Brazilian rain forest!

Cassidy actually demanded that I detail in a memo the various aspects of my job and the hours I worked. He was behaving like a time and motion expert. I ask you? Football managers don't work forty-hour weeks. It's a seven-days-a-week job, often sixteen to eighteen hours a day. There was no way that I was going to start trying to justify my existence to him. Neither was I prepared to discuss team matters with all and sundry. Meetings chaired by the chief executive were the order of the day. All heads of department were requested to attend and talk about what was happening in their areas, such as catering and ticket sales. Just imagine what would have happened had I gone along with what I perceived to be Cassidy's power trip. The whole world would have known the innermost secrets of the dressing room – including our rivals.

Not only could I not have fully trusted certain other employees with loose tongues, I couldn't even trust the chief executive. Documents were being leaked to the press and a whispering campaign was being orchestrated from within. Who was responsible for this utterly unacceptable state of affairs? No prizes for guessing. What Cassidy could not seem to grasp was the fact that he was talking to friends of mine and openly discussing my situation at the club. Those friends included certain members of the press and they were keeping me abreast of developments behind the scenes. One day I actually took Cassidy aside and told him, rather forcibly, that I knew what he was up to. I told him if he had something to say, he should have the courage and decency to do so to my face. Whenever I attempted to seek clarification of my position from the board, I was stonewalled, but I only had to pick up a newspaper to find out what was going on behind my back.

On the morning of our final league game of the season, when we had to beat St Johnstone at Perth to qualify for Europe, details of a leaked document appeared on the front page of the *Scottish Sun*. The memo, drawn up by Cassidy, set out details of how a change of manager would be handled with maximum damage limitation to the club. Strangely, the identity of the newspaper's mole was never discovered. Now, there was a real surprise! Mind you, as one prominent sports journalist quipped at the time, Celtic had so many leaks that if it had been a ship it would have been renamed the *Titanic*.

However, I was determined to go down with my ship. Walking out was never an option, because that would have meant quitting and I have never been a quitter at anything, especially where Celtic is concerned. The end was nigh, though, and I received a telephone call from Ian Archer, a highly respected sports writer and close personal friend, detailing Cassidy's strategy. Ian painted a clear picture, having been informed by Cassidy of the exact scenario which was due to unfold in the coming days.

Ian, who sadly passed away a couple of years ago, informed me that the following Wednesday, 22 May, was earmarked as D-Day, so I telephoned my lawyer for guidance and he advised me to get in touch with my accountant, Frank Walker, as he felt it would be more beneficial to have a money man on hand when the axe fell. Frank immediately agreed to put himself on stand-by and I then approached Cassidy and asked him exactly what game he was playing. I also told him I was fully aware of the agenda he had drawn up. He denied any knowledge of what was going on, but I had been assured that if Kevin Kelly returned from a trip with the Celtic Boys' Club to France in time, Wednesday had definitely been designated the big day.

In an effort to make life difficult for Cassidy and the board, I hit on the idea of disappearing for a couple of days and told John Kelman, the chief scout, and Benny Rooney, who was in charge of the reserves, that I wouldn't be contactable for the following day as I would be on the golf course. The pair of them agreed to deny any knowledge of my whereabouts and the scene was set for a hanging without the accused being present. However, just as I was about the leave Celtic Park, Cassidy approached me to say that he had just newly learnt that a board meeting had been set for 10 a.m. the following day.

It turned out to be a very brief meeting. The chairman, Jack McGinn, expressed deep regret that the board had been forced to take such a 'painful' decision, but added that they felt it had been unavoidable, based on results. A short statement was passed to the waiting pressmen, to the effect that the club had decided to terminate my employment. Jack also said that he would discuss a settlement over the course of the next few days, but I wasn't having that. 'No way, Jack,' I replied. 'That matter has to be attended to here and now.' So, off I went to phone Frank Walker and he promised he would be at the ground in a matter of minutes.

Imagine my shock when I walked back into the boardroom to discover my assistant, Tommy Craig, occupying the seat I had just vacated. I am not naive enough to imagine that Tommy had not already been sounded out about succeeding me prior to my sacking, at least in the short term, but a wee bit of dignity and class would not have gone amiss.

Jack McGinn then informed me that the press were keen to talk to me, but I answered by telling him that he had invited the journalists to the ground so he should be the one to face them. As it happened, I partially relented and agreed to speak with a couple of sports writers whom I knew well, but I was not about to parade myself in front of the TV cameras and the world at large. As I made my way out into the car park, having agreed the terms of my compensation, I refused to let my emotions show. The *Scottish Sun* ran a headline the next day proclaiming, 'The Day They Made The Big Man Cry', but I bit back the tears – publicly at least. I even managed to make a joke, by telling a group of journalists and supporters, who were gathered at the front door of the stadium, that I had half-expected to see a guillotine erected in the forecourt. I also urged the fans to carry on supporting the team, because they supported the best team in the world and the players needed their continued backing.

Inwardly, though, I was heartbroken. That day was the lowest point in my life. I had no qualms about the directors deciding that I was no longer the man for the job, but I don't think I deserved to be sacked in that manner. The fact is, if a manager fails to produce results he deserves to be kicked into touch. If the board wanted shot of me, all they had to do was come and say to my face that my time was up. All the manipulation and conniving was so unnecessary. I was very disappointed by the directors' treatment of me, but I was not surprised. I felt the people running Celtic at that time had lost the ability to behave with dignity.

Celtic is a club that has always demanded loyalty and called on its employees to display allegiance, but they haven't always given it in return. I was a player for eighteen years and manager for a further nine, yet in my last season I spent almost every weekend being told by my friends and acquaintances that Cassidy was spouting off about me. I felt that the board never treated me with the respect I deserved and I was never part of things. It was as if I was kept at arms length.

However, while I was hugely emotional, I also experienced a sense of relief that the lies and back-stabbing were at an end. I also recall thinking how Big Jock must have been truly remarkable to have put up with the treatment he received over the course of thirteen years, even given the wonderful way Celtic fans react to success and really show their appreciation.

When I drew up outside my home and opened the car door, a neighbour came rushing across to say that she had just heard of my fate on radio and offered her commiserations. 'They are just bastards, Billy,' she said. 'Bastards!' Somehow, I made it through the front door before bursting into tears.

# CHAPTER 22

# LIFE GOES ON

I don't mind admitting that I remained bitter for some considerable time following my dismissal as Celtic manager. My bitterness had nothing to do with being sacked. My view has always been that if you aren't producing the goods, the people paying your wages are entitled to say that enough is enough and show you the door. But as I have said I was both deeply hurt and angry at my treatment by the Celtic directors. I felt I was entitled to be treated with some dignity after the length of my playing and mangerial career, although I couldn't claim to have been surprised at the manner of my removal.

Celtic at that time were bereft of common courtesy. With Cassidy pulling the board's strings, Celtic was no longer the club I had once known. My affection for the club has never altered. I am a Celtic man through and through and I always will be. No one individual could ever turn me against the club, no matter what they did to me, but I was in a state of shock, I suppose. I was a lost soul, seemingly without a purpose in life. I remember one evening, shortly after I was sacked, going to bed and reflecting that I had not done a single worthwhile thing from the moment I had got up that morning.

Being manager of Celtic had been much more than just a job to me.

It was a vocation. The position carried massive responsibility and could never be defined by the number of hours you worked. Some days, I was lucky if I saw my wife and children for ten minutes out of twenty-four hours, but I didn't mind. I was still only fifty-one when I left Celtic and I have always been the sort of person who needs to be on the go all the time. I have never found it easy to relax, but for a time I was like a cat on a hot tin roof.

Initially, I didn't know if I wanted to go back into the game. I was thoroughly disillusioned and disgusted, but gradually the bitterness began to fade. I had more important considerations in my life than the people who ran Celtic Football Club. Several factors were responsible for my mood beginning to lighten, the most significant of them being the birth of our first grandchild, James, in May 1991. That was a truly uplifting experience and having a grandson took my mind off the events of the previous couple of months. Liz and I decided to book a holiday in Spain for ourselves, my daughter, Libby, and James, who was only six weeks old at the time. A prominent Glasgow businessman and dyed-in-the-wool Celtic fan, Bernard Corrigan, was kind enough to offer us the use of his apartment at Arroya De La Miel, near Benalmadena, and it proved to be a most pleasant and relaxing couple of weeks.

I returned vowing to get my life back in order and I took tremendous solace from the many letters of support and encouragement I had received from Celtic supporters. There had been an almost daily deluge of mail and most of it was positive. The fans were terrific, but that didn't surprise me in the least. There has always been a strong bond, because I am one myself, and I think they know that, because my relationship with the supporters remains close to this day.

On the day of my sacking, I recall receiving a letter from a lady requesting my signature on various bits and pieces of memorabilia. I saw no reason not to comply with her wishes and duly autographed the photographs and programmes she had sent. Some time later I received a second letter, in which she expressed her embarrassment. She had absolutely no need to feel that way as she hadn't realised what Cassidy and company were up to, but I appreciated the fact that she had taken the trouble to offer condolences.

While the backing of the supporters helped pull me round, I knew that I couldn't live on fresh air alone and that I would have to seek some sort of gainful employment, but when the offer of a job came, it was from an unusual source. The *Sunday Mail* newspaper contacted me with the suggestion that I might fancy the idea of writing a Saturday football match report. Why not, I thought. I have always enjoyed a good relationship with the members of the sporting press and I had spent many hours in their company over the years. From Celtic's earliest days in Europe, the press travelled with the team and the players formed a bond with most of the journalists. It was perhaps easier back then, because there were few demands on the hacks to produce exclusives exposing the peccadilloes of the players.

It was the late Ian Archer who described himself and his colleagues as fans with typewriters and I felt it an apt description. I have often felt that sports writers are not dissimilar to footballers in that they work in a high profile environment and are called on to express themselves in a forthright manner. I think journalists are also similar to players in that they are cheeky and argumentative among themselves at times and are capable of falling out and then just as quickly falling back in with each other. We were the same as players. There were never any lasting grudges. I have also always believed that the only people you can be cheeky with are your friends. Outsiders wouldn't understand or accept such behaviour.

Having chosen to stay away from Celtic Park in the period immediately following my sacking, I was very reluctant to return until the *Sunday Mail* came on the scene. At first I was uncomfortable with the idea of reporting games from the Celtic Park press box, but it didn't take me long to get over my initial apprehension. After all, I reasoned, what did I have to feel guilty about? I knew I would not have a problem looking the chairman, Jack McGinn, straight in the eye, or any of the other Celtic directors for that matter. Cassidy I did not consider even to be worth my contempt.

I also had an opportunity to return to the game when Ian Gellatly, the Dundee secretary and previously chairman of the club, called out of the blue and asked if I was interested in becoming manager. I was flattered and agreed to travel to Tayside to meet Ian for a working breakfast to discuss the offer in more detail. However, I quickly realised that it would be the wrong move at that time – for me and the club. The night before I was due to meet Ian, I lay wide awake, tossing and turning, and the conviction grew that I would be taking the job for the sake of returning to football and for the money. I knew that my heart wouldn't be in it. So, I telephoned Ian the following morning and thanked him for his interest, but explained that it would be wrong for all concerned. I was glad, on reflection, that I turned Dundee down, because I had taken the Aston Villa job without thinking deeply about what I was doing and had almost instantly regretted my decision. It's hopeless when you are in a job you are not enjoying. That's when everything starts to go wrong and it invariably ends in tears.

I was also still unsure whether I wanted to have such a direct involvement in the game. I felt it important not to rush in, because there was still an element of disillusionment. I had to be comfortable with whatever decision I took. So, instead of heading for my dad's home town, in 1992, when a pub became available just a short walk from Hampden Park, I elected to enter the licence trade instead. The Madeira in Torrisdale Street became McNeill's Bar and I began a whole new career as a publican. I had owned a small pub in Bellshill years before, so I knew it was hard work, but my mum, Ellen, had run the place for me, so I couldn't claim to be much of an expert. On the other hand, I knew how to pull a pint and I have never been scared of hard work, so I threw myself into the role with gusto. The fact that I had become landlord of a Celtic-orientated pub helped, of course.

Running a pub is a combination of hard work and unsocial hours, but I enjoyed it in the main during the ten years we owned McNeill's Bar, before we sold up in 2002, by which time the profit margins had become less and the hours longer. My daughter, Carol, assumed the role of manager for a time, but the family in general mucked in and helped out when required. I have always felt that going into the pub trade was the right move for me at the time. It took me out of myself and, having a predominantly Celtic clientele, meant that there was never any shortage of football talk, which I thoroughly enjoyed. Looking back we had some great times.

I also became a member of the Glasgow Vintners Association, a body made up of publicans. Basically, the aim of the association is to arrange various social events for its members, such as golf outings, and it was like being a member of a football team again. You have to develop a thick skin to cope with the banter, but I enjoyed that aspect and I remain close to several of the people I got to know. I am happy to say that I am still a member, even though I no longer have any involvement in the trade.

Although I was the boss, I never abused the privilege of being able to call the shots when it suited me, but the luxury of working flexible hours meant that I was also able to develop my TV and radio work, in addition to my newspaper column in the *Scottish Sun* newspaper. It was great seeing the game from another angle, but I already had experience of how the media operates. In my capacity as a TV and radio summariser, I had been fortunate enough to be present at the World Cup finals of 1982, 1986 and 1990, and I regarded that as a great honour. Having been denied the opportunity to play in the World Cup finals, being part of the greatest football show on earth was the next best thing. I doubt that there is a more electrifying sporting event and I love the hype and buzz surrounding the World Cup.

I also had the good fortune to be present at the 1992 European Championship finals in Sweden and the 1998 World Cup in France. Sweden was an especially enjoyable experience for me, coming, as it did, just a year or so after my dismissal as manager. There was an opportunity to stay at the same hotel as the rest of the press guys and the social aspect was far from dull. The journalists work hard, but they also know how to let their hair down and I was included in evening visits to the finest restaurants and pubs of Gothenburg and Norrkoping. I also found it interesting learning at first hand how they tackle what is often a difficult job, striking the correct balance between reasoned criticism of players and managers' tactics. I had crossed swords with most of the press lads at some time in the past, because of differences of opinion, but I am glad to say that there was no lasting animosity in the majority of cases.

The Scottish press crops must also have considered me one of the lads, though, because I was asked to play for them in a game against their Dutch counterparts. It turned out to be one of the last times I pulled on a pair of football boots. My right knee was already knackered and my final 'international' appearance didn't help improve its condition. I have had the knee cleaned out several times, but it appears that I am going to require more detailed surgery to repair the years of wear and tear. I keep putting it off in the hope that the problems will disappear, but I'm afraid that I've been kidding myself on.

It's hardly surprising the number of ex-players who suffer from similar problems. I'm sure it has a lot to do with the fact that greater pressure was put on the players of my generation to carry on regardless. Allan McGraw, who played for Morton and Hibs and later went on to become manager at Cappielow, is a classic example. Allan had something like twenty cortisone injections in the same knee and now requires the use of two sticks to get about. It's a real shame and Allan's case reflects badly on the medical profession at that time, in that no individual should apparently have more than two cortisone injections in the same part of their body. Clearly, if Alan had been aware of the long term damage that was being done to his knee, he would never have allowed it to happen, but he accepted the treatment in good faith in the belief that he was doing his best for his club. Not that he's the type to complain. Allan was a prolific goal-scorer and nowadays he's a committed golfer who is out on the course almost daily, in spite of the pain and discomfort he suffers.

I know from personal experience that players used to regularly camouflage injuries, because our livelihoods depended on us playing, but, thankfully, there is little likelihood of the same thing happening in the modern game, because clubs can no longer afford to take a chance on the long-term fitness of players worth millions of pounds.

While I was fairly content with my lot in the years after I left Celtic, I would be lying if I said that I didn't harbour the hope that one day I would get the call inviting me back to Celtic Park to take up a role behind the scenes. I hold the view that the game has a tendency to disregard people who could be of value to it through their knowledge and experience of football, but when Celtic did eventually make me an offer of part-time employment, it wasn't the one I had been hoping for. David Kells, who was a prominent member of the club's commercial division, asked if I would become the match-day host of the newly opened Captain's Table Restaurant. On the basis that something is better than nothing, I went along to check out the set-up – only to discover that I had apparently lost my place in history.

Fergus McCann, who had by this time become chairman, was giving me a conducted tour of the restaurant and pointing out the various past captains of Celtic, whose portraits adorned the walls. Imagine my surprise when I noticed that there was no likeness of B McNeill Esq to be seen anywhere. It was one thing getting the sack, quite another to become Celtic's forgotten man! So I said to Fergus, 'Tell me, what have you got to do to get your picture on the wall?' 'Be the skipper of Celtic' he replied. 'That's amazing,' I said. 'I thought I had been captain here from 1963 to 1975.' It was a lesson in just how important – or unimportant – you can become in the greater scheme of things, but, in fairness, the situation was quickly rectified and I took my place alongside the others.

However, it still hurt a little. I also feel that Celtic could have made much greater use of the Lisbon Lions in the way that Rangers recognised John Greig's contribution. Greigy was a marvellous servant and he was eventually brought back to Ibrox in a public relations role, even though he had previously been sacked as manager. Not only was Greigy's worth recognised in terms of his ability to relate to the supporters as an ambassador for the club, he is today a Rangers director and an example of the value former players can have in promoting a club.

I could never complain about the treatment I've received from other clubs when it came to requesting match tickets, though. I've always been looked after and I appreciate the kindnesses that I have been shown by former rivals. And the one thing I've never done is abuse my position as a former Celtic player and manager. No one could ever point a finger and accuse me of cashing in on my past. I have two season tickets for Celtic Park and I use them as often as I can.

# CHAPTER 23

# HEART OF
# THE MATTER

'Billy McNeill Dies On Operating Table' – these were the words that haunted me when I was woken early on the morning of Saturday 8 March 1997. I had quickly dropped off to sleep the previous evening from the effects of the pre-med I had been given to prepare me for open-heart surgery at Glasgow's Ross Hall Hospital. Unfortunately, the drugs had not prevented me from dreaming and in my dream I saw the unwelcome newspaper headline staring back at me. It did nothing to ease my sense of dread at what lay ahead.

Happily, my dream did not turn out to be prophetic. I survived my triple bypass operation and lived to tell the tale. Some time later, when I told my good friend, Mike Jackson what I had dreamed, he asked, 'Was it front page or back page news?' I had to laugh, but I didn't see any humour in my situation when I was given the news a month earlier that I had a dickey ticker. Until that moment, I had always imagined that I was pretty much indestructible. I am a proud big bugger and the idea that there was anything seriously wrong with me seemed absurd, but suddenly I was facing the biggest fight of my life. Was I scared? You bet.

The first indication I got that there might be a problem of some sort was during a trip to London the previous December, to watch Benny Rooney's actor son, Kevin, appear in a new stage play. Benny, a friend of many years standing, his wife, Marion, Liz and I and another couple, Angus and Sally MacLean, were staying at the St Ermins Hotel, but when we left the theatre there was a shortage of taxis. Eventually we managed to hail one to take our wives back to the hotel and the three of us decided to start walking. We hadn't bothered with overcoats, despite the time of year, but it wasn't especially cold. However, I began to experience a slight discomfort in the left side of my chest and shoulder, similar to the sensation you get when you lie at an awkward angle in bed. To be honest, I didn't think it was any big deal and I didn't even bother to mention it to the other two. Eventually we managed to hail a cab and when we arrived at the hotel we headed straight for the bar. By then I had forgotten all about the mild sensation I had felt earlier.

But when it happened a couple more times I began to wonder. Then, towards the end of January, it happened two days in succession and I told Liz. Her advice was to contact the family doctor, Jack Mulhearn, and fix an appointment for a check-up. Jack was also the Celtic team doctor and he agreed to see me more or less straightaway, so he could run a few tests, including an ECG. Nothing out of the ordinary showed up, but, rather than take any chances, Jack referred me to a heart specialist, Frank Dunn, for further checks. I was linked to a variety of monitors and told to run on the treadmill. Now, as a player I had regularly done an extra hour pounding away on the Celtic Park treadmill after training and never experienced a problem. In fact, it had become something of an addiction, because I had always been very proud of my fitness levels, but this time was different. I began experiencing pain in my chest and Frank immediately ordered that the machine be switched off.

The tests had shown that I had a couple of arteries that had narrowed, but I was told at that point that medication might sort the problem out. However, an angiogram revealed that the situation was a little more serious than that. Basically, I had two choices – either having what amounted to a balloon inserted to enlarge the arteries or a bypass. Talk about being spoiled for choice! Whatever I decided, I was advised to have corrective treatment as soon as possible. The surgeon, Mr Davidson (I never did discover his Christian name), advised me that surgery was his preferred option, because the balloon treatment tended to be a temporary answer only. I took his advice. At least I was assured that the problem had been detected early and that my ticker was in excellent shape otherwise, but try telling that to someone who regarded himself as a perfect physical specimen!

I still couldn't believe what had happened to me, but the realisation dawned fully less than a fortnight later when I checked into Ross Hall. Prior to my hospitalisation I had been prescribed a course of aspirin and beta-blockers and immediately developed the most God-awful rash. When I telephoned Jack Mulhearn to tell him, he reacted by saying that I had better hope it wasn't the aspirin that was causing the problem, because that might present certain difficulties. Thankfully, it was the beta-blockers. I don't mind admitting that I felt real fear as I lay in my hospital bed, waiting to be operated on. That was the worst time, because, for all that I had been given assurances that the surgery had a high success rate, and I also had a couple of pals who had undergone bypass surgery, it is not without certain risks.

So, when Liz came to visit me on the Friday evening I was in no rush to see her leave. We chatted for a while about practical matters and she was her usual positive self, telling me how I would soon be back on my feet and fighting fit once more. It must have been a tough time for my wife and kids, but they didn't show it too much. As a family we had been fortunate up to that point not to have faced any major health crises, so it was a new experience for us all. Thank heaven they didn't know about my premonition! Otherwise, they might have tried to call the whole thing off, but, thankfully, my worst fears proved unfounded.

It was Scottish Cup quarter-final day, but Dundee United versus Motherwell and Morton versus Kilmarnock were just about the last thing on my mind while I was being wheeled into the operating theatre. Celtic had beaten Rangers, 2–0 two days earlier but, for once, the outcome of an Old Firm game had not been uppermost in my mind. However, perhaps on reflection, Celtic's success was a positive omen, for I was determined to make it a winning double.

Not that I was aware of what was happening once the anaesthetist had inserted the point of his needle into my hand and told me to count down from ten. The next thing I knew I had come to in the high dependency unit. I had a tube inserted in my mouth to assist my breathing and was wired to a bank of monitors, but I was remarkably alert, all things considered. I also made up my mind that my recovery began there and then. So, without further ado, I signalled to a nurse and indicated that I wanted to phone home and reassure my wife and family that I was OK. The nurse explained that I might find it somewhat problematic making myself understood with a tube protruding from my mouth, but she managed to get clearance to remove the apparatus and I made my call.

I didn't instantly recognise the voice at the other end. It was my son Martyn's girlfriend, now wife, Yvonne, and she asked who was calling. 'It's Mr McNeill, Yvonne. Is Mrs McNeill there?' I asked. As it happened, Liz had gone to visit a friend after being advised by the surgeon to delay coming to the hospital as the sight of patients hooked up to the various pieces of equipment in an intensive care unit can be quite alarming. So, I asked Yvonne if she would get Liz to give me a ring when she returned home, but Martyn returned first, after dropping his mum off at her friend's, and when Yvonne relayed the message that I had phoned he thought she had lost her marbles. 'Don't be daft,' he said. 'My dad's just had a major operation.' Poor Yvonne!

Maybe I was just lucky, but probably the fact that I was a non-smoking former professional sportsman contributed to my recovery. Even though I didn't have the best diet in the world and enjoyed a drink, I was pretty fit for my age. I had just turned fifty-seven a few days before going under the knife, but my general fitness was good. I had remained active into my fifties and had taken part in the occasional old crocks game. I was warned that it was normal for someone who has undergone major heart surgery to suffer a reaction of some sort during their period of recovery, but I was fortunate in that I didn't experience any noticeable set-backs at the time.

However, I was told by the surgeon that it was not at all uncommon for someone who has undergone bypass surgery to experience difficulty concentrating. I can vouch for that. While I never was very good at fixing my mind on a subject for hours on end, nowadays I am lucky if I can get through two pages of a book without losing the thread of the story. I was also told that I might become more emotional and that has proved to be the case, too. It's not unusual for me to be watching a soppy old movie on TV and to feel the tears well up, but I can live with such inconveniences. It's a small price to pay for enjoying good health.

I was also overwhelmed by the volume of letters and get well cards I received from the general public. Most of them were from Celtic supporters and I was deeply touched at the depth of feeling. So many bunches of flowers arrived at the hospital that we could have gone into the florist business. Instead, once my private room was overflowing with all sorts of blooms, Liz made sure that the surplus was distributed throughout the hospital.

I remember at the time feeling very humble that my wellbeing clearly meant so much to so many people. It was a very emotional time and the public's response meant a great deal to me. So, too, did the reaction of the football world at large. I received a steady stream of phone calls from people in the game and I was amazed to learn that so many former players had undergone similar surgery. However, for all that you might imagine that the stresses and strains of management had been a contributory factor in my condition, the surgeon dismissed the idea.

Among the telephone callers was Graeme Souness, my old Rangers adversary. Graeme had already undergone open-heart surgery and he'd had the misfortune to be rushed back into hospital after suffering complications following his initial release. 'Do as the doctors tell you,' advised Graeme. 'Don't be like me. I thought I knew best and ended up with a problem. Mind you, could you really blame me when I had a new, beautiful young wife to go home to?'

I was resigned to having to endure a period of recovery, but I determined to make it as short as humanly possible, so, to that end, I launched myself on the comeback trail. There were a few shocks in store, though. For a start, I had shed a stone in weight and was back down to my playing weight of twenty-two years earlier. The first time I took a shower after being allowed out of bed was also a rather strange experience. There I was, standing under the spray, doing my level best to try to stop the water bouncing off my chest in case I did myself damage!

But, in most senses, the recovery process was right up my street. I viewed it as being like pre-season training. That's the most challenging period for any footballer trying to get back top peak fitness and I have always loved a challenge. Within a couple of days of my operation I was allowed to do a circuit of the hospital corridors and I tackled the task with gusto. So much so that when I went racing past the nurses' station, one of them said to me, 'Mr McNeill, please slow down. You're blowing all my papers off the desk.'

Less than a week after my operation I was allowed home, with the instruction to take it easy, but I never have been very good at putting my feet up and doing nothing. That made me a bad patient. I wasn't supposed to leave the house for a day or so, but within a couple of hours I was badgering Liz to be allowed to go for a short walk, because I felt like a caged animal. Liz relented, but it proved to be a shorter walk than I had planned. I made it only as far as the end of our street, before I was ordered back. I realised there and then that I wasn't super-human after all. I had also been given a series of exercises to do and that suited me. Gradually, I began to feel stronger and it was no longer any sort of challenge to walk to the end of the street and back.

In addition to Liz, Mike Jackson was a key player in my recovery. Mike would collect me by car and we would drive to one of Glasgow's many parks and walk for hours on end. On one occasion, we were caught in a snowstorm a long way from shelter and Mike's car. But those walks were essential for me. Glasgow is known as 'the dear green place' and there couldn't have been many patches of green grass that we didn't trample over.

Golf has always been a big passion of mine and I was keen to start swinging a club again, but I was warned by the doctors not to overdo things at first. I was advised to play a couple of holes at most and build up from there. However, the first time I visited my club at Haggs Castle, with Martyn, I think we played fourteen or fifteen holes before I saw sense. By that stage Martyn was panicking, but I was so pleased with myself that I just smiled and told him to shut up.

My family have always been very important to me and we are a close-knit unit, but I think the experience of seeing their old dad flat on his back brought us even closer together. Liz and the kids were very protective towards me. They shielded me from any outside pressures. My doctors had said that home wasn't necessarily the best place to continue a recovery programme and had encouraged me to remain in hospital for as long as possible, but they need not have worried. I was left in peace, even if my wife and kids were keen to fuss over me.

The other Lisbon Lions were almost as bad. They were like a bunch of mother hens clucking round their chick. Whenever we got together they were scared to let the wind blow on me. Just a few months after my operation we celebrated the thirtieth anniversary of our European Cup win and the team was invited to Las Vegas by one of the many North American Celtic Supporters' Associations. Fortunately, I managed to obtain medical clearance to make the trip, but hardly a moment passed without one of the lads asking me how I was feeling.

Jimmy Johnstone was especially attentive. One evening we were invited to one of the many casinos and ended up having a few drinks too many. Jinky, never the best at holding his drink, became increasingly emotional and eventually there was just the two of us sitting on high stools at the bar, with the wee man telling me what a great bloke I was. Jinky's always fancied himself as a bit of a singer and next thing I knew he was holding my hand and telling me he was going to do a Bon Jovi number especially for me. Bon Jovi? I had never even heard of them. Undeterred by my show of ignorance, Jinky launched into song. What the locals made of our touching scene I hate to think, but we certainly attracted a few strange looks.

We were also taken to visit a ranch and invited to go horse riding. Needless to say, the owner selected the biggest horse he could find for me, a beautiful white stallion, but I could have done without him shouting out, 'A white stallion for King Billy!' The sight of the former captain and manager of Celtic riding a white horse would not have found favour with the supporters. Mind you, I'll bet the Rangers fans would have enjoyed the moment!

STV were also keen to make a documentary of the Lions, thirty years on, and they arranged for us to return to Seamill, where we had prepared for the final, prior to travelling to Lisbon. The memories and the booze flowed and we were all nursing hangovers the next day when we boarded a coach to take us to a country club near Blanefield, in Stirlingshire, where we were to join our wives for a celebration party. Rather unwisely, the organisers also provided a case of champagne to make the journey go with a swing and by the time the coach was driving along Maryhill Road in Glasgow we were once again feeling no pain.

Mind you, Bertie Auld still had his wits about him and he suddenly ordered the driver to stop so he could visit his old mum. Bertie had been brought up in Maryhill and had clearly been hit by a wave of nostalgia, but as soon as Bertie alighted from the coach we instructed the driver to close the door and proceed as originally planned. So we reached Blanefield one Lion short, but Bertie, being Bertie, eventually arrived by taxi a couple of hours later, having done his duty and a good deal more sober than he had been when we last saw him disappearing up a close.

The comradeship of my former team-mates and the support of my wife and family was vitally important to me at that time. So, too, was my faith. It is not something I like to talk about too openly, because I believe religious belief is a private matter for the individual concerned, but I derived an inner strength from my faith and it helped me through what was a difficult and testing time in my life. No doubt some cynics will scoff at the notion that faith plays a part in the recovery process following major surgery, and I respect their right to an independent view, but I talk from personal experience and make no apology for raising the subject. In the years since I was given the grim news that I required an operation to rid me of what was clearly a potentially fatal heart condition, I have had the good fortune to enjoy excellent health, but I have never taken my health for granted. None of us knows what lies around the corner, so it's important to enjoy the moment and appreciate what we have.

I emerged from my experience with a slightly different view of life. I also became far more appreciative of the marvellous work done by those in the medical profession. Some people are often too quick to criticise. The media often highlights mistakes and it's right that they should be brought to the attention of the public to try to ensure that there is no repeat when a patient's life is at stake. However, thousands of people every day in this country leave hospital with reason to be grateful to those who administer to the sick, and the doctors and nurses who cared for me at Ross Hall were an example of the wonderful job those in the medical profession do.

# CHAPTER 24

# FAMILY MATTERS

N early seven years after being shown the door by Celtic, on 7 February 1998 I returned to the dug-out one last time – as manager of Hibs. It was a purely one-off visit and there was no happy ending when my former club, Aberdeen, beat us, 3–0, at Pittodrie. The situation had arisen when Jim Duffy had been sacked as manager and replaced by Alex McLeish. There was a transitional period to allow Big Eck to tidy up matters at Motherwell, before making the switch to Easter Road, and I stepped in because a month earlier I had been invited by Jim to return to the game as Hibs' football development manager. It was an offer I jumped at.

Basically, Jim wanted me to attend to the more mundane aspects of his job, to enable him to concentrate his energies on overseeing matters on the training ground. Administration wasn't Jim's strongest suit and he felt, with my experience, I was ideally suited to assume that role. Part of my remit was to assess possible transfer targets and to act as a middle man between Jim and the board, but, while I relished having a direct involvement in the game again, I was also realistic enough to know that lack of resources dictated that we wouldn't be in a position to sign most of the players Jim identified. I pointed this out to him, but he was happy for me to carry on anyway.

However, I had been at Hibs only two or three weeks when the board decided that the club required a change of direction and chose to replace the manager, so I was thrust into the role of caretaker boss. It felt strange to be in charge of a team, even on a temporary basis, and I certainly didn't want to be seen dancing on Jim's grave, but it was exciting to be back dealing directly with players and I quickly realised that I had lost none of my enthusiasm. I was travelling daily to the capital from my home on the south side of Glasgow and I quite enjoyed the time spent alone in my car, turning over various scenarios in my mind. I also took a keen interest in overseeing the club's scouting system and liaising with the managing director, Rod Petrie.

When Alex arrived, though, he brought his own entourage with him and I was surplus to requirements. In fairness, Alex welcomed my involvement at the club and encouraged me to stick around, but I didn't feel that it was right or proper to cast my shadow over team affairs. I told Rod that I didn't feel that there was a really worthwhile role for me in the greater scheme of things and he reluctantly agreed that I was probably correct in my assessment of the situation.

Rod's a shrewd big fellow and I think he recognised earlier than most the problems football was about to face. He realised that the game couldn't continue down the path it had been following for years and he began taking positive steps to cope with the difficulties that were starting to arise. I believe it was because of Rod's foresight that Hibs have managed to avoid going into free fall in the same way other clubs have done of late, even though it was a close call. I am also glad to say that we parted on good terms when, after just a few months, my comeback ended.

Although I was at Easter Road for only a short time I might have had a far longer association with Hibs had circumstances been different. A long time before – fourteen years earlier to be exact – Hibs had made me an attractive offer to return to Scotland. It was October 1984 and I was manager of Manchester City when the then Hibs chairman, Kenny Waugh, approached me. I was sorely tempted, but resisted the offer, largely on the grounds of loyalty to Peter Swales and City.

Following my brief sojourn in the capital, I concentrated my efforts on being a publican, coupled with my roles as a newspaper columnist and TV pundit, and I suspect that my wife and family were secretly quite pleased that my football comeback had turned out to be relatively short-lived. Not that Liz has ever been anything other than fully supportive of whatever decision I have taken. They say that behind every successful man is a strong woman and my wife has been a rock since the day and hour I met her in 1961.

When we first knew each other, Liz was a dancer and I was a professional footballer. That meant we had plenty of time to be together and the financial resources to do most things we wanted to, so life was idyllic. Marriage is a wonderful institution, but it is not without its difficulties at times, and Liz has coped admirably with the demands of life as the wife of a football player and later club manager. In those professions you need the backing of someone who is caring, supportive and without self-interest. I have been extremely fortunate that my wife was happy to assume the role of running the household and looking after the family.

It can't be easy being the wife of a prominent sportsman. In addition to taking responsibility for running our home, Liz also had to pamper me to an extent. In my opinion, rest is a key element in the wellbeing of a football player, because fitness is vitally important, so there were times when I effectively had to put myself first and my family second. I can't have been easy to live with at times, either. While I endeavoured to draw a line between football and my family, it was impossible not to bring my troubles home with me on occasion. The pressures of football management are such that the job is bound to impact on your home life. It's fine when the team is winning, but defeat invariably makes you tetchy and argumentative. However, Liz was always good at spotting my mood and ensuring that I was given sufficient space to chill out.

I have never found it easy to unwind, though. I can't ever seem to relax completely and I prefer to be on the go all the time. I am also a bit of a perfectionist and I hate it when something isn't done properly, but Liz has always been able to cope with my foibles. She has been a great foil for me and ensured that I've never got carried away. She has kept me in my place and in touch with reality and I am eternally grateful for the support my wife has given me through the highs and lows.

Happily, there were many more highs playing for, and managing, a club of the status of Celtic. We have also been able to enjoy a reasonable lifestyle, because of the rewards the game brought. While the demands of management are such that time becomes a priceless commodity, I was fortunate as a player to be able to spend valuable time with my kids as they were growing up. I remember the sense of pride and enjoyment when Liz dressed the girls in identical outfits when we were on holiday. I also used to love having a kick-about with Martyn and I recall when Susan, our first born, arrived in the world on New Year's Day 1965, being terribly excited and dashing to the hospital in the early hours of the morning to see my daughter for the first time. For once, an Old Firm game was of secondary importance – even though Rangers beat us, 1–0, later that same day. Thirteen months later, on 4 February 1966, we suddenly had a family of three when the twins, Carol and Libby, were born.

All five of our children have different personalities, but Liz and I are proud of each of them. Susan has always been conscious of her responsibilities as the eldest. She is employed as a stock controller and is hardworking and conscientious. She and her husband, Phillip, don't have any children, but they are great with their nieces and nephews.

Carol is easy-going and more laid back than her twin sister, Libby. She's the type who, if you ask to borrow five pounds, will hand it over happily, even if that's all the money she has in her purse. I am reminded of my mother when I'm with Carol. She's got a caring side to her nature and enjoys a good laugh. Carol, who is employed in pre-school work, is good value in any company and always up for a bit of fun. Libby is sharp and intelligent and works for the Allied Irish Bank. She's a hard worker with a strong personality and was an excellent gymnast as a youngster.

Paula, the youngest of our daughters, was born four years after the twins, on 26 March 1970, and, like Susan, is very conscientious in her outlook. She's always been a bit of a pet, but has shown herself to be a very responsible mother. Matthew, Paula's son, is probably subjected to greater discipline than our other grandchildren, but his mum and dad, Charlie, dote on him all the same. Paula is also a working mother, employed by social services.

Martyn is the baby of the family. Born on 23 December 1975, he became a father himself earlier this year when he and his wife, Yvonne, presented us with our sixth grandchild. Liz and I never set out with the express purpose of having five kids and it wasn't the case that we kept trying for a boy. Martyn just happened along, but I must admit that I'm delighted that we were blessed with a son. He's a good lad and a bright fellow, who has always enjoyed messing his sisters about, and I like to think that the pair of us get on very well – more like pals than father and son.

I suppose I tried to be a disciplinarian with my kids, as my father had been with me. I don't mean that I operated a strict regime and was always on at them, because children have to be allowed certain freedoms to express themselves and their personalities, but I have always placed great store in respecting other people's property and values and, I guess, when I look at them now, I did a reasonable job. As an only child, I never knew what it was like to have brothers and sisters and I didn't understand when my friends talked about what their relationships with their siblings meant. However, I have been able to observe the closeness that exists within my own family and I'm pleased to say that a bond is evident between all of them.

I'm sure it won't surprise anyone to learn that the McNeills are a football family. Paula is the only exception. She has never really been a fan, but her sisters certainly are and they have an impressive knowledge of the game. However, at no time did I actively encourage my son to follow in my footsteps, because I believed that if he had shown an aptitude to make it as a footballer, it would have happened naturally.

For most people football is a recreational pastime to be enjoyed with their pals. Only a small percentage of youngsters ever make it into the professional ranks and it's important that parents allow their kids to enjoy the game, in the knowledge that if the talent is there it will show up sooner rather than later. However, I would be lying if I didn't admit to having harboured the hope that Martyn might turn out to be good enough to earn his livelihood from the game. Indeed, there was a period when he played for a local boys' team in Manchester and showed promise as a defender, but he was unable to advance beyond a certain level. Martyn still plays five-a-side with his mates and thoroughly enjoys himself, but he was the only one of our kids who never saw me play, other than in film clips. In fact, rugby eventually became Martyn's preferred sport at school and he was an accomplished player, fearsome when making challenges. I think he must take that aggressive streak from his mother!

When I became actively involved in the political scene at an age when most men are giving serious consideration to winding down and taking life a bit easier, to some extent Liz was left holding the fort again. I have always taken a close interest in politics, but I didn't foresee the day when I would become engaged in matters of government. However, out of the blue, a couple of years ago, I received a telephone call from John Swinburne, who had been commercial manager and, more recently, a director of Motherwell, a position he continues to hold. John informed me that he was forming his own party and wanted to meet with me to outline his plans. John's a real character and I agreed to listen to what he had to say.

He said that it was his intention to start up the Senior Citizens Unity Party and stand as a candidate in the Scottish Parliamentary elections to champion the pensioners' cause. Among John's aims is to see an increase in the old age pension and free TV licences for the over-sixty-fives. Those are the sort of issues that are close to my heart, because I have always felt that as a nation we underplay our responsibility to the older members of our society. It used to annoy the hell out of me when I watched my own parents being taxed and losing out on certain other benefits, because my dad received a pension from the army. He was entitled to that after giving twenty years of loyal service to his country, yet he didn't reap the same benefits as certain others of his generation. People are quick to praise the members of our armed forces when there is a conflict and they are called on to help protect this country's interests, but they are just as quick to forget about our soldiers, sailors and airmen in peacetime. In general, most other European countries appear to have a greater respect for their senior citizens and acknowledge that they have a responsibility to look after them.

John explained that his aim was to improve the lot of the average pensioner and the longer I listened to what he had to say, the more impressed I was. In an effort to get his party off the ground, John was keen to enlist my support in the belief that I could help raise the profile of his campaign. Given my own views and beliefs, I readily agreed. Initially, I attended various meetings, basically to offer moral support to

John, but as his campaign intensified in the build up to the 2003 elections, I became increasingly more absorbed in the whole business of politics. I can't say with any certainty that my involvement made a significant difference to John's prospects, but I was delighted when he was elected as MSP for Central Scotland. It was a remarkable achievement considering that the Senior Citizens Unity Party was only a few months old when John won the seat, but he has made it clear that it has never been his ambition to compete on equal terms with the established political parties. John sees himself more as a nuisance figure, badgering away at the big guns in an effort to pressurise opponents into doing more to assist the elderly in enjoying a better standard of living.

Apparently, I am third in line to succeed John, in the event of him being forced to step aside, but I have no wish to become a politician, for all that I respect the need for people to devote their lives to working on behalf of their fellow citizens, in the knowledge that society would be in an even bigger mess without them. If truth be told, I would far rather spend time on the golf course than sitting in the new Scottish Parliament debating various affairs of state. Golf remains a passion, but it has become increasingly more difficult for me to achieve a decent score because of the problems I experience with my knee. My wife keeps pointing out that I can no longer manage to press my knees together and I was given a further reminder of this fact when a lady I had never met before approached me at Glasgow Airport and declared, 'Heavens, Billy, I never realised how bow-legged you are!' Glaswegians are never slow to express themselves and I couldn't help laughing at her mix of cheek and humour.

I am very fond of the people and the city and the warmth Glasgow generates. Glasgow may have an unwanted reputation in some respects, but it's been my home for most of the past forty years and more and I wouldn't live anywhere else.

# CHAPTER 25

# THE ROAD AHEAD

I have never given up hope that football might still have a role of some description for me to play in terms of influencing the future of the game. I would welcome the opportunity, but I somehow doubt that it's going to happen now. Football has been my life and it has provided me with a whole host of wonderful experiences and memorable moments. Most would settle for simply meeting their heroes. I was fortunate enough to play with, and against, many of mine and perhaps become a hero to other generations myself. What more could I have asked for?

I also have the friendship of my surviving Lisbon Lions team-mates. Ours is a special and unique relationship and one that has deepened as the years have passed. We are still a team and continue to offer one another support when it is needed – and we haven't forgotten how to enjoy ourselves when we get together – but football has moved on since 1967.

At long last Celtic has a stadium to be proud of and one that befits the reputation of the club. The former Celtic Park held great memories, but it had become a relic of the past. Fergus McCann is rightly credited with having saved the club from going into liquidation in 1994 and, for creating the wonderful stadium that is now in place, he is fully deserving of great praise. Without him, God alone knows what would have happened to Celtic. Fergus also provided the platform for Celtic to build a solid base and eventually achieve season tickets sales in excess of 50,000. That is guaranteed income and vital in giving financial security – if, indeed, there is such a thing in football these days.

However, the disappointing aspect of Fergus's time at Celtic Park is that he left having taken a lot of money from the supporters, through share issues. The intention was to put the club on a much stronger footing, not to provide Fergus with a wealthy lifestyle. In the final analysis, I believe that Fergus benefited much more than he was entitled to, but that should not detract from the part he played in the club's advancement over the past decade, as the transformation in Celtic's fortunes has been truly remarkable.

Of course, under Martin O'Neill the team has enjoyed extraordinary success; the type the fans craved and reminiscent of the levels Big Jock sought to achieve. Much credit has to be given to the present board of directors, who have worked hard to create a situation where Celtic have been able to compete with their principal rivals to acquire the services of quality players. No one can say with any certainty how long the club will be able to maintain its drive in its present environment, and without the resources enjoyed by the top clubs in England it is going to be extremely difficult for Celtic to maintain the progress that has been made in Europe.

We always had to lift our game when we entered the European arena, but, I believe, balanced against that was the fact that football domestically was much more competitive in our day. So, the present squad has had to raise its standards more than we did. For Celtic to reach the UEFA Cup final in May 2003 was a quite remarkable feat. However, while I confess that there may be an element of defensive pride in this statement, I am forced to point out that when I and my team-mates won the European Cup, every team at that time were champions of their respective leagues. I am a huge fan of the present Champions League set-up, but every team is no longer a national league champion and it is not a Champions League in the truest sense. It cannot be, when you have teams who have finished second and third, and in some cases even fourth, competing for the biggest prize in European football.

As a consequence of countries like England and Italy having three or four teams in the Champions League, the UEFA Cup has been deprived of greater status, but it remains a hugely competitive tournament for all that. That's why O'Neill and his players were deserving of the greatest praise. The incredible response of the supporters was also further clear evidence of what European football means to Celtic fans. They went to Seville in their tens of thousands and left a lasting impression. There is a romanticism associated with Celtic playing in Europe and the 2002–03 season emphasised that.

Nine of the McNeill household and other family members travelled to Spain for the final and we had a marvellous few days. Losing to Porto could not detract from the size of the achievement. There was the obvious disappointment of defeat, but it was not so great that it obscured the enjoyment factor. The supporters appreciated the lengths the team had gone to make the dream happen and there was no sense of disillusionment.

But what is the future for Celtic in Europe? I used to wish for a British league of some description, while, at the same time, recognising that to be part of such a set-up would inevitably incur some loss of national identity, and I have not changed that view. Without being members of the Premiership or whatever, I don't think Celtic – and Rangers – can realise their full potential, because both clubs have outgrown Scottish football, but I am less convinced than I once was that this will eventually happen. Frankly, I can't imagine UEFA endorsing the concept of teams from one country becoming members of a league in another, although UEFA have indicated that they are keen to develop the Champions League concept.

I see that as being a secondary competition, in the sense that we will continue to have national leagues, and UEFA may well choose to operate a two-tier system, but it is not only Scotland where the game is dominated by two clubs. A similar situation exists in other countries and even the Premiership has become the province of a handful of clubs. Which clubs other than Arsenal, Manchester United and Chelsea can realistically expect to be crowned Premiership champions?

Any extension to the Champions League set-up would, of course, impact on the domestic game as a whole. Scottish football is already in a parlous state and can ill afford any further body blows, but is it feasible for the Old Firm to operate two teams, one for European and one for domestic competition? Perhaps. Certainly, the loss of the Old Firm altogether would have a dramatic effect on the long-term prospects for Scottish football. What is definitely required is a more competitive league and supporters would no doubt welcome the prospect of Aberdeen, Hearts and Hibs, for example, slogging it out in a more evenly contested title race, featuring what would effectively be the Old Firm's second strings.

However, I fear that there is an inevitability that some clubs will go to the wall. It does not require a degree in mathematics to work out that any club paying out 105 per cent of its overall income on players' wages is courting disaster in the longer term. Having said that, I believe it is wrong to force players to take massive pay-cuts. Once a contract has been agreed it should be honoured. Each of us makes financial commitments according to our circumstances and it's unreasonable to expect any individual to accept a sudden and dramatic change in his earnings.

Football has had a wake-up call and there is a need for realism. Sometimes I think the game is its own worst enemy, in as much as it doesn't utilise the expertise of former professionals. Too many have been lost to the game when they had something positive to offer. It never ceases to amaze me how successful businessmen become involved in football and immediately lose sight of reality. They oversee developments they would never allow to happen in the real business world. Directors must be able to provide the necessary funding to match their aspirations, but there must also be a greater appreciation of the realism of their situation. Those running football clubs cannot expect miracles. Managers can only operate effectively within the financial constraints placed on them. There is far too often an unrealistic expectancy on the part of directors and supporters.

Hopefully, if the current crisis leads to clubs being forced to develop youngsters it will result in the game as a whole benefiting. The way ahead in my view is the development of home-spun talent, but we will not reap the rewards of such a policy if these youngsters cannot see a clear path to first-team football stretching out before them. Bosman made it far too easy for foreign players to come into our game. In most cases they did so because they were being offered better wages than they could earn in their own country. While some enhanced Scottish football, others have been motivated simply by the financial rewards. Consequently, because of the influx of those players we have sacrificed the development of our own kids, as it has been easier to acquire the ready-made article.

Youth development is a difficult and time-consuming exercise, because it takes a long time for a youngster to mature into a first-team player, but I personally welcome the notion that it is the only way ahead for Scottish football, because it will inevitably lead to higher standards. My son, Martyn, is involved in football agency work and I assist him in that role. Already Martyn has several highly promising young clients and I am encouraged by the thought that more and more clubs are recognising the validity of this approach.

Unfortunately, there is little room for optimism when it comes to our national team. Scotland's international stock is at rock bottom and shows few signs of improvement. I welcomed Berti Vogts's appointment as Scotland coach and made my approval public, but the team has not developed in the way I had hoped. Indeed, there has been no advancement in any shape or form that I can see. In fairness to Vogts, there was an appalling dearth of natural talent at his disposal in the first place, but I am not altogether sure that he fully appreciated the importance of the national team to the football public in Scotland. We are a passionate race and respond accordingly to the success or failure of the national team. Conceding four goals to Wales, five to France and six to Holland suggested to me that out shortcomings were not just down to bad luck. The structure is clearly flawed.

International football is also making far too many demands on the clubs. The SFA has to bear in mind the fact that the clubs pay the players' wages and it is they who suffer in the event of their player sustaining a serious injury, as in the case of young John Kennedy of Celtic. Vogts got carried away with playing meaningless friendlies that had the effect of further eroding confidence. It seems to have been a case of quantity rather than quality. At this moment in time, the prospects of Scotland making it to the 2006 World Cup finals in Germany appear slim, but I shall go on hoping, because I remain passionate about our national team.

I am also still as much in love with football as I was on the first day I walked through the front door of Celtic Park, at the start of what was a wonderfully rewarding career that has given me so much. However, I now have more time to devote to enjoying the pleasures of my family, in particular my six grandchildren. Liz and I have been blessed. The eldest of them, James, is thirteen and is growing into a fine young man. His brother, Gerrard, is a year younger, while the third of Libby's brood, Abby, is eight. Carol's daughter, Alexandra, is ten years old, while Paula's little one, Matthew, recently began school after turning five. Sean, Martyn's son, who was born in March this year, is the latest addition to the family. Some days, when the six of them invade our lovely home in Newton Mearns, I wonder how Liz copes, but, like me, she loves having the grandchildren round. They help keep us young.

Mind you, I doubt that I'll ever begin acting my age. The idea of sitting by the fireside, puffing on a pipe and letting the world slowly drift by is never one that has appealed to me. Offhand, I can't think of many ambitions that remain unfulfilled. I've been extremely fortunate and I have few regrets, but I like to think that I still have something to offer. Football has been good to me and I am not ready to switch off just yet. Anyhow, I wouldn't know how to sit back and relax. I haven't stopped for the past fifty years and I've no intention of slowing down. This is one Lion who intends to keep on roaring for a while longer.

# STATISTICS

## BILLY MCNEILL

- William McNeill, born Bellshill, 2 March 1940
- Career: Mossend Primary School, Hereford Schools, Our Lady's High. Blantyre Vics to Celtic 20 August 1957 £250. Retired 3 May 1975. Appointed Clyde manager 1 April 1977; Aberdeen manager 9 June 1977; Celtic manager 29 May 1978; Manchester City manager 30 June 1983; Aston Villa manager 22 September 1986 to 8 May 1987; Celtic manager 28 May 1987 to 22 May 1991; Hibernian Football Development Manager 1998

### Honours:

- 29 full Scottish caps, 3 goals; 5 Under-23, 9 Scottish League appearances. Scottish Football Writers Association Player of the Year 1965. Awarded MBE 1974

### Other playing honours:

- 9 Scottish League Championships; 7 Scottish Cups, 6 Scottish League Cups, 1 European Cup

### Managerial honours:

- 5 Scottish League Championships; 3 Scottish Cups, 1 Scottish League Cup

## APPEARANCES FOR CELTIC

| Season | League Cup | | Scottish League | | Scottish Cup | | European Cups | |
|---|---|---|---|---|---|---|---|---|
| | Apps | Goals | Apps | Goals | Apps | Goals | Apps | Goals |
| 1958–59 | 17 | – | – | – | 6 | – | – | – |
| 1959–60 | 19 | – | 7 | – | 6 | – | – | – |
| 1960–61 | 31 | 1 | 8 | – | 4 | – | – | – |
| 1961–62 | 29 | 1 | 6 | – | 6 | – | – | – |
| 1962–63 | 28 | 1 | 7 | – | 6 | – | 1+ | – |
| 1963–64 | 28 | – | 4 | – | 6 | – | 8# | – |
| 1964–65 | 22 | – | 6 | 1 | 6 | – | 2+ | – |
| 1965–66 | 25 | – | 7 | – | 10 | – | 7# | 1 |
| 1966–67 | 33 | – | 6 | – | 10 | 2 | 9* | 1 |
| 1967–68 | 34 | 5 | 1 | – | 10 | – | 2* | – |
| 1968–69 | 34 | 3 | 7 | 3 | 9 | – | 6* | – |
| 1969–70 | 31 | 5 | 5 | – | 11 | 2 | 9* | – |
| 1970–71 | 31 | 1 | 8 | 1 | 10 | – | 5* | 1 |
| 1971–72 | 34 | 3 | 6 | 1 | 8 | – | 7* | – |
| 1972–73 | 30 | – | 7 | 1 | 10 | – | 4* | – |
| 1973–74 | 30 | – | 5 | – | 11 | – | 7* | – |
| 1974–75 | 30 | 1 | 4 | – | 9 | – | 2* | – |
| | | | | | | | | |
| Totals | 486 | 21 | 94 | 7 | 138 | 4 | 69 | 3 |

| * | European Cup |
|---|---|
| + | Fairs Cup |
| # | Cup-Winners' Cup |

## OTHER MATCHES

World Club Championship 3 (1 goal)
Glasgow Cup 20 (2 goals)
Glasgow Charity Cup 3

## SCOTLAND APPEARANCES

1961 v England, Republic of Ireland, Republic of Ireland, Czechoslovakia, Czechoslovakia, Northern Ireland
1962 v England, Uruguay
1963 v Republic of Ireland, Spain, Wales
1964 v England, West Germany
1965 v England, Spain, Poland, Finland, Northern Ireland, Poland (1 goal)
1967 v USSR
1968 v England, Cyprus (sub)
1969 v Wales (1 goal), England, Cyprus (1 goal), West Germany
1972 v Northern Ireland, Wales, England

Top photo in plate section two, page seven.

Back row, from left to right: Tommy Gemmell, Margaret Haddow (a close friend of the late Jimmy Steele), Benny Rooney, Willie O'Neill, John Hughes, Neil Mochan jnr., Bertie Auld, Joe McBride, Jim Craig, Charlie Gallagher, Bobby Lennox, Stevie Chalmers and Bobby Murdoch.

Front row: Jimmy Johnstone, John Fallon, Billy McNeill, Ronnie Simpson, Sean Fallon, John Clark and Willie Wallace.

# INDEX

Note: 'BM' denotes Billy McNeill. References to countries, cities, towns, etc., are to football teams unless otherwise indicated. Subheadings for individuals are filed in chronological order.